D0394484

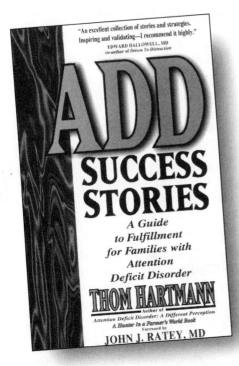

ADD Success Stories

A Guide to Fulfillment for Families with Attention Deficit Disorder

Thom Hartmann

Foreword by John J. Ratey, M.D.

The first specific guidebook on how to be "successful in the world" as a teenager or adult with ADD.

ADD Success Stories is filled with real-life stories of people with Attention Deficit Disorder (ADD) who achieved success in school, at work, and in relationships. This book shows children and adults from all walks of life how to reach the "next step" — a fulfilling, successful life with ADD.

Read this book and discover

- which occupations are best for people with ADD

- how parents of ADD kids successfully juggle work and parenting

- how ADD students are thriving - from kindergarten to medical school

- how ADDers and their spouses can find happiness in their relationships

$11.95, Trade paper, 272pp, ISBN 1-887424-03-2

Available at bookstores everywhere or call (800) 233-9273 to order

Bulk discounts for ADD groups are available at (800) 788-3123

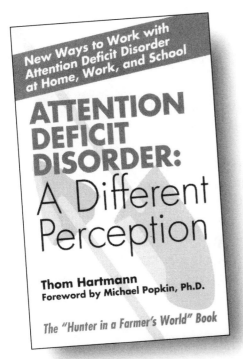

Attention Deficit Disorder

A Different Perception

Thom Hartmann

Foreword by Michael Popkin, Ph.D.

Thom Hartmann sees ADD sufferers as "hunters" —
totally focused on movement, constantly monitoring
their environment, exhibiting incredible bursts of
energy. These "hunters" find themselves in a
contemporary society of "farmers" (cautious, slow
and steady workers).

As many as 20 million Americans may suffer from ADD.
This is the first book to explain that ADD may be
beneficial. It identifies ADD individuals who changed
the world, like Ernest Hemingway, Thomas Edison, and
Benjamin Franklin. Hartmann, the father of an ADD
child, explains how adults and children with ADD can
adapt and function more creatively and productively. His
remarkable "hunters in a farmer's world" theory was
profiled in *Time* magazine.

$10.95, Trade paper, 162pp, ISBN 1-88733-156-4

Available at bookstores everywhere or call (800) 233-9273 to order
Bulk discounts for ADD groups are available at (800) 788-3123

Also by Thom Hartmann
published by Underwood Books

ATTENTION DEFICIT DISORDER
A Different Perception

ADD SUCCESS STORIES
A Guide to Fulfillment for Families
with Attention Deficit Disorder

BEYOND ADD
Hunting for Reasons in the Past & Present
(Fall 1996)

THINK FAST!
The ADD Experience

Edited by
Thom Hartmann & Janie Bowman
with **Susan Burgess**

Underwood Books
Grass Valley, California
1996

THINK FAST! The ADD Experience
ISBN 1-887424-08-3 (trade paper)

Copyright (c) 1996 by Mythical Intelligence, Inc.

Distributed by Publisher's Group West

Volume discounts are available to ADD groups:
call (800) 788-3123 and ask for customer service

Manufactured in the United States of America

10 9 8 7 6 5 4 3 2

Book design by Don Arnoldy
Cover by Arnie Fenner/Spectrum Design

The ideas in this book are based on the respective authors' personal experiences with ADD, and as such are not to be considered medical advice. This book is not intended as a substitute for psychotherapy or the medical treatment of Attention-deficit Hyperactivity Disorder and the various medications described herein can only be prescribed by a physician. The reader should consult a qualified health care professional in matters relating to health and particularly with respect to any symptoms which may require diagnosis or medical attention.

For the members of the ADD Forum on CompuServe,
their families, and the professionals
who work with them.

Your gifts of compassion and understanding
will forever change the way others view
differences in style of attention.

Preface

WELCOME to our community. While that may seem like an odd opening for a book, it's just the right thing to say because this book is an anthology of articles and experiences from the world's largest interactive ADD Support Group, the ADD Forum on CompuServe.

The ADD Forum has over 55,000 members in more than 27 countries, and is accessible by a local phone call for over 96% of the U.S. population and in 140 foreign countries.

With thousands logging on to the forum each week and as the home of the most active membership of any ADD group in the world, we are, indeed, a global community.

People can "talk" daily in real time, either privately or in our conference rooms. It's not unusual to see people who've become online friends—but who live in widely disparate parts of the globe—discussing their lives, trials, and triumphs.

We also have an active message area where people can post messages in specific areas of interest, from pharmacology to relationships to alternative therapies. These messages are woven into 'threads,' like a family tree of continuing dialogue and group conversation. They often make for lively discussions, as you'll see.

Our libraries are permanent storage areas for information about ADD that people can read or retrieve to their computers. With just a few strokes of the keys people can quickly access articles by forum members, including professionals, or read forum discussions about subjects such as parenting, education, careers, therapy, medications and relationship issues.

This sort of electronic community is rapidly coming to fill the void left by the disintegration of small-town America, and it's a marvelous replacement. People of all ages, races, genders, appearances, body types, abilities and disabilities interact on the level playing field of cyberspace.

Although I've never met most of our members in person, I feel closer to many of them than I do to my own neighbors here in suburban Atlanta. For example, I carried on lively and fascinating discussions with CompuServe's Issues Forum Manager Georgia Griffiths for years before I learned one day that she was both blind and deaf from birth. Yet, despite this, she has reached out and touched millions of people through her work on CompuServe, and is considered a friend by thousands.

The ADD Forum provides a unique opportunity to share information and experiences from people of many diverse backgrounds: from ADD adults, to parents of ADD children; from professionals in the field to those who have an academic interest in the subject.

This book is one of the most thorough and detailed overviews of ADD available in the world. By reading the articles, words and thoughts of a great number of these people, you'll become familiar with virtually every viewpoint on the topic, from the most scholarly to the most personal to the most conventional.

We invite you to sit back, relax, and join our experts, curmudgeons, skeptics, cheerleaders and ordinary folks as we share the ADD experience with you.

—Thom Hartmann

Foreword

WHAT'S LIFE LIKE with ADD and ADHD? This book may help you find some answers.

You've heard about Attention Deficit Disorder and Attention Deficit Hyperactivity Disorder—perhaps on network television shows like 20/20; perhaps in Time magazine or Wired; or if you live outside the United States, on the Australian TV Australian TV show called Beyond 2000. Maybe your child's teacher said your youngster has it. Or, maybe you wonder if you do.

So what is it? If you have it, or live with it, what do you do about it?

ADD/ADHD is a set of traits having to do with span of attention, impulsiveness and restlessness.

With insight and information, these traits can often be turned into real assets; without it, such insight and knowledgeif not, life can be an endless series of problems ranging from barely noticeable to debilitating.

THINK FAST! THE ADD EXPERIENCE contains a wealth of answers filled with insight and wisdom, collected into the world's largest anthology of experiences and articles on ADD. Many, but not all, of the more than 75 writers are members of the largest support group in the world for ADD: the 55,000-plus online members of the ADD Forum, on the CompuServe Information Service.

ADD: A syndrome looking for a cause

Experts are still hard at work seeking the causes—and defining the symptoms—of ADD and ADHD. As you'll see, views abound.

In general, though, they agree that most people with ADD share a common set of symptoms including distractibility, impulsiveness, frequently 'tuning out' when others are talking, a search for high stimulation, and hypersensititivity, and so on.

Thought at one time to be merely a 'behavior problem,' ADD/ADHD was re-defined in the 1950s as 'minimal brain damage'—and metamorphosed during the next 40 years into today's Attention Deficit Disorder and Attention Deficit Hyperactivity Disorder. Both are conditions, or syndromes, marked by attention differences from today's the 'normal' person. Attention Deficit Hyperactivity Disorder includes a physical tendency toward 'wigglesomeness' or restlessness.

The collective attention of experts and laymen alike is now focusing on the term 'disorder.' More and more, the concept of ADD as a disorder is being qualified by inclusion of a string of positive qualities—such as creativity, high intelligence, ability to do many things at once, an aptitude for small business entrepreneurship, and a powerful intuitive sense.

On the negative side are things like disorganization, distraction, forgetting, difficulty completing tasks, an unreliable time sense, collection of 'clutter.' For those who are hyperactive as children and restless as adults, add a troublesome inability to sit still.

The symptoms can show up as a dislike for center seats on a plane (because you can't get up easily to walk around); dislike of paperwork (booooooorrrrring); a preference for short, easily completed projects; a love of travel; social difficulties; music running continuously in your head. Or, hypersensitivity to repetitive noise or rough cloth; the ability to concentrate so completely as to seem oblivious to the rest of the world; being distractible in a flash from one thought to another; lightning associations between thoughts; gifted children; impulsive decisions; a huge appetite for stimulation; often being late; difficulty with transitions; mercurial moods.

What to do about ADD?

What if this sounds like you or someone you know? What next?

You have lots of useful options, from developing your own coping strategies to medication to therapy to finding a coach who will assist you much as a football coach supports his team. Doctors, therapists, social workers, counselors, parents and lots of other experts in this collection of opinions, theories and discussions will give you their viewpoints.

Parents as experts? You bet!! Parents who become aware their child has ADD become experts, often better versed in the topic than many educators or members of the health care community. As you'll see, children become experts too, once they are invited to participate in their own coping strategies.

Parents frequently become advocates for their children, drawing on a considerable body of already-developed knowledge. A lot of it is available in the ADD Forum's libraries. Sharing with other parents online has helped many a child get a better deal from the school system.

Discovering reflections of 'yourself' as you learn about the syndrome is often an 'AhHA!' experience of foundation-rattling proportions. Some people grin in sheer delight as they see themselves mirrored with uncanny accuracy: 'At last!!' they exclaim, 'So that's why I'm this way!'

They begin to read voraciously, gulping down every bit of information on store bookshelves, in magazines, and online. They absorb coping strategies, join networked support groups in person or online, zoom off to a doctor for formal diagnosis. (Nobody can beat the speed of an ADDer on the track of vital information or working under a tight deadline!)

Some, though, seem to prefer wearing ADD or ADHD like a badge, using it to excuse themselves from life's routine responsibilities. Others, whose first glimpse of ADD is from a position of 'woe is me, I'm a victim' or, a 'you're a deficient, disordered specimen', may hide in denial and fright, steadfastly refusing to poke their heads out to see how they can improve their lives.

But this book isn't about how to be a victim; it's about how to make the most of life.

Thousands of people with ADD, and their relatives, spouses and friends, choose to share their experiences with others in national and international support groups in person or through online computer networks like the ADD Forum, The groups provide an extended family, a place to release the burdens of daily life, find praise and support—and soak up the balm of acceptance and appreciation for what each member offers the support community.

Cooperation and Support On-Line

The ADD Forum on CompuServe is an astonishingly friendly place where the spirit of cooperation and support thrives.

Listen to Kimmery Mackie as she describes her experience with the forum after joining in July, 1995:

> Hi Everyone!
>
> Just feeling a little melancholy tonight. So I thought I would just tell everyone how great you all are.
>
> In my whole life I have never found as many super people as the ones that I have met here. I have only been in this forum for a little over a month now and I feel like I know quite a few of you like an old friend.
>
> From the very first day I posted my cry for help you have all given the kindest and best advice. And overwhelming support.
>
> For any newcomers that may be reading this, I would like to say, you have found your information highway home. The members here welcome everyone with open arms and kind words. Stick around and you will see.
>
> Again thank you to everyone and I hope we have many more years together!
> God Bless,
> Kimmery

The experience of ADD is one often best shared with others—though the impulse is sometimes to travel the highway alone, unencumbered, free.

Carol Yudis regained a sense of her self with the ADD Forum, as she explained to Sherry Griswold . . .

> Sherry,
>
> I believe that this forum means a lot of things to a lot of people, me included.
>
> This has been the toughest year with Brandon since he was born, and after joining last February I have managed to keep it together. Not that I wasn't together before I joined however, there was a huge void in my life.I provided Brandon with everything he needed, also Steve and my other two children, but I had nothing left for myself.
>
> Finding this forum has filled that very empty void. I now have extremely compassionate, caring people to express my feelings with; knowing that they really do understand. We come here because we want to be here; and in one way or another we are all the same.
>
> It really does help keep my head on straight, not to mention providing me with the one missing piece, information! And, I do agree Sherry, helping and listening to others manages to ease the weight of the world off our shoulders too.
>
> I never imagined that I would have such a large family! (grin!)
> Carol

About this book

Most of the forum discussions you'll read (called 'threads' because they are a series of linked messages) have, of course, been edited to fit the book. A few folks have chosen pseudonyms.

Among their many qualities, ADDers are known to discuss most anything at great length, with a great many sidetracks and sometimes-convoluted complexity.

To keep messages in some kind of order on the forum, a volunteer group called 'sysops,' or systems operators, make sure the messages tidily connected and change their locations on the message board as needed. The message board itself is divided into topics just like a large bulletin board. If you have a message to post about parenting, for instance, you would post it in one of the parenting sections. Generally within hours you have a response from someone who has something to say on your topic.

In the forum libraries, where files are held for a year or more, you can research almost anything on the topic of ADD and ADHD—and copy those files to your own computer at home or work where they can be printed out on your printer. The world's foremost authorities on ADD have files in the forum libraries waiting for you to read them.

CompuServe itself, with more than 3.7 million members worldwide, provides easy-to-use software to access its more than 1,600 forums. Call 1-800-848-8990 to sign up for membership and receive the software. Or, once you get online, you can locate one of the 'autopilot' programs that lets you designate the places you'd like to visit, scoop up messages and files, and go back offline—all in a few minutes' time with no manual intervention from you.

Now, think fast! Zzooooom—off into the pages of this book to hear the inside story of The ADD Experience, from people around the world who are living it even as you read this—and discussing it online.

—Susan Burgess

Contents

The ADD Experience

Introduction by Dave deBronkart

THE ADD EXPERIENCE has changed a lot in the last few years.
As recently as 1993 the established wisdom said "Your brain doesn't work right; its chemistry is wrong." As ADD hit the public awareness in the 1990s, its image was influenced by media coverage such as *Newsweek's* sensational article (July 26, 1993). Featuring a heavily retouched photo of a boy screaming in an orange fog, the piece used terms like "a devastating lifelong condition" and it cited a variety of horror stories.

The article barely mentioned, near the end, that "most [ADDers] are spared long-term problems." And of course it never mentioned any *successful* ADDers.

The outlook is different today.

Today we're redefining the ADD experience. More and more people are acknowledging the natural differences between individuals, and looking at things in a different way. And we have many successful role models.

In the medical community, the media's depiction of failure was lampooned by the emergence of Harvard Medical School faculty members, Edward M. Hallowell, M.D., and John J. Ratey, M.D., both ADDers. (Can you be mentally defective and wind up on the faculty of the world's top medical school?) At conferences, Hallowell and Ratey began handing out free copies of their paper "What's It Like To Have ADD," containing remarks such as "I resent the term 'attention deficit.' " Their popular book DRIVEN TO DISTRACTION continues to be a mainstay of support for the ADD community.

Meanwhile entrepreneur and author Thom Hartmann published his first book, ATTENTION DEFICIT DISORDER: A DIFFERENT PERCEPTION—the first ever

---

Dave deBronkart is a successful ADD adult who didn't discover the trait until he was 42. A black-belt troubleshooter in computerized graphic arts, public speaker, software writer and head of his training firm The Competence Group, he's known for his ability to analyze complex problems from several angles at once—sometimes indulging in three-day sleepless binges. Dave can be reached at CompuServe 76702,1140.

to point out the possibility of a natural *healthy* brain state called ADD, and the first book to publish a list of positive ADD role models throughout history.

People have flocked to this optimistic view in droves. The old negative paradigm has been busted open. Today, ADD articles in major magazines include clear reference to the new view. In June 1994 *Time* magazine prominently mentioned Hartmann's "controversial but appealing theory," and way-hip *Wired*, a widely read computer magazine, declared "ADD should be dubbed the official brain syndrome for the information age."

So yes, thank you, the ADD experience is different today. We've come to under-stand that the fast-moving mind can be well adapted to the right setting. If a restless kid learns fine in a less-boring setting, does the kid have a learning disability? Evidently not; perhaps the conventional classroom has a teaching disability: the kid *is* able to learn, but some classrooms are unable to teach to his particular learning style.

The same thinking applies to careers. We've learned to let each person choose a career that makes sense—and in the ADD experience, that means finding a job that brings excitement, variety, the opportunity to move around, and often a tight deadline orientation. Anything but monotony! Witness the life experience of Thomas Edison, who by today's standards, would probably be diagnosed ADD.

Many professionals and entrepreneurs with ADD consider it an asset because they've learned to harness the incredible energy it gives them. At the same time they adapt to their individual needs by staying away from jobs with requirements that drive them nuts: endless paperwork, sitting at a desk all day, and so on. Often, such adaptations alone are enough to make them successful in their careers and family.

Careers such as technical troubleshooting, sales, newspaper reporting, acting, and creative arts are now recognized as well-suited to the ADD experience. And if a job does require paperwork and administration, then many find a good methodical partner to handle it for them.

Can ADD be a pain in the neck? Sure. But today the leading authorities are saying words like "Embrace your true nature" (Hallowell/Ratey) and "Three quarters of the problems in an ADD life come not from the ADD but from being misunderstood" (Lynn Weiss). The emphasis is not on "What's 'wrong' with me" but on "What am I really like?"

That's why this opening section of THINK FAST! THE ADD EXPERIENCE includes Hallowell's "What's it like to have ADD?" Also in this section, you'll read the words of many other perceptive ADD adults as they share their insights into what life is like —in their experience, in the discussion titled "You know you have ADD when . . ." The section closes with an online group chat about the life of Edison, who was restless, impulsive, couldn't sit still, couldn't wait his turn in school . . . you get the picture.

It's no coincidence that the discussions in this section are often funny. Humor works best with a quick mind, and that's easy for a person whose motto is "Think Fast!" And *that* is the heart of The ADD Experience.

What's it like to have ADD?
by Edward M. Hallowell, M.D.

WHAT IS IT LIKE to have ADD? What is the feel of the syndrome? I have a short talk that I often give to groups as an introduction to the subjective experience of ADD and what it is like to live with it: Attention Deficit Disorder. First of all I resent the term. As far as I'm concerned most people have Attention Surplus Disorder. I mean, life being what it is, who can pay attention to anything for very long? Is it really a sign of mental health to be able to balance your checkbook, sit still in your chair, and never speak out of turn? As far as I can see, many people who don't have ADD are charter members of the Congenitally Boring.

But anyway, be that as it may, there is this syndrome called ADD or ADHD, depending on what book you read.

So what's it like to have ADD? Some people say the so-called syndrome doesn't even exist, but believe me, it does. Many metaphors come to mind to describe it. It's like driving in the rain with bad windshield wipers. Everything is smudged and blurred and you're speeding along, and it's reeeeally frustrating not being able to see very well. Or it's like listening to a radio station with a lot of static and you have to strain to hear what's going on. Or, it's like trying to build a house of cards in a dust storm. You have to build a structure to protect yourself from the wind before you can even start on the cards.

In other ways it's like being super-charged all the time. You get one idea and you have to act on it, and then, what do you know, but you've got another idea before you've finished up with the first one, and so you go for that one, but of course a third idea intercepts the second, and you just have to follow that one, and pretty soon people are calling you disorganized and impulsive and all sorts of impolite words that miss the point completely. Because you're trying really hard. It's just that you have all these invisible vectors pulling you this way and that which makes it really hard to stay on task.

Plus which, you're spilling over all the time. You're drumming your fingers, tapping your feet, humming a song, whistling, looking here, looking there, scratching, stretching, doodling, and people think you're not paying attention or that you're not interested, but all you're doing is spilling over so that you can pay attention. I can pay a lot better attention when I'm taking a walk or listening to music or even when I'm in a crowded, noisy room than when I'm still and surrounded by silence. God save me from the reading rooms. Have you ever been into the one in Widener Library? The only thing that saves it is that so many of the people who use it have ADD that there's a constant soothing bustle.

What is it like to have ADD? Buzzing. Being here and there and everywhere. Someone once said, "Time is the thing that keeps everything from happening all at once." Time parcels moments out into separate bits so that we can do one thing at a time. In ADD, this does not happen. In ADD, time collapses. Time becomes a black hole. To the person with ADD it feels as if everything is happening all at once. This creates a sense of inner turmoil or even panic. The individual loses perspective and the ability to prioritize. He or she is always on the go, trying to keep the world from caving in on top.

Museums. (Have you noticed how I skip around? That's part of the deal. I change channels a lot. And radio stations. Drives my wife nuts. "Can't we listen to just one song all the way through?") Anyway, museums. The way I go through a museum is the way some people go through Filene's Basement. Some of this, some of that, oh, this one looks nice, but what about that rack over there? Gotta hurry, gotta run. It's not that I don't like art. I love art. But my way of loving it makes most people think I'm a real Philistine. On the other hand, sometimes I can sit and look at one painting for a long while. I'll get into the world of the painting and buzz around in there until I forget about everything else. In these moments I, like most people with ADD, can hyperfocus, which gives the lie to the notion that we can never pay attention. Sometimes we have turbocharged focusing abilities. It just depends upon the situation.

Lines. I'm almost incapable of waiting in lines. I just can't wait, you see. That's the hell of it. Impulse leads to action. I'm very short on what you might call the intermediate reflective step between impulse and action. That's why I, like so many people with ADD, lack tact. Tact is entirely dependent on the ability to consider one's words before uttering them. We ADD types don't do this so well.

I remember in the fifth grade I noticed my math teacher's hair in a new style and blurted out, "Mr. Cook, is that a toupee you're wearing?" I got kicked out of class. I've since learned how to say these inappropriate things in such a way or at such a time that they can in fact be helpful. But it has taken time. That's the thing about ADD. It takes a lot of adapting to get on in life. But it certainly can be done, and be done very well.

As you might imagine, intimacy can be a problem if you've got to be constantly changing the subject, pacing, scratching and blurting out tactless remarks. My wife has learned not to take my tuning out personally, and she says that when I'm there, I'm really there. At first, when we met, she thought I was some kind of nut, as I would bolt out of restaurants at the end of meals or disappear to another planet during a conversation. Now she has grown accustomed to my sudden coming and goings.

Many of us with ADD crave high-stimulus situations. In my case, I love the racetrack. And I love the high-intensity crucible of doing psychotherapy. And I love having lots of people around. Obviously this tendency can get you into trouble, which is why ADD is high among criminals and self-destructive risk-takers. It is also high among so-called Type A personalities, as well as among manic-depressives, sociopaths and criminals, violent people, drug abusers, and alcoholics. But is also high among creative and intuitive people in all fields, and among highly energetic, highly productive people.

Which is to say there is a positive side to all this. Usually the positive doesn't get mentioned when people speak about ADD because there is a natural tendency to focus on what goes wrong, or at least on what has to be somehow controlled.

But often once the ADD has been diagnosed, and the child or the adult, with the help of teachers and parents or spouses, friends, and colleagues, has learned how to cope with it, an untapped realm of the brain swims into view. Suddenly the radio station is tuned in, the windshield is clear, the sand storm has died down. And the child or adult, who had been such a problem, such a nudge, such a general pain in the neck to himself and everybody else, that person starts doing things he'd never been able to do before. He surprises everyone around him, and he surprises himself. I use the male pronoun, but it could just as easily be she, as we are seeing more and more ADD among females as we are looking for it.

Often these people are highly imaginative and intuitive. They have a "feel" for things, a way of seeing right into the heart of matters while others have to reason their way along methodically. This is the person who can't explain how he thought of the solution, or where the idea for the story came from, or why suddenly he produced such a painting, or how he knew the short cut to the answer, but all he can say is he just knew it, he could feel it. This is the man or woman who makes million dollar deals in a catnap and pulls them off the next day. This is the child who, having been reprimanded for blurting something out, is then praised for having blurted out something brilliant. These are the people who learn and know and do and go by touch and feel.

These people can feel a lot. In places where most of us are blind, they can, if not see the light, at least feel the light, and they can produce answers apparently out of the dark. It is important for others to be sensitive to this "sixth sense" many ADD people have, and to nurture it. If the environment insists on rational, linear thinking and "good" behavior from these people all the time, then they may never develop their intuitive style to the point where they can use it profitably. It can be exasperating to listen to people talk. They can sound so vague or rambling. But if you take them seriously and grope along with them, often you will find they are on the brink of startling conclusions or surprising solutions.

What I am saying is that their cognitive style is qualitatively different from most people's, and what may seem impaired, with patience and encouragement may become gifted.

The thing to remember is that if the diagnosis can be made, then most of the bad stuff associated with ADD can be avoided or contained. The diagnosis can be liberating, particularly for people who have been stuck with labels like "lazy," "stubborn," "willful," "disruptive," "impossible," "tyrannical," "a space-shot," "brain damaged," "stupid," or just plain "bad." Making the diagnosis of ADD can take the case from the court of moral judgment to the clinic of neuro-psychiatric treatment.

What is the treatment all about? Anything that turns down the noise. Just making the diagnosis helps turn down the noise of guilt and self-recrimination. Building certain kinds of structure into one's life can help a lot. Working in small spurts rather than long hauls. Breaking tasks down into smaller tasks. Making lists. Getting help where you need it. Whether it's having a secretary, or an accountant, or an automatic bank teller, or a good filing system, or a home computer—getting help where you need it. Maybe applying external limits on your impulses. Or getting enough exercise to work off some of the noise inside. Finding support. Getting someone in your corner to coach you, to keep you on track. Medication can help a great deal too, but it is far from the whole solution. The good news is that treatment can really help.

Let me leave you by telling you that we need your help and understanding. We may make mess-piles wherever we go, but with your help, those mess-piles can be turned into realms of reason and art. So, if you know someone like me who's acting up and daydreaming and forgetting this or that and just not getting with the program, consider ADD before he starts believing all the bad things people are saying about him and it's too late.

The main point of the talk is that there is a more complex subjective experience to ADD than a list of symptoms can possibly impart. ADD is a way of life, and until recently it has been hidden, even from the view of those who have it. The human experience of ADD is more than just a collection of symptoms. It is a way of living. Before the syndrome is diagnosed that way of living may be filled with pain and misunderstanding. After the diagnosis is made, one often finds new possibilities and the chance for real change.

The adult syndrome of ADD, so long unrecognized, is now at last bursting upon the scene. Thankfully, millions of adults who have had to think of themselves as defective or unable to get their acts together, will instead be able to make the most of their considerable abilities. It is a hopeful time indeed.

You Know U Have ADD When . . .

One day a group of forum members began discussing what it was like to have ADD. It quickly blossomed into a light-hearted and enlightening exchange which became a classic in the forum libraries.

Hi Everyone . . .
I heard (Dr. John) Ratey a few weeks ago—nice slide show with his presentation (keeps the brain from wandering).

No doubt I have it, but am reluctant to get "labeled" by using my health plan for diagnosis, treatment. I will try coaching with organization skills and more *exercise*, which Ratey harped on- I agree, for I rode extensively with a bike club 8 yrs ago, but along came the kid, etc., and now I just do short rides with her..

You know you have ADD when:
- ☛ The bolts you got for some project idea are still in the bag you bought them in and now you can't find the bag . . . after 2 weeks . . .
- ☛ You forgot you bought some needed parts, buy them, and find you already had them . . . arggh!
- ☛ It takes longer to get the tools together for a job than to do the job, so you move on to something with more "priority."
- ☛ You never clean up after doing a project because you were distracted into something else.
- ☛ You haven't a clue what is on a videotape (still lying around) because you forgot to label it . . . and when you view it to check and the kid wants something, you get distracted, come back, and don't remember you had the tape in the machine.
- ☛ You find food in the microwave the next morning because you were distracted away yesterday and forgot you had put it in.

—So am I forgetful? I remember what I do read or see on TV; I remember phone numbers from years ago; I remember what someone did last week when they've forgotten- So *distraction* is the key!

(You can't forget what you never put into memory to begin with!!!)

—*Michael G. Benthin*

You know you have ADD when . . .

☞ You go to get something from the bedroom, and by the time you get there you forget what you were going for.

☞ You go to pick up your kid from some activity, and when you get there, you remember that they are at home asleep.

☞ You call someone on the phone to ask them a question and by the time they answer (1 ring), you forgot what you were going to ask.

☞ You make yourself a list of things to do, and then you forget where you put it.

☞ You take your shopping list with you and you forget to look at it.

☞ You park your car at the store, and then forget which car you drove.

Hey, I like this thread . . . let's see how many we can get altogether.

—*Janet Whipple*

You know you have ADD when . . .

You finally sit down to organize the file that you knew that you should have started months ago, only to find that you *did* start it months ago, with extensive notes to prove it, but now you don't remember what conclusions you reached at the time .

—*Ben Greenberg*

You know you have ADD when . . .

☞ You get in the car and can't find your keys and then discover they are still in the door. (or someone tells you that there are a set of keys in your trunk lock).

☞ You fill your own gas tank and drive off without the gas cap . . . again.

—*Harry Baya*

You know you have ADD when . . .

☞ You go to pick up your kid at his friend's house; you realize you have driven right by the house. You turn around, and arrive at home . . . still without the kid!!

—*Deb Land*

Gee, after reading all these, I can certainly relate, and then again, realize I'm not as bad as some!

Yes I've driven right by the house where I was to pick someone up, but at least I finally realized it and didn't drive home!

No, my big problem with lists (like market) is *finding the d*mn lists*—they magically vanish between being written and pushing the cart.

You know you have ADD when . . .

☛ Your environs adhere to the *horizontal filing system*—every horizontal surface has something on it you planned to put away somewhere, and when it gets five deep, it's time to start cleaning up (if the spouse didn't throw it all in a box already!!!!!!)

—Michael G. Benthin

How about this one . . .

☛ You go to the store to get something *specific*, then buy a whole bunch of other stuff, and forget to buy what you originally went to the store for (until you get home, that is).

—Bob Frazier

The store experience is familiar.

Years ago, maybe 15, a friend asked me to remember that we had put a bag under the seat of the car when we left it. I made a really strong effort to remember this.

So now, I go in the store, I realize I may be forgetting something I really meant to buy and I ask myself, "What do you want to remember?" And, you guessed it, I remember that silly bag from 15 years ago.

I find writing things down helps a lot . . . sometimes. The problems are: I forget to write it down; I forget that I wrote anything down; I forget to take the note with me when I need it; I take the note and forget to look at it; I take the note, read it, and then forget before I actually do it. But, praise the universe, sometimes I write it down, take the note, read it, and actually *do it*. I can't say I'm getting better at it . . . but I do enjoy those experiences.

I designed a memory watch band that had little color markers with two positions for each. The idea was that you pushed a marker up when you had something specific to remember. It would be like tying a string on each finger. What I do now is I put my college ring on another finger. Someday I will probably lose that ring because of that. I never did anything with the watch band idea.

—Harry Baya

You know you have ADD . . .

☛ When you are headed for church and drive to school instead.

—Sherry Griswold

You know you have ADD . . .

- When your daughter calls from church and asks why both Mom and Dad left (in separate cars) without her.
- You make plans to meet your Significant Other at a restaurant after [you] both get out of work, but end up at two different restaurants.

Don George

You know you have ADD when . . .

- You are halfway to work when you realize that you changed jobs two months ago and the new job is in the opposite direction.
- You know what a psychopharmacologist is.
- You clean up a pile of papers and discover an open book on memorization techniques that you had completely forgotten you were reading weeks ago.
- You know who Thom Hartmann, Ned Hallowell, and Peggy Ramundo are.
- You cut a presentation short to run home because you don't remember turning the lawn sprinkler off—and then discover you forgot to turn it on.
- You always park in the same place so you will know where your car is.
- The best conversation you had all day was with yourself.
- You carefully pack as much into the dishwasher as you can, put in the detergent, latch the door then come back at dinner time to find you forgot to turn it on.
- You wash a load of clothes twice because you can't remember if you put detergent in the first time.
- You are introduced to someone and two seconds later you don't know their name.
- The relaxing sound of trickling water you hear is the humidifier overflowing onto the floor. Again.
- You realize that awful odor is a pan of water boiled dry. You put on another pan of water and 30 minutes later notice that odor again .
- "The chicken can't remember why she crossed the road" actually makes sense to you.
- The last time you were early for anything, you had forgotten to set the clock back one hour.
- You are going to do something about procrastinating. Someday.

☞ You finally remember to do a small task, get the needed tools together, congratulate yourself for getting it together, and discover that you had already done it.

☞ You are on a first name basis with the people at every customer service desk in town because you have left your checkbook, coupons, purchases, etc., so often.

—*Gary Brown*

I did this one just this morning!
　You know you have ADD when . . .

☞ You go to take your meds, you have your Adderall in one hand and a glass of water in the other hand. You drink all the water, then are startled to find the Adderall is still in your hand!

—*Deb Land*

Many times I have placed my morning dosages of Wellbutrin and some vitamins in a small jar I use to keep them together before taking, and then later in the day find that they are all still in the jar! My doctor is not amused. At least I have learned to put the rest of the day's doses in another container so I can figure out how many I have taken that day and how many remain. I found myself unable to do this from memory.

　I need a system to keep track of whether or not I gave the cat his morning insulin shot. I don't think I have ever messed this up, but have come close. It calls for a hyperfocused reconstruction of my time in the kitchen earlier that day.

　By the way, does anyone consistently return to the space where their car was parked *the day before*, after leaving school or work?

—*Rob*

ADD: The Edison Trait

Did Thomas Edison have ADD? Forum members joined then-Forum Manager Dave deBronkart, who has a keen interest in the topic, as he explored the life of Thomas Edison in this March 17, 1994 forum conference. The conference was moderated by Karen Sanders, mother of an ADD child.

Karen (Host) Welcome everyone to the conference. Our guest is Dave deBronkart. Dave is a sysop of the ADD forum, and has been studying the life of Thomas Edison.

Dave, ADD has been called the Edison Trait—when Edison was a kid did he show ADD traits?

deB (Guest) Sure did! [Note: I want to acknowledge that this whole "Edison trait" idea first came to me from Thom Hartmann while he was writing his first book. I was at first skeptical, so I did some digging, and the more I learned, the more I found out how right Hartmann was about this. That's what led me to the information below.]

An important point needs to be made at the outset: as Hallowell points out in his book, "It's dangerous to diagnose the dead" (grin), because you can't tell what they were actually like. But especially in the case of ADD, which is a strictly behavioral diagnosis, based solely on observed behaviors, it's not unreasonable (imo) to ask, "Given what we know of this person's life, would a clinician today diagnose the same person as having ADD?" In Edison's case, there's little doubt.

Steven Foust deB, can't we also make judgments on them based on autobiographical (or biographical) works?

deB (Guest) Yes, that's the whole point: the only resource we really have, in something like ADD, is the available written record.

Karen (Host) Did Edison have an autobiography?

deB (Guest) Edison didn't have an autobiography, and one challenge is that most of his biographies are mostly legend, constructed by his second wife whom he married at age 38.

Dave deBronkart (76702,1140) says his main interest in ADD is in finding ways to harness the trait's strengths.

Steven Foust How would an autobiography be "weighed" vs. a biography?

deB (Guest) Good question, Steve. In Edison's case, one would have to be extra careful of an autobiography, because as with many good entrepreneurs, he was a bit of a huckster.(grin) But . . . there's one biography that stands out as well-researched . . . the one by Robert Conot . . . for instance, it's the only one that points out that he was NOT known as Thomas, any time in his life, until his second wife took over—he was known by his middle name, Al (for Alva). That's how distorted his public image is.

Karen (Host) Did Edison concentrate on one area, or was he "all over?" Did he limit his work?

deB (Guest) Nope, he didn't limit his work. Let me go back to your first question . . . for the record, his childhood is full of instances that would today be cause for an ADD diagnosis (if not conduct disorder): He set the family barn on fire "to see what it would do;" he went swimming with a friend in a waterhole, and when the friend disappeared underwater, he didn't know what to make of it so he went home; in school, he was fidgety; blurted things out, wouldn't wait his turn, wouldn't listen when he was supposed to, was puny and uncoordinated; was razzed and bullied by classmates.

Karen (Host) How much formal education did he have?

deB (Guest) (Most of these, by the way, are from Conot, which is the biography that claims to be well researched.) Formal education: three different schools, plus home schooling, up to age 11—*not* abnormal for someone in those days, in fact this is an example of how Edison promoted his own false legend: he claimed to have had almost no formal schooling, when in fact he had a typical amount, and continued to take classes (e.g. at Cooper Union in NYC) as an adult. But that doesn't change the key diagnostic point: he couldn't stand to sit still and learn by rote, he *had* to be doing things himself, hands-on.

Karen (Host) He always emphasized the positive and self-promoted. If he was ADD, how did he manage to be productive?

deB (Guest) HEY! I resent that question! (grin) *I'm* ADD, and I just had a heck of a productive day, despite having had only 1.5 hrs of sleep last night (on an airplane all night), and having had 3.5 hrs sleep/night for the 2 previous nights. In fact, today I got as much done as I do in some weeks. And I wrote a program for a client, on a rush basis, that worked on the first try, and solved the guy's problem.

Karen (Host) Allow me to restate: How did he marshal his creativity?

deB (Guest) Now, to answer your question:(grin)
First, he was a classic example of someone who needed a partner in order to produce. His mind spewed out ideas faster than he himself could turn them into experiments. Only when he had partners capturing them did his phenomenal patent rate occur: 75/year, at times.
Second, he refused to work normal hours: He often went to bed when the sun came up, *if* he came to bed. (He was also a major sugar-and-caffeine junkie, by the way.)

Morgan I'm curious about what form these productive partnerships took. How did they work?

deB (Guest) Good question. He had two partners, when he was at his best: One made good drawings of the ideas, the other made working models that could be perfected. (In other words, he stumbled onto the method of having someone else fill in the skills he lacked: team building.)

Steve Simon All of the famous "ADD" people in history seem to have been ADHD. Do you know of any of these famous folks who were ADD without the hyperactivity?

deB (Guest) Good question, Steve—don't know, off the top of my head.

Karen (Host) Yes, was Edison more ADD or ADHD?

deB (Guest) The record of his adult life doesn't talk much about fidgetiness.

Morgan Was he the one who worked out the form of the partnerships or was he helped into it perhaps by his wife or another interested party?

deB (Guest) Definitely NOT by his first wife, but in fact his second wife did remake his life, including changing his public image to the point of changing his publicly known name! But for the first 30+ years, he was aggressive, the one who started things.

Karen (Host) Edison seems to qualify as ADDult by his impulsiveness!

deB (Guest) Yes, in fact, the ways in which he matches today's entrepreneurs are pretty amusing. I've known a few entrepreneurs, and to a one, they hate paperwork, tend to deal with finances by ranting and raving, can be *brutal* as supervisors, offering not much more of a supervisory palette than "Whip 'em into a frenzy" (grin), and all that applies to Edison, in spades, except his supervisory palette may have been more limited.(grin)

Karen (Host) Do we know much what Edison thought his strengths were?

deB (Guest) Huh! Good question. Let me think about it. (He had a huge ego, that's for sure.)

Susan B. What was that about his publicly known name?

deB (Guest) He was born Thomas Alva Edison, and according to Conot he was known by his middle name (Al) all his life, until his second wife, at age 38, decided to remake his public image. Thus, everything you have ever read or seen that talks about Thomas Edison is a derived secondary product of the PR machine surrounding him in the second half of his life!

Susan B. Thanks. (grin)

deB (Guest) For instance, the movie "Young Tom Edison" is a total crock: there *was* no "Tom Edison" until middle age.

Now I want to start tying this in to ADD, okay?

Now, the question arises: so what if he was ADD? Well, a couple of things. First, what if a kid with exactly that activity profile were plopped into today's school system, where he wasn't allowed to hit the road at age 11, as Edison did (getting a job on a train, eventually living in 17 cities in 11 years), but instead was made to sit still the whole time, with diagnoses etc. etc. etc.?

This is not an academic question, it's dead serious. What would have happened if impulsive young Edison had been put in a hammerlock and/or sat on [as happens to some ADD kids today]?

Morgan I suspect we'd be living in a vastly different world. Thomas Edison would have remained Al Edison, denied the opportunities he seized to use the gifts of ADD to all of our advantages.

deB (Guest) PRECISELY.

Morgan Scary . . . and there are other little Al Edisons out there being beaten down by the system.

deB (Guest) Let me point out that the kid who DID emerge was hardly an angel . . . my point isn't that leaving someone to his/her own devices produces flowers (grin) . . . He was geeky, annoyed people with his constant practical jokes, didn't know when to shut up, ruined his workplace often by dismantling things, spilling battery acid, etc. The point, to the contrary, is that the strengths flourished only because they weren't squashed, because instead he ended up with enough breathing room to be as he was and not get shot in the process.(grin)

Karen (Host) But Edison never tried to change himself, that we know of? Or "medicate."

deB (Guest) No, to the contrary, didn't medicate except sugar and caffeine. But that was major, evidently: his whole life, his lunch was nothing but apple pie and coffee, dinner too, often. No evidence of any drug abuse.

Steven Foust How can we be sure, since at that time certain drugs (cocaine) were not outlawed yet?

deB (Guest) (Alcoholism in his family.) Good question, Steve—I don't know of evidence either way.

Karen (Host) He created opportunities for himself by forging partnerships, and creating friendships with the likes of Henry Ford. What else did he do to help himself?

deB (Guest) Hmmmm . . . good question. I don't know that any business per se came out of liaisons with Ford and the like.

Susan B. Have you looked at any other inventors re: ADD?

deB (Guest) No, I haven't personally, but Thom and Hallowell both point to Ben Franklin.

Karen (Host) What else about Edison's ADD can we learn from?

deB (Guest) I think his life would have been easier if he'd been conscious of his limits and accepted help: for instance, money was a constant PITA to him. But, like many forum members, he felt he *should* be able to manage it, so bills would pile up while he had plenty of money in the bank, until people were suing him, then he'd go on a binge, answering all his mail and writing checks for days, and, sometimes, since he never knew how much he had, he'd run out, and then he'd go into a frenzy to finish some invention and sell it to get cash.

Karen (Host) Your point is we should take help when we need it.

deB (Guest) Yes, thanks for saying it concisely.(grin)

Morgan Seems to me that one thing he did really well was to accept his own rhythms in regard to time so that he could be so incredibly productive, letting himself go on work binges when he had the flow, and crashing when it was over.

deB (Guest) (oooo, nice point!) Yes! in fact, Morgan, I'm just realizing something myself: I *wish* I could always be productive by being short on sleep but I'm just figuring out that what it does is to "tank up" by getting a couple of good nights' sleep first, *then* go on a low-sleep binge.

Deidra/FL Sorry I missed the beginning, did he work strange hours? i.e., was he a night owl?

deB (Guest) Sure did! — he was lousy as a supervisor, because he often went home when everyone else was arriving, constantly worked through the night, would nap, sometimes, under a staircase, spreading out newspapers as a mattress, or he'd just crawl up on a lab bench and sleep there. Sometimes he'd work 36 hrs. straight, or more, with just these naps, then go home and topple into bed, with his good suit still on, stained with chemicals.

Karen (Host) It's hard to advise people to work strange hours, but maybe we all need to "go with the flow" whenever we can. Wonder if he ever said "That's the way I am."

deB (Guest) Excellent point, Karen! In fact, the Conot biography has several cases where he demonstrates what we now call "expert blaming" skills, a not uncommon ADD trait: For instance, "You cannot expect a man [this in a letter to his investors] to invent all day and all night, and then still have energy left to worry about details like finance.") (grin)

Susan B. (grin) worry about finance!!!

Karen (Host) The downside is he must have had disappointments in his life, eh? (If people can learn from Edison's life, maybe we can learn from his disappointments.)

deB (Guest)   Yes, many disappointments: For one thing, he was a lousy husband, and a fairly detached parent. He seemed self-centered (something that screams out repeatedly from Hallowell's pages), but wasn't selfish, was very generous, yet wasn't nurturing to wife or kids. Also had many, many ideas and companies that didn't pan out.

Morgan   So he had it figured out that financial genius wasn't likely to go with his kind of genius?

deB (Guest)   No, he *didn't* figure it out . . . he thought "Since I'm smart, whatever the problem is, it must not be ME."(grin) (Sound familiar to any parents out there?)

Morgan   Ah.

Karen (Host)   You've made some great points, Dave, about learning from Edison's life . . . any other hints?

deB (Guest)   Any other hints: yes . . . "beware your own style's hazards." Several of his relatives were alcoholics, and one nephew, who showed promise of being as clever as Edison himself, was very high-stimulus-seeking, and got into a wild crowd in Paris, and ended up dead as a result of too many risky activities.

Karen (Host)   How tragic!

deB (Guest)   Who knows what the guy would have invented . . . he was just 22 or so when he died, I think, though Edison had already put him in charge of some things.

Karen (Host)   What was Edison's lifespan?

deB (Guest)   Almost 80, I think. I'll look it up. Yes, 84. 1,093 patents.

Karen (Host)   What a life of accomplishment!

Susan B.   Would you summarize the positive things about ADD that we can learn from Edison's life?

deB (Guest)   Sure, thanks—then we can wind this up.

First, if we accept that Edison was ADD, as all the evidence suggests, then it's pretty evident that the "bing-bing-bing mind," or, as he put it, "My kaleidoscopic brain," was pivotal in his creativity:

constantly thinking of things, putting ideas together, cross-pollinating from one project to another. At one point he had over 100 experiments going at once.

Next, and perhaps most important, is that he didn't put his effort into dwelling on what he *couldn't* do. Rather, he focused his energy on finding those"islands of competence," as one of the ADD docs says at conferences, and nurturing them.

This reminds me of the parable at the start of last year's great little book SOAR WITH YOUR STRENGTHS. In the parable, a rabbit and duck go to school together. The rabbit loves school the first day, where they teach running, but when they cover flying on the second day, the rabbit breaks a leg. And what does the school do? They set up a remedial flying program for him. (big grin)

Susan B.   (grin) Cool!

deB (Guest)   Far more sensible is to focus on your strengths, if you can do fine just as you are! Put your mind on what works, and make the most of it—as Edison did.

Karen (Host)   Thank you for being our guest.

deB (Guest)   Thanks for moderating!

Different Perceptions of ADD

Introduction by Richard E. Reither, M.A., M.F.C.C.

A S THE NAME of what we now call Attention Deficit Hyperactivity Disorder (ADHD) changes, so does the information available to professionals and parents alike. Over the years, the name has indeed changed several times. As recently as ten years ago, if one were to have asked the average person what an attentional disorder was, the answer would have been a blank look.

Today, ADHD is rapidly becoming a more common term, due in large measure to national exposure from radio and TV talk shows, educational books aimed at parents and educators and of course the CompuServe Information Service ADD Forum. The evolution of ADHD is changing as new theories are created which challenge or augment our current knowledge.

This section of THINK FAST! presents three different ways of viewing what ADD is. First, author Thom Hartmann's use of cultural anthropology to explore an altogether new way of viewing the ADHD person has been met with widespread hope and excitement, in that it de-emphasizes pathology and focuses on the strengths of the individual. Next, Russell A. Barkley's expansion of Jacob Bronowski's work serves to further hone our understanding of ADHD symptomology by focusing more on the concept of response inhibition rather than inattention. Finally, printed here for the first time, new author Carla Nelson's

Richard Reither (76600,716) is a licensed Marriage, Family and Child Therapist in Fresno, CA. In private practice for the last ten years with a focus on the assessment and treatment of adults and children with learning and attention differences, he is a frequent guest lecturer on LD and ADHD subjects for school districts, organizations and the local CH.A.D.D. chapter.

theory of the multidimensionality of ADHD very ably points to the complexity of the condition. Since we still know relatively little of how the brain works, it stands to reason that only the surface has been scratched on this puzzling neurobehaviorial experience.

As a result of new theories emerging from varied sources around the country and the world, our understanding of this fascinating and frustrating condition will be greatly expanded in the years ahead. With greater understanding will come better treatments and a wider acceptance among the medical and academic communities toward that which, at least for now, is called ADHD.

Are You a Hunter or a Farmer?
by Thom Hartmann

> *The creatures that want to live a life of their own, we call wild. If*
> *wild, then no matter how harmless, we treat them as outlaws, and*
> *those of us who are 'specially well brought up shoot them for fun.*
> —Clarence Day, *This Simian World*, 1920

Disassembling ADD

At its core, ADD is generally acknowledged to have three components: distractibility, impulsivity, and risk-taking/restlessness. (If you throw in hyperactivity, you have ADHD—Attention Deficit Hyperactive Disorder—which, until recently, was considered to be "true" ADD, but is now viewed as a separate condition. ADHD is the disorder that children were believed to grow out of sometime around adolescence, but it appears that most ADHD kids simply become adults with ADD as the hyperactivity of their youth sometimes diminishes.)

Distractibility is often mischaracterized as the inability of a child or adult to pay attention to a specific thing. Yet people with ADD can pay attention, even for long periods of time (it's called "hyperfocusing"), but only to something that excites or interests them. It's a cliché—but true—that "there is no ADD in front of a good video game."

It's also often noted by ADD experts that it's not that ADDers can't pay attention to anything: it's that they pay attention to everything.

A better way to describe the distractibility of ADD is to call it scanning. In a classroom, the child with ADD is the one who notices the janitor mowing the lawn outside the window, when he should be listening to the teacher's lecture on long division. The bug crawling across the ceiling, or the class bully preparing to throw a spitball, are infinitely more fascinating than the teacher's analysis of Columbus' place in history.

While this constant scanning of the environment is a liability in a classroom setting, it may have been a survival skill for our prehistoric ancestors.

Copyright © 1995 by Mythical Intelligence, Inc.

Excerpted from ADD SUCCESS STORIES: A GUIDE TO FULFILLMENT FOR FAMILIES WITH ATTENTION DEFICIT DISORDER by Thom Hartmann. Underwood Books, Inc. ISBN: Hardcover 1-887424-04-0 $24.95, Softcover 1-887424-03-2 $11.95

Thom Hartmann (76702,765) is the Primary Sysop for the ADD Forum on CompuServe and parent of an ADD teenager. He is the founder (along with his wife, Louise) and former Executive Director of the New England Salem Children's Village in Rumney, New Hampshire, a residential treatment facility for children in the White Mountains. He's also the author of ATTENTION DEFICIT DISORDER: A DIFFERENT PERCEPTION published by Underwood/Miller, and FOCUS YOUR ENERGY published by Pocket Books.

A primitive hunter who didn't find that he easily and normally fell into a mental state of constant scanning would be at a huge disadvantage. That flash of motion on the periphery of his vision might be either the rabbit that he needed for lunch, or the tiger or bear hoping to make lunch of him. If he were to focus too heavily on the trail, for example, and therefore miss the other details of his environment, he would either starve or be eaten.

On the other hand, when the agricultural revolution began 12,000 years ago, this scanning turned into a liability for those people whose societies moved from hunting to farming. If the day came when the moon was right, the soil was the perfect moisture, and the crops due to be planted, a farmer couldn't waste his day wandering off into the forest to check out something unusual he noticed: he must keep his attention focused on that task at hand, and not be distracted from it.

Impulsivity has two core manifestations among modern people with ADD. The first is impulsive behavior: the proverbial acting-without-thinking-things-through. Often this takes the form of interrupting others or blurting things out in conversation; other times it's reflected in snap judgments or quick decisions. Another aspect of impulsivity is impatience.

A prehistoric hunter would describe impulsivity as an asset because it provided him with the ability to act on instant decisions, and the willingness to explore new and untested areas. If he were chasing a rabbit through the forest with his spear, and a deer ran by, he wouldn't have time to stop and calculate a risk/benefit analysis: he must make an instant decision about which animal to pursue, and then act on that decision without a second thought.

Thomas Edison eloquently described how his combined distractibility and impulsiveness helped him in his "hunt" for world-transforming inventions. He said, "Look, I start here with the intention of going there" (drawing an imaginary line) "in an experiment, say, to increase the speed of the Atlantic cable; but when I have arrived part way in my straight line, I meet with a phenomenon and it leads me off in another direction, to something totally unexpected."

For a primitive farmer, however, impatience and impulsivity would be a disaster. If he were to go out into the field and dig up the seeds every day to see if they were growing, the crops would die. (The contemporary manifestation of this is the person who can't leave the oven door shut, but has to keep opening it to check how the food's doing, to the detriment of many a soufflé.) A very patient approach, all the way down to the process of picking bugs off plants for hours each day, day after day, would have to be hard-wired into the brain of a farmer. The word "boring" couldn't be in his vocabulary: his brain would have to be built in such a way that it tolerated, or even enjoyed, sticking with something until it was finished.

Restlessness, risk-taking, or, as described by Drs. Hallowell and Ratey, "a restive search for high stimulation," is perhaps the most destructive of the behaviors associated with ADD in contemporary society. It probably accounts for the high percentage of people with ADD among the prison populations, and plays a role in a wide variety of social problems, from the risky driving of a teenager to the infidelity or job-hopping of an adult.

Yet for a primitive hunter, risk and high-stimulation were a necessary part of daily life. If hunters were risk- or adrenaline-averse, they'd never go into the wilds to hunt: for a hunter, the idea of daily risking one's life would have to feel "normal." In fact, the urge to experience risk, the desire for that adrenaline high, would be necessary among the members of a hunting society, because it would propel their members out into the forest or jungle in search of stimulation and dinner.

If a farmer were a risk-taker, however, the results could lead to starvation. Because decisions made by farmers have such long-ranging consequences, their brains must be wired to avoid risks and to carefully determine the most risk-free way of doing anything. If a farmer were to decide to take a chance and plant a new and different crop—ragweed, for example, instead of the wheat that grew so well the previous year—it could lead to tragic dietary problems for the tribe or family.

That genetic predispositions to behavior can be leftover survival strategies from prehistoric times is a theme most recently echoed in the March 27, 1995 *Time* magazine cover story on the brain. It pointed out that craving fat, among some people in parts of the world that experienced periodic famine, would ensure the survival of those who were able to store large quantities of this nutrient under their skin. "But the same tendencies cause mass heart failure when expressed in a fast-food world," the authors point out.

Even the genetic inclination to alcoholism may have positive prehistoric roots, according to evolutionists Randolph Nesse and George Williams in their book WHY WE GET SICK. The persistence of an alcoholic in the face of social, familial, and biological resistance and disaster, they say, reflects an evolutionary tenacity to go after neurochemical rewards despite obstacles. This tenacity may in some way be responsible for the continued growth, survival, and evolution of our species.

So the agricultural revolution brought us two very different types of human societies: farmers and hunter/gatherers. They lived different lives, in different places, and those persons in farming societies with the ADD gene were probably culled out of the gene pool by natural selection. Or they became the warriors for the society, now hunting other humans as tribes came into conflict. In some societies, such as Japan and India, this was even institutionalized into a caste system, and history is replete with anecdotes about the unique personalities of the warrior castes such as the Kshatriya in India and the Samurai in Japan.

Where have all the hunters gone?

If we accept for a moment the possibility that the gene that causes ADD was useful in another time and place, but has become a liability in our modern, agriculture-derived industrial society, then the question arises: why isn't there more of it? How did we reach a point in human evolution where the farmers so massively outnumber the hunters? If the "hunting gene" was useful for the survival of people with it, why have hunting societies largely died out around the world? Why is ADD only seen among 3 to 20 percent of the population (depending on how you measure it and whose numbers you use), instead of 50 percent or some other number?

Recent research from several sources point out how hunting societies are always wiped out by farming societies over time: fewer than 10 percent of hunting society members will normally survive when their culture collides with an agricultural society. And it has nothing to do with the hunter's "attention deficits," or with any inherent superiority of the farmers.

In one study (reported in *Discover*, February 1994), the authors traced the root languages of the peoples living across central Africa. They found that at one time the area was dominated by hunter-gatherers: the Khoisans and the Pygmies. But over a period of several thousand years, virtually all of the Khoisans and Pygmies (the "Hottentots" and the "Bushmen" as they've been referred to in Western literature) were wiped out and replaced by Bantu-speaking farmers. Two entire groups of people were destroyed, rendering them nearly extinct, while the Bantu-speaking farmers flooded across the continent, dominating central Africa.

The reasons for this startling transformation are several:

First, agriculture is more efficient at generating calories than hunting. Because the same amount of land can support up to ten times more people when farming rather than hunting, farming societies generally have roughly ten times the population density of hunting societies. In war, numbers are always an advantage, particularly in these ratios. Few armies in history have survived an onslaught by another army ten times larger.

Second, diseases such as chicken pox, influenza, and measles, which have virtually wiped out vulnerable populations (such as native North and South Americans who died by the thousands when exposed to the diseases of the invading Europeans), began as diseases of domesticated animals. The farmers who were regularly exposed to such diseases developed relative immunities. While they would become ill, these germs usually wouldn't kill them. Those with no prior exposure (and, thus, no immunity), however, would often die. So when farmers encountered hunters, they were killed off just by exposure to the Farmer's diseases.

And finally, agriculture provides physical stability to a culture. The tribe stays in one spot, while their population grows. This provides them with time to specialize in individual jobs: some people become tool- and weapon-makers, others build devices which can be used in war, and others create governments, armies, and kingdoms. This gives farmers a huge technological advantage over hunting societies, which are generally more focused on day-to-day survival issues.

So now we have an answer to the question: "Where have all the hunters gone?"

Most were killed off, from Europe to Asia, from Africa to the Americas. Those who survived were brought into farming cultures either through assimilation, kidnapping, or cultural change, and provide the genetic material that appears in that small percentage of the people with ADD.

Further evidence of the anthropological basis of ADD is seen among the modern survivors of ancient hunting societies.

Cultural anthropologist Jay Fikes, PH.D., points out that members of traditional Native American hunting tribes behave, as a norm, differently from those who have traditionally been farmers. The farmers, such as the Hopi and other Pueblo Indian tribes, are relatively sedate and risk-averse, he says, whereas the hunters, such as the Navajo, are "constantly scanning their environment and more immediately sensitive to nuances. They're also the ultimate risk-takers: they and the Apaches were great raiders and warriors."

A physician who'd recently read my first book, and concluded that he saw proof of the Hunter/farmer concept in his work with some of the Native Americans in Southwest Arizona, dropped me the following unsolicited note over the Internet:

"Many of these descendants of the Athabaskan Indians of Western Canada have never chosen to adapt to farming. They had no written language until an Anglo minister, fairly recently, wrote down their language for the first time. They talk 'heart to heart,' and there is little 'clutter' between you and them when you are communicating. They hear and consider everything you say. They are scanning all the time, both visually and aurally. Time has no special meaning unless it is absolutely necessary (that's something we Anglos have imposed on them). They don't use small talk, but get right to the point, and have a deep understanding of people and the spiritual. And their history shows that they have a love of risk-taking."

Will Krynen, M.D., noted the same differences when he worked for the Canadian government as the doctor for several native North American tribes, and during the years he worked for the Red Cross as a physician in Southeast Asia. After reading my first book, he wrote:

"I've worked among indigenous hunting societies in many parts of the world, from Asia to the Americas. Over and over again I see among their adults and the children that constellation of behaviors we call ADD. In those societies, however, these behaviors are highly adaptive and actually contribute to their societies' success.

"Among the members of the tribes of northern Canada, such as the caribou hunters of the McKenzie Basin, these adaptive characteristics—constantly scanning their environment, quick decision-making (impulsiveness), and a willingness to take risks—contribute every year to the tribe's survival.

"These same behaviors, however, often make it difficult for tribal children to succeed in western schools when we try to impose our western curriculum on them."

But what sent humankind onto the radical social departure from hunting to farming? Few other animals, with the exception of highly organized insects such as ants, have any sort of a society that is based on anything that looks like agriculture.

J. Bronowski, in THE ASCENT OF MAN (Little, Brown 1973), points out that 20,000 years ago every human on earth was a hunter and forager. The most advanced hunting societies had started following wild herd animals, as is still done by modern Laplanders. This had been the basis of human and pre-human society and lifestyle for several million years.

Until 1995, the earliest hard evidence of human activity (and hunting activity at that) came from the Olduvai Gorge in Tanzania, Africa, with fragments of stone tools and weapons that dated back 2.5 million years. More recently, University of Southern California anthropologist Craig Stanford is quoted in the *Chicago Tribune* (reprinted 5/1/95 in the *Atlanta Constitution*) as saying that recent research he conducted in Africa indicates that early hominids may have been tribally hunting as early as 6 million years ago.

So for 6 million years we and our ancestors were hunters, and suddenly, in a tiny moment of time (10,000 years is to 6 million as less than 3 minutes is to a 24-hour day) the entire human race veered in a totally new direction.

The reason, according to Bronowski and many anthropologists, probably has to do with the end of the last ice age, which roughly corresponds to the beginning of the agricultural revolution. (Bronowski and most authorities place the agricultural revolution as occurring roughly 12,000 years ago.) At that time, mutated grasses appeared simultaneously on several continents, probably in response to the sudden and radical change in climate. These grasses were the first high-yield, edible ancestors of modern rice and wheat, and provided the humans who lived near where they appeared with an opportunity to nurture and grow these staple foods.

Those people with the Farmer-like patience to grow the crops evolved into the farming societies, and ridded their ranks of the impulsive, sensation-seeking Hunters among them. Those persons who were not patient enough to wait for rice to grow maintained their hunting tribes, the last remnants of which we see today in a few remaining indigenous peoples on the earth. (The Old Testament, for example, is in large part the story of a nomadic hunting tribe moving through the wrenching process, over several generations, of becoming a settled farming tribe.)

The need to reduce uncertainty

Another aspect of the way ADD plays out in a cultural context could be set in the framework of the need to reduce uncertainty in life, referenced by various psychological theorists from Adler to Jung.

For those Hunters with a highly-variable sense of time, reducing uncertainty in the environment takes the form of acting now, responding immediately to each change in the environment. For those Farmers, however, who experience a linear sense of time, reducing uncertainty takes the form of trying to stabilize things. These people will, as surely as the tide, eventually try to get rid of people who like to change things.

Thus, because Hunter-like people are the agents of change, once the change they create is adopted by the "stables" (Farmers), this latter group will historically isolate them, kill them off, or exile them. Britain did this with the undesirables they sent to America and Australia, and some schools do this socially in ghettoizing ADD children.

Hunters and Farmers in Modern Society

This gives us another insight into the role of the leftover Hunters in our modern society.

Certainly, most of society is set up to reward Farmer-like behavior. Our schools are still based on an agricultural model of long summer vacations left over from times past when the children were needed to bring in the crops. Stability is cherished, but job-hopping and other forms of social instability are viewed as alarm flags to prospective employers or spouses.

The industrial revolution, much like the agricultural revolution, further extended the culture-shift that caused ADD to suddenly fall "outside the template," by introducing mechanization using repetitive (farming) techniques. This helps explain why the "factory" model of modern public schools so often is anathema to ADD children, and why experience-based school environments are so useful for ADD kids.

At first glance, it would seem that being a Farmer in today's society would be very desirable. The checkbook gets balanced, the grass is mowed regularly, and the bolt gets put on the screw at the factory, day in and day out.

But it's often the Hunters who are the instruments of social change and leadership. Societies with few Hunters among them require cataclysmic events to stimulate change.

Japanese society, for example, which had been agricultural for thousands of years, was essentially stagnant until Admiral Perry parked his Black Ships off the coast and threatened war if the Japanese wouldn't let him trade with them.

That signaled the end of a major era in Japanese society. The virtual destruction of Japan during World War II brought about the second great change in their society. It's interesting to note that in the Japanese language there's no word that cleanly translates into "leadership." The notion of standing apart from the crowd, going your own way, and challenging existing institutions is totally alien to Japanese culture.

Virtually all the major changes in that very Farmer-like society were brought about by the invading barbarians (the translation of the Japanese word gaijin, which also means foreigner), and happened from without.

On the other hand, the leader in innovation in the world is the United States. We invented the transistor, although the careful and methodical Japanese refined it. The same applies to radio, television, VCRs, plastics, and on and on. We even invented a form of government which is now duplicated all around the world.

And who are we here in America that we would be so innovative? We are the Hunters: the misfits of British society who were daring and brave and crazy enough to undertake the crossing from Europe to America to conquer a new land. And those Americans not descendants of the first wave of British immigrants or prisoners are the offspring of later adventurers from the rest of Europe, Africa, and Asia.

Society needs its Hunters, no matter how much it tries to suppress them in its institutions and schools. ADD Hunters like Edison and Franklin were responsible for massive social, cultural, and technological change, and even today we find a disproportionate number of high-stimulation- seeking persons among the creative ranks, in every discipline from the arts to politics to the sciences.

For example, Wilson Harrell, former Publisher of *Inc.* magazine and former CEO of the Formula 409 Corporation, and author of the book FOR ENTREPRENEURS ONLY (Career Press, 1994) is one of America's most famous entrepreneurs. After reading the first draft of my book, FOCUS YOUR ENERGY, he wrote:

> For generations, we entrepreneurs have been asking ourselves: "Was I born this way, or was it the circumstances of my childhood that led me to the entrepreneurial life? Was it destiny or accident?" . . .
> [Now we know that] entrepreneurs are entrepreneurs because, down

through the eons of time, we have inherited the Hunter genes of our ancestors. . . .

Until I read Thom's books, I believed that entrepreneurship was inspired by an insatiable desire for freedom. It's so wonderful to know that it's more, much more. That we are born. That we are genetically bound together. That we can and will pass these incredible genes on to our children and their children's children. That, in spite of politicians and Farmer bureaucracies, the entrepreneurial spirit will live on.

Wilson Harrell views ADD as a net positive, in that it sparks the entrepreneurialism which has made our nation great.

In India there also appears to be a very different view of ADD than is conventional in the United States. During the monsoon season of 1993, the week of the Hyderabad earthquake, I took a 12-hour train ride halfway across the subcontinent to visit an obscure town near the Bay of Bengal. In the train compartment with me were several Indian businessmen and a physician, and we had plenty of time to talk as the countryside flew by from sunrise to sunset.

Curious about how they viewed ADD, I said, "Are you familiar with the personality type where people seem to crave stimulation but have a hard time staying with any one thing? They hop from career to career, and sometimes even from relationship to relationship, and never seem to settle down to one thing?"

"Ah, we know this type well," one of the men said, the other three nodding in agreement.

"What do you call it?" I asked. "Very holy," he said. "These are old souls, near the end of their karmic cycle." Again the other three nodded agreement, perhaps a bit more vigorously in response to my startled look.

"Old souls?" I said, thinking that a very odd description for what we call a disorder.

"Yes," the physician said, taking his turn in the conversation. "In our religion, we believe that the purpose of reincarnation is to eventually free oneself from worldly entanglement and desire. In each lifetime we experience certain lessons, until finally we are free of this earth and can merge into the oneness of what you would call God. When a soul is very close to the end of those thousands of incarnations, he must take a few lifetimes and do many, many things, to clean up the little threads left over from his previous lifetimes."

"This is a man very close to becoming enlightened," the first businessman added. "We have great respect for such individuals, although their lives may be difficult."

Another of the businessmen raised a finger and interjected: "But it is the difficulties of such lives that purify the soul." The others nodded agreement.

"In America we consider this a psychiatric disorder," I said. All three looked startled, then laughed.

"In America, you consider our most holy men, our yogis and swamis, to be crazy people, too," said the physician with a touch of sadness in his voice. "So it is with different cultures. We live in different worlds."

In the Hunter/warrior societies of northern India and Europe, religious rituals were developed which would teach focusing and concentration. These include saying the Rosary in the Roman Catholic tradition, with the beads serving to provide a form of biofeedback, constantly reminding the person to not allow their mind to wander. In Hinduism prayer beads called a Mala are often used, which help in Mantra meditation where a single sound (such as "Om") is repeated over and over again.

That the Hunting societies, with their culturally-ingrained prevalence of ADD-like behaviors and highly distractible people, would create concentrative religious rituals to teach them to focus makes perfect sense. Focusing is something which doesn't come naturally to their people, so it's evolved as a learned behavior in the culture.

In traditionally agricultural societies, however, the meditative techniques are quite different.

From Trungpa Rimpoche and Oesel Tensig I learned Vipassana, or mindfulness, and practiced the technique for ten to fifteen hours a day at Karme Choeling. In this Tibetan Buddhist system, the goal is not to concentrate the mind on one point, but to empty the mind and be fully aware. It's practiced with the eyes open; whenever a thought arises which may become the focus of concentration, we visualized it as a bubble we would mentally reach out and pop as we noted to ourselves that we were thinking. This released the thought and returned the mind to empty awareness.

The goal of this form of meditation is not focus, but its opposite. As Berkeley-based Chilean psychiatrist Claudio Naranjo wrote in his 1971 essay *On the Psychology of Meditation*, Vipassana and Zen represent "the negative way" form of meditation, and come from the East. Mantra, rosary, mandala, and prayer represent the opposite, Western "concentrative or absorptive meditation."

Thus, the agricultural societies of southern Asia, farmers for millennia with a highly focused society and people, naturally developed cultural rituals which train awareness and distractibility. These systems teach them to resist their natural impulse to concentrate their attention.

A view ranging from world history to entrepreneurship to religion and culture shows the distinctions between Hunters and Farmers. And we see that the institutions of contemporary Western society are rooted in the agricultural/ industrial model, making misfits of Hunters. However, there's room for both Hunters and Farmers in this world, and, for both to succeed, we each must learn to honor the other, and not try to position either as being somehow superior or inferior.

Is ADD a "Disorder"?

Viewing ADD from this historical view presents us with both risks and opportunities.

The primary opportunity is to use a model or paradigm for describing ADD that's not disease-based and doesn't imply brain damage or what many children interpret as some type of retardation. This is particularly useful for adolescents, for whom issues of self-esteem are crucial. Before any form of therapy can work, from counseling to medication, a person must have hope; this model restores self-esteem, thus empowering individuals to change.

The risk is that some in our society will use the Hunter/farmer model as a rationale to deny help to those with ADD. "If it's not a disorder but just a difference," they'll say, "then why should we pay for special programs in our schools, and why should our insurance pay for medications and therapy?"

But acknowledging a possible source for ADD in our gene pool is not the same thing as denying the damage that ADD can do, or the challenges it presents to an individual in modern society. There's nothing incompatible with a child or adult declaring their "Hunter ancestry" and also taking medication or getting therapy. Those afflicted with sickle-cell anemia don't avoid therapy just because they're less likely to get malaria if they were to return to Africa. If any sort of an adaptation is a liability in modern society, we must treat it as such, in a straightforward fashion, without trying to rationalize about or avoid discussing the modern maladaptiveness of it.

In this context, the Hunter/farmer model gives us new insights into why certain medications work to reduce the "symptoms" of ADD, and provides models to restructure school and work environments to better accommodate the unique needs of people with ADD.

Paradigm or Science?

Whether the Hunter/farmer model as a way of viewing ADD is ultimately demonstrated to be good science or not may be less than vital. For the moment, it provides us with a way to view this condition that leaves self-esteem intact, accurately models and predicts how and why medications are helpful, and reframes our techniques for working with Hunter-type individuals in schools, the workplace, and in relationships.

Like the (as yet unproved) electron-flow model for explaining electricity, the Hunter/farmer paradigm allows us to get our hands around a phenomenon, to wield it to our benefit, and to empower the lives of people.

If ADD is part of our genetic heritage, it cannot be an excuse for a person's failings. It's merely an explanation, one that then provides the first steps toward overcoming those obstacles which, in the past, so often caused failure.

A New Theory of ADHD
by Russell A. Barkley, PH.D.

T HE CURRENT CLINICAL CONSENSUS HOLDS that ADHD is comprised of three primary symptoms: inattention, impulsivity, and hyperactivity. Inattention is often stressed as a primary feature of the disorder. Yet research on ADHD often finds that inattention is not reliably found in children with ADHD or does not distinguish the condition from other psychopathological disorders. This is not to say that those with ADHD are not observed to be "off-task" more, lower in persistence of effort, and less able to continue responding to assigned work—they surely are. It is to say that formal laboratory measures of various components of attention do not reliably find the problems of those with ADHD to be in the realm of attention. Instead, the most consistent findings show a primary deficit in behavioral or response inhibition, the ability to delay responses, or the tolerance for delay intervals within tasks. Thus, the primary component of ADHD is more one of disinhibition or poor delay of response than inattention. Most investigators working in the area of ADHD with whom
I have spoken seem to agree with this assessment of the extant literature and its conclusions.

Assuming for now that poor response inhibition or inability to delay response is the major hallmark of ADHD, how does this explain the myriad problems those with ADHD encounter in their academic, social, familial, emotional, occupational, and other domains of adaptive functioning? Why is such a deficit so debilitating to the successful adaptive performance of the individual in meeting the demands of daily social life? And how would this explain the poor organization and planning, poor sense of time management, deficits in mental arithmetic computation, delayed self-directed speech, immature social communication with peers, heightened emotionality, diminished problem-solving ability, limited sense of self- awareness, and delayed moral development, to name but a few of the deficits noted in ADHD children?

From THE ADHD REPORT, Volume 1, Number 5, 1993, pp. 1-3 Used by permission. Copyright © 1994 Guilford Publications, 72 Spring St, NY, NY 10012. 1-800-365-7006.

Russell A. Barkley, PH.D. is Director of Psychology and Professor of Psychiatry and Neurology at the University of Massachusetts Medical Center. He is the author of four books on ADD, including ATTENTION DEFICIT HYPERACTIVITY DISORDER: A HANDBOOK FOR DIAGNOSIS AND TREATMENT *(Guilford, 1990) and* RAISING A CHILD WITH ADHD: A PARENT'S HANDBOOK *(Guilford, 1995). Dr. Barkley can be reached at the University of Massachusetts, Dept. of Psychiatry, 55 Lake Avenue, Worcester, MA 01655. For information on The ADHD Report, contact Guilford Publications at 1-800-365-7006.*

I believe that an answer may rest within a theory proposed by Jacob Bronowski (1967/1977) over 25 years ago concerning the evolution of human language from other forms of primate social communication that led to several unique features of human language and cognitive abilities. [Bronowski was a distinguished mathematician, physicist, philosopher, and science writer most widely known for his book THE ASCENT OF MAN and the public television show based on this work in the late 1970s.] Like any new and useful theory, this one should better explain the findings in the literature on ADHD, accounting for findings not easily explained by existing theoretical models, such as those stressing attention. Moreover, it should direct our research and clinical attention to new areas worthy of exploration not previously thought relevant to ADHD. I believe that my extrapolation of Bronowski's theory to ADHD meets these requirements and provides a deeper understanding of the difficulties faced by those with ADHD in meeting the demands of daily adaptive functioning. It also seems to suggest that the impact of ADHD on daily living may be more pervasive than was once believed.

Bronowski's theory of delayed responding and language

Bronowski cogently argued that a major advancement in the evolution of human communication arose initially as an increase in the simple capacity to delay responses to a signal, message, or event. The human capacity to delay responding vastly exceeds that of our nearest primate relatives by a quantum leap. This capacity to inhibit initial reactions to events, arising primarily from the expansion of the frontal lobes, permitted the later development of four uniquely human mental abilities: separation of affect, prolongation, internalization, and reconstitution. If ADHD represents a relative deficit in the development of delayed responding or response inhibition in the individual, as I believe, then these four mental processes should also be less proficient and less likely to guide or inform ongoing adaptive behavior than in those not deficient. The evidence that they are is quite compelling.

Separation of Affect

Bronowski argued that the delay in human responding permits the referral of the incoming signal, message, or event to more than one brain system at a time, allowing simultaneous processing of the event by multiple reference centers—the primary advantage of a large brain, he proposed. In so doing, humans are able to split the signal separately into its affective charge and its information or content. This capacity to separate feeling from fact, affect from content, and form from substance, permits humans to deal with the content of the message alone. All other species respond to these two features of a signal or message immediately and in total. Affect and content are one in the signal and in the response to it. In humans, the response delay permits the splitting of both the signal and the response to it into the separate features of content and affective charge. The ability to separate affect from informational content in signals and response permits humans the power of objectivity, perspective, logic, and rationality, as we ordinarily think of these attributes. It also ultimately underlies the human capacity for conducting science.

If those with ADHD are less able to delay or inhibit responses to momentary signals or events, we should find them less able to utilize this downstream capacity for the separation of affect and thus less likely to have it inform and guide their ongoing adaptive behavior.

They should react more often to the affective charge of a message or event than do others, and respond with greater intensity and range of affect as well. In short, they should prove more emotionally reactive to social situations than those without ADHD.

They should also prove less objective in their assessment of the situation, more self-centered (less perspicacious), and less "scientific" or logical in their reactions to social situations, particularly those imbued with more affective signals than usual. I and many others have been struck by just these social limitations in the behavior of those with ADHD seen in clinical situations. Yet minimal research exists on the issue.

Prolongation

Bronowski reasoned that response delay also permits the signal to be more strongly and symbolically fixed mentally (working memory) through language and imagery. This has the effect of sustaining the mental existence of the stimulus during the delay long after the external event has passed into nonexistence in real time. This symbolic fixing of the signal permits time to refer or compare it with memory of other such events from which emerges our sense of past or hindsight.

From this referencing backward in time and the manipulation of our recall of these past events in working memory derive our imagination and our sense of the future. The latter likely arises from our use of past events in memory to conjecture hypothetical futures. The consideration of such hypothetical futures leads to the formation of plans that propose action at a future time. Through our communication with others we can then exchange such proposals or messages for future action—an ability seen in no other species.

To summarize, the delay in responding permits a stronger, more lasting mental fixing of the signal from which springs hindsight, imagination, forethought, and our general sense of time—capacities apparently unique to our species.

Again, my extension of this theory to ADHD would indicate that those with the disorder should be less proficient in the utilization of these capacities in view of their inability to delay responding. Failing to delay precludes the adequate usage of these mental abilities to glean information than can inform or guide ongoing adaptive behavior.

After all, what is the point of using such capacities if the response to the signal or event is already released? It is too little, too late to guide adaptive behavior. If true, my application of this theory to ADHD points to a diminished sense of, or window on, time and its utilization in guiding behavior, a diminished sense of hindsight and forethought and their governance of current behavior, and a diminished capacity in those with ADHD to fix signals in working memory. Could these deficiencies explain why those with ADHD show less learning from past experience (hindsight), greater forgetfulness (fixing of the signal), less concern for future events, and a diminished sense of time in the guidance of ongoing adaptive behavior? Might it also explain the diminished capacity for performing mental calculations? I know of no research on these issues yet am impressed with how often I find such problems in the clinical presentation of my cases and how responsive ADHD adults are to my inquiring about them.

Internalization

Bronowski theorized that the imposition of a delay between signal and response permits humans to use language not only as a form of communication with others, as it is used by other species, but as a means of communicating with oneself. In this process language is turned on the self and eventually internalized, permitting us the powers of reflection, rule formation, and the governance of behavior by such rules (plans, propositions for action) and, more generally, self-control.

This capacity for rule creation and rule-guided behavior, as Steve Hayes (1989) argued, frees humans up from the control of behavior by the moment (contingency-shaped behavior) or immediate context, and brings their behavior under the control of agnate, rules, plans or proposals for action. In so doing, behavior becomes less variable, less subject to control by spurious or superstitious momentary consequences, more future oriented, less emotional (due to less exposure to contingency-shaping that results in more emotional reactions), and better suited to mediating long delays in schedules of consequences (deferred gratification). We can exchange these rules with others, providing the foundation for the transmission of culture (morals, mores, norms, policies, laws, and the wisdom acquired from past generations) to new generations.

Applying Bronowski's theory to those with ADHD suggests that their inability to delay responding should result in less mature self-directed speech, diminished reliance on internalized language to control behavior, less utilization of reflection, diminished control of behavior by proposals for action (rules and instructions), especially in reference to a future time, and poorer self-control in general. That moral development would be more delayed in those with ADHD is an obvious consequence as well. Behavior in those with ADHD should be more variable, more controlled by momentary context, more emotional and contingency-shaped, less directed to future consequences, and less able to mediate delays between responding and later consequences. Again, this seems to fit with research findings on self-directed speech, rule governance, and moral development in children with ADHD, and squares beautifully with what I see clinically as well.

Reconstitution

Finally, Bronowski proposed that from the delay in responding and the internalization of language it permits, we derive the abilities of analysis and synthesis. That is, we can deconstruct events and signals into parts, progressively redistributing them into particulars (objects, properties, actions) and progressively generalize their hortative content (proposals for action). We can then reassemble these particulars into entirely new outgoing messages. This not only underlies our dramatically superior powers of generative language but also of analysis and creativity (synthesis)—powers vastly expanded through this process of reconstitution.

My generalization of this model to ADHD instructs us to consider whether those with ADHD are less able to utilize these capacities in daily ongoing adaptive behavior than others. Are they less analytical, less capable of problem-solving on demand, and less given to synthesis or less creativity in coping with daily events? I am not sure, and minimal research exists on the issue. It seems highly worth a look.

Conclusion

My adaptation of Bronowski's theory of delayed responding to ADHD, in which an impairment in inhibition likely exists, seems to provide a more elegant explanation of existing research findings, a deeper appreciation for the pervasive impact of the disorder on daily life, and exciting suggestions for numerous future research explorations. Mind you, it is not that those with ADHD are incapable of separation of affect, prolongation, internalization, and reconstitution, but that the inability to delay response results in less utilization of, and reliance upon, these downstream mental abilities in informing and guiding ongoing responses. Improve the capacity for delay and these downstream mental functions should act more proficiently, providing forward information to guide ongoing adaptive behavior. Evidence from recent studies (Berk & Potts, 1991) on stimulant medication suggests just such an improvement in these mental abilities when inhibition is increased by medication. And so it is not that those with ADHD do not think before they act so much as they act before permitting time to think. Rabelais was right: "Everything comes to those who can wait."

References

Berk, L. E., & Potts, M. K. (1991). *"Development and functional significance of private speech among attention-deficit hyperactivity disorder and normal boys."* JOURNALS OF ABNORMAL CHILD PSYCHOLOGY, 19, 357-377.

Bronowski, J. (1967). *"Human and animal languages."* TO HONOR ROMAN JAKOBSON (Vol. 1). The Hague, Netherlands: Mouton & Co.

Bronowski, J. (1977). *"Human and animal languages."* A SENSE OF THE FUTURE (pp. 104 – 131). Cambridge, MA: MIT Press.

Hayes, S. (1989). RULE-GOVERNED BEHAVIOR: COGNITION, CONTINGENCIES AND INSTRUCTIONAL CONTROL. New York: Plenum.

Rhythms of the Racing Brain
by Carla Berg Nelson, Sysop, CompuServe ADD Forum

Introduction

Ask someone with ADD if his problem is getting too turned on or too unplugged, and he will probably scratch his head. In terms of things that excite him, he is prone to be over-engaged, over-aroused, overactive, or "hyper." In terms of things that leave him cold, he is under-aroused, inattentive, and "hypoactive" instead. In this sense, everyone with ADD experiences both under and over-attentiveness, both under and over-arousal, and both hypo- and hyperactivity.

It's as if the engines in our brains came factory-equipped with only two options: full speed ahead or full stop. We spend our lives careening between going too fast and too slow. We can only zoom in or zone out, turned on or turned off.

Harvard physicians Edward Hallowell and John Ratey in their book DRIVEN TO DISTRACTION were the first to clearly describe the stimulus-driven dynamic that makes us this way. Whatever the differences across the ADD spectrum, a "pull to the stimulus" propels us all. Without this stimulus fuel, our brains sputter and stall.

All brains respond to stimulation, of course. What sets us ADD "Hunters" apart from our non-ADD "Farmer" counterparts is how much we need, how often we need it, and what happens if we can't find it. Our quest for stimulation is as potent as an addiction, both in how it drives us and what it takes to change it.

We are lucky to live at a time when it is finally becoming clear how potent this force can be, when it is being discussed that our roving minds have as much to do with the nature of our brains as the nature of our characters.

But less clear and less often discussed is what distinguishes one type of ADD from another. Many ADDers—and their physicians—still don't see that ADD can be a problem of thinking too much as well as thinking too little, that people like us can be driven by hyperactive bodies and hyperactive minds.

Part One: The Limits of our Labels

If there ever was a clinical label open to misunderstanding, it is "Attention Deficit." Throughout its genesis as a diagnostic entity—from "Minimal Brain Damage" (1950s) to "Hyperkinetic Disorder of Childhood" (1960s) to the current "Attention Deficit and/or Hyperactivity Disorder" (1990s)—clinicians have been in conflict about what it means and where it applies and the public has been confused.

The child who can't sit still. The adult who can't concentrate. The chronically preoccupied who procrastinate. Overactive bodies with underactive minds. Underactive bodies with overactive minds. Any and all the above have been called "ADD" by different clinicians at different times.

Should this label apply to everyone who suffers from chronic inattention or only to some? The continually conflicting experts still haven't come to consensus. And the public is still confused.

For decades, ADD was seen as a combination of physical overactivity and mental underactivity that restless young males were supposed to outgrow. Over time it became clear that a large number of children, both male and female, shared the same problems with inattention—even if they did not share the same outwardly active bodies. As the clinical lens widened, it also became clear the symptoms did not just disappear when childhood ended.

ADD "without hyperactivity" was added to the Diagnostic and Statistical Manual (DSM-III) in 1980, and that designation evolved into the term "Predominantly Inattentive" in 1994 (DSM-IV). With this wider view, increasing numbers of children and adults are being diagnosed and treated.

Thus official wisdom now says an ADDer may be hyperactive and inattentive, or just inattentive. But you have only to look at my two offspring, both diagnosed and both helped by stimulant medication, to know the ADD spectrum does not "just" end there.

TWO SCATTERED LIVES

There is little question my son and my daughter both qualify as "chronic inattentives." Their lives are full of scatter: Forgotten assignments, lost possessions, horribly messy rooms, horribly messy binders. Nothing is finished unless you remind (or threaten)—and as often as not, not then. Even though able and willing, both struggled with incompletion and failure at school starting with the first homework assignment. Reward, penalty, pleasure, pain, none of it made much difference. Year after year, the scatter grew.

With a such long history of under-attentive restlessness and such a clear gap between capability and performance, both my two were rather easily diagnosed after I finally learned about ADD and sought out an experienced specialist. But in every other aspect, their paths diverge. As much as they are alike, they couldn't be more different in processing styles and temperaments, even though they both have the same "Non-hyperactive-Inattentive" diagnosis.

She is super-sensitive; he is super-mellow. She locks onto thoughts and won't let go. He rarely locks on to anything except high stimulation play. It takes an Act of Congress to change her mind. He usually can be persuaded by a smile. Both of them must pedal hard to get their brains in gear, but once engaged, her mind zooms into overdrive while he has to continue to push his to reach cruising speed and keep pushing to stay there. She struggles to gear down and switch her focus to something less absorbing. He struggles to focus on anything that requires extended thinking. Yet they both register well to the right on the bell curve of intellect.

Beyond their inattentive behaviors, the only core symptom these two really share is being stimulus-driven. Neither can sustain an effort without a source of incredibly keen engagement. But everything else about how they operate, including response to medication, says they come to that end by different routes.

Millions who look like my under-focusing son are being diagnosed and helped with medication and accommodations at work or school. Untold numbers of adults and children who look like my over-focusing daughter are being told "not ADD" and turned away, or told they're "only" depressive and given prescriptions that may worsen their attentional problems. Unless, that is, they find a savvy specialist who already knows over-focusing and under-focusing can both be shades of ADD.

Goodness knows how many millions more fall in the middle, like me, their mother, a mix of his temperament and her processing style; over-focused cognitively, but under-focused everywhere else.

Untold numbers of people like me who are also told "not ADD," and advised to "try harder," or "try therapy." Unless, that is, they also find a savvy specialist who knows that continuous cigarettes, coffee and colas may serve as self-medicating stimulant substitutes; someone who already grants the whole of what the DSM implies.

ZOOMING OUT FOR A WIDE-ANGLE VIEW

I've spent three years focusing on attention deficits, listening to and learning from countless personal stories, assisting ADDers around the country as a sysop (system or forum operator) on CompuServe's ADD Forum, exposed to expert opinions of all stripes, from the most conservative to the most radical, reading popular books and medical texts and studies old and new, and comparing it all to what I learned at Berkeley.

It took all that time and all that input before I was willing to say that the constellation of attentional styles I saw in my family might reflect something more than our personal differences. By then, I'd seen the same patterns countless times in thousands of case histories.

I researched and queried until I could explain what I observed. I took off the clinical labels to look at the process of thinking itself. That developed into a system for modeling the speed and strength of our processing styles and the interplay of different stimulus sources. (This paradigm will be presented in a separate series of more "technical" papers.) Once I reapplied clinical labels, I saw my diagrams had been depicting an ebb and flow of brain activity driven by the interplay of attention and arousal. Then I began to chart the effects of over and under-arousal combined with over- and under-focusing.

Bit by bit, a different vision of ADD came into view. It was not a fixed spectrum along a scale of either physical or mental activity, but a range of inattentive states driven by the interaction of attention and arousal; a dynamic, sometimes volatile, mental state that shifted its weight between "overthinking" and "overdoing" depending on the nature of the person and the nature of the activity.

In a very real sense, it is both an attention deficit and an attention surplus. Whether it represents too much or too little focus depends on the angle you choose.

Small wonder patients (and professionals) have been confused.

PART TWO: Toward a 'Unified Theory' of ADD?

SPEEDING BODIES AND MINDS

I agree with the clinicians who find "over- and under-focusing" a very useful way to depict the breadth of ADD, because it makes it clear that "inattention" can result from thinking too much as well as thinking too little. The harder you focus on a single thing, the less you attend to everything else, while the less focused you are, the less you attend to everything in general. Thus you can be persistently inattentive from either over- or under- focusing and thus do over- and under-attentiveness both produce attention deficits.

In simpler terms, you could say the under-focused are propelled by racing bodies, while the over-focused are driven by speeding minds. One is fueled by the physical stimulus of action or sensation, the other is propelled by the cerebral stimulus of ideas or emotions.

Both types are run by racing brains that take constant infusions of highly charged stimulus fuel—that's what makes them both ADD. But each takes a different kind of propellant to energize. One uses the body to power the mind; the other uses the mind to power the body:

1. The Speeding Body: Kinetic Energy
Do you need action or danger to keep your attention tuned in? If so, it may be that your racing ADD brain is powered by "kinetic" energy—the energy of mo-

tion. You are quick to move, but slow to ponder. Overactive kinetically, compelled to keep moving, you struggle to stay plugged in to any task that requires sustained cerebral "thought energy." If it is hard to switch off your body and turn on your mind, you may be this mentally "under-focused" type.

2. The Speeding Mind: Cerebral Energy
Are you quick to think but slow to move? Prone to ponder too much and do too little? If so, your racing brain may be powered by "cerebral" energy, the energy of thought, which means your most powerful stimulus fuel comes from ideas and emotions. Overactive mentally, compelled to keep thinking, your struggle is to find the "oomph" to follow through, or to detach and switch your focus to something else. If you find it hard to turn off your ideas or turn down your feelings, you may be this mentally "over-focused" type.

A State of Flux in our Brains
It is our tendency to be chronically over- or under-engaged in both our bodies and minds, expressed as too much or too little attention and too much or too little activity, that is our common core symptom. This swing of attention, this flux of excess mental and physical energies, is what sets us apart and makes us feel different. The flux itself makes us ADD.

Prior efforts to categorize the hues of ADD have tended to emphasize either the body (hyperactive) or the mind (inattentive). But to see the whole spectrum of possibilities that appear in real life, we must consider what happens in both our minds and our bodies at the same time. Only then does it become apparent that attention deficits can result from either mental or physical hyperactivity.

People on both ends of the spectrum can be restless, distractible and inattentive to a disabling degree thus fulfilling what is sometimes called the "Holy Trinity" of the diagnosing manual. Both are equally ADD. But they arrive at that state from opposite directions.

All ADDers share a compelling, perhaps even insatiable, need for high arousal to keep their brains switched on. But the racing body of the under-focused type arouses kinesthetically, while the racing minds of the over-focused type are powered by cerebral stimulation. In clinical terms, you could say this means they are prone to hypercerebration or hyperkinesthesia.

Being physically overactive, the under-focused type, when very aroused, lean toward excess movement (hyperkinesis). The mentally overactive (hypercerebral), are compelled to engage their minds instead. Over-aroused, they can become what you might call "hyper-emotive" or "hyper-cognitive," locked on to feelings or ideas.

Some ADDers experience both physical and mental over-activity; they are chronically over-focused and over-aroused at the same time. But the racing minds of the over-focused tend to be hypersensate instead of hyperkinetic.

A Collection of Missing Links?

Physician Marcel Kinsbourne of Harvard has written that the hypersensitive shade of over-focusing may be the "missing link on the spectrum between autism and normality." He is not the only expert to have considered links between ADD and other pathologies.

Other clinicians have speculated about connections with dyslexia and other learning disorders, as well as psychiatric disorders such as depression, traumatic stress, obsessive-compulsiveness, opposition-defiance and manic-depression. Many have also noted how often ADD occurs with the tics and compulsions of Tourette's Syndrome.

I suspect they all may be correct, in a sense. ADD, as I see it, is a condition of flux provoked by extremes of mental and physical energy, a core perturbation of internal equilibrium that may ripple out into other disorders depending on the rest of a person's biology and life experience.

That's not to say I think everyone with ADD is a "pale shade" of mentally ill or a pale shade of autistic, just that it seems very likely there are some common physiological roots. Which roots are involved for a given individual, and whether they branch into other pathologies, depends on where that person stands on the entire grid of ADD.

Laid out whole, I believe the entire ADD spectrum is exactly that—a grid, a matrix of possibilities based on different combinations of different types of over- and underactivity. That grid just might represent the intersection of several spectrum disorders and be a collection of "missing links."

Three Types of ADD

When I began to sort and compare ADD subtypes, it seemed to me there were two hues of hyperactivity—physical and mental—with over- and under-focusing at opposite poles. But Kinsbourne's account of a subtype that was over-focused to the extreme was one puzzle piece that helped me to see there are actually three shades of ADD—three different attentive types: under-focused, over-focused plus a chronically "hyper-focused" type.

Choosing labels to name these possibilities and illustrate their differences wasn't easy. But since attention is most often viewed in terms of mental energy, as a cognitive function, I chose to contrast the three in terms of their cerebral activity.

If hyper-focused is one extreme on a scale of cerebral energy, it makes sense to call the other end hypofocused. In between these poles, there is a mixed-focus type with an "ON/OFF" bipolar quality that switches between thinking too much and thinking too little in response to arousal. After I modeled these three, Tom Allen, a forum member and an EEG specialist, told me about three similar patterns seen in the brain waves of ADDers: one with a mind that gets stuck "ON", one that gets stuck in "OFF" and a third that switches between "ON" and "OFF."

Busy brains take flight

To see which type applies to specific individuals, you must look more closely at their styles and behaviors to see if they are wrestling with an overactive mind or body, or both. Below is a more detailed description of each type and highlights of some of their challenges.

Type 1: Hypofocus "Impulsive Explorer"

Excitement seeking engagement: In terms of cognitive energy, the under-focused Type 1 appears under-aroused and hard to engage. But when it comes to pleasure or play, they are ready to get up and go. They have pent-up excitement looking for a place to happen. Even if not hyperkinetic in the clinical sense, their strongest stimulus source is kinesthetic. Engagement is virtually effortless when it involves rapid activity or bodily sensation. If excited, they are also classic cases of impulsivity, prone to act without thinking first. Russell Barkley has described this inability to delay response as being "disinhibited."

Cognitive amplification required: Impulsive Explorers may rarely read books unless pressed, but that's not to say they are not intellectually curious. They may be highly curious, even fanciful (like the cartoon strip "Calvin & Hobbes") or mischievous (like Dennis The Menace). But only with intense interest or rapid activity can they make their brains sit still to input much detail. Without keen engagement of some sort, there is not enough "stimulus gain" to overcome weak cerebral focus, and without that big stimulus push they can't focus their thinking, even if they want to comply. This chronic struggle to sustain cerebral activity is what defines them as "under-focused."

Rapid, intense sensation-seekers: Time and again, I've seen the same pattern in forum members—intelligent, curious folk who quickly fade unless the pace is quick and the stimulation lively. It might be the pleasure of praise, the tension of conflict, the bounce of laughter or the excitement of drama, but it takes a steady flow of keen sensation to keep them tuning in. It's as if any cognitive activity needs to be amplified to overtake the kinetic energy that propels their minds to keep moving. If I remove the physiological labels and think in metaphors, I imagine this type as a bumble bee, a whirring hum of excited brain energy held aloft by the speed of its wings.

(Continued on overleaf)

The chart below is a summary of the three focusing styles in both "technical" and "plain English" terms:

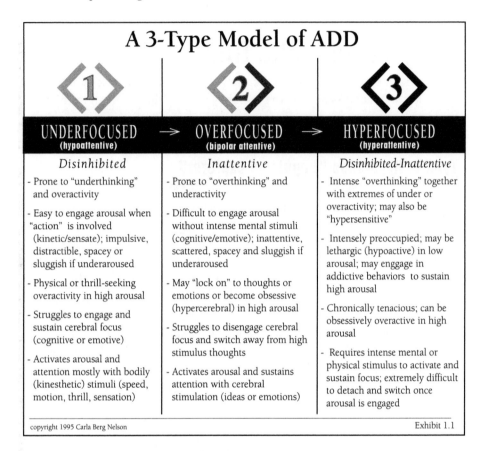

A 3-Type Model of ADD

⟨1⟩	⟨2⟩	⟨3⟩
UNDERFOCUSED → (hypoattentive)	OVERFOCUSED → (bipolar attentive)	HYPERFOCUSED (hyperattentive)
Disinhibited	*Inattentive*	*Disinhibited-Inattentive*
- Prone to "underthinking" and overactivity	- Prone to "overthinking" and underactivity	- Intense "overthinking" together with extremes of under or overactivity; may also be "hypersensitive"
- Easy to engage arousal when "action" is involved (kinetic/sensate); impulsive, distractible, spacey or sluggish if underaroused	- Difficult to engage arousal without intense mental stimuli (cognitive/emotive); inattentive, scattered, spacey and sluggish if underaroused	- Intensely preoccupied; may be lethargic (hypoactive) in low arousal; may enggage in addictive behaviors to sustain high arousal
- Physical or thrill-seeking overactivity in high arousal	- May "lock on" to thoughts or emotions or become obsessive (hypercerebral) in high arousal	- Chronically tenacious; can be obsessively overactive in high arousal
- Struggles to engage and sustain cerebral focus (cognitive or emotive)	- Struggles to disengage cerebral focus and switch away from high stimulus thoughts	- Requires intense mental or physical stimulus to activate and sustain focus; extremely difficult to detach and switch once arousal is engaged
- Activates arousal and attention mostly with bodily (kinesthetic) stimuli (speed, motion, thrill, sensation)	- Activates arousal and sustains attention with cerebral stimulation (ideas or emotions)	
copyright 1995 Carla Berg Nelson		Exhibit 1.1

THREE TYPES MIX IN A MATRIX

All of us with ADD know our attention fades when we are understimulated. Our overactive parts become less active and our underactive parts become even more sluggish. This is what lies beneath our hyper- and hypoactivity.

Arousal is both an internal and an external force. It comes from within as a result of our brain biology, and from without, as a result of the environment. Some of us are easily aroused; others require considerable effort. But, being ADD, all of us need high arousal in order to sustain our efforts. ADDers who are predisposed to low arousal by their biology are especially dependent on their environments to provide the stimulus push they need to sustain activity. These low arousers may appear chronically lethargic. Those who are predisposed to high arousal, on the other hand, may find it easy to find stimulation, but live their lives bouncing from one high-stim activity to the next.

Type 2: Mixed Focus "Restless Seeker"

Engagement seeking excitement: Where an Impulsive Explorer needs to dampen arousal to sustain focus, a Restless Seeker, or Type 2, must amplify his in order to activate. This type is specially prone to chronic under-engagement. But when he does find something stimulating to captivate his wanting-to-be-active mind, he can rapidly swing from inattention to over- focusing. From a cerebral point of view, his problem is with sustaining arousal more than sustaining attention, for once he engages, his mind zooms into overdrive, so much so he may get "stuck," unable to think about anything else but the idea or emotion at hand.

A push-me-pull-me bipolarity: Being arousal-driven, the attentions of a Restless Seeker are especially prone to be what clinicians call "context-dependent," or contingent on the environment. Under-aroused, they space out; over-aroused, they can't unhook their thoughts. This constant push and pull between extremes of mental over- and underactivity makes this type "bipolar" in its cerebral energy, as shown by the marked contrast in behavior at different levels of engagement. Under-aroused or understimulated, the Type 2.1 is a persistent procrastinator, paralyzed by boredom. Over-aroused or over-stimulated, you see the Type 2.3 (or what Lynn Weiss also calls a "conscientious controller") whose persevering tenacity on highly charged issues shades closer to the obsessiveness of a chronically hyper-focused Type 3.

Inconsistently compulsive: The drive of a Restless Seeker is subject to interruption as soon as arousal fades. To keep arousal amplified, this type is also especially prone to "self-stimulate" with conflict or worry. The Type 2.1, or the Persistently Preoccupied Procrastinator, is the hardest to arouse and engage, and is the least attentive of the Restless Seekers. The absent-minded professor or the preoccupied poet with writer's block could both be this type. The Type 2.2 Restless Seeker, nicknamed the Compulsive Creator, is in between. Also compulsively driven, but less easily aroused, he is more likely to channel excessive energy into being overextended, instead of over-anxious. The Compulsive Creator is often over-invested in career, causes or hobbies to keep arousal raised, and may achieve a great deal professionally yet still be a persistent procrastinator everywhere else. A very aroused Type 2.3, the "Inconsistent Perfectionist," may exhibit perfectionism from intense over-focusing, yet lack the kinetic energy to follow through consistently, and thus is vulnerable to chronic self-defeat and frustration. When I think of a Restless Seeker metaphorically, I see a butterfly, an ebb and flow of fast and slow motion that rises and falls, flutters, then rests.

(Continued on overleaf)

The matrix below depicts this range of possibilities by describing each of the three types at different stages of engagement, from Level 1 (low arousal) to Level 3 (hyperarousal). Thus Level 1.1 depicts a Type 1 who is under-aroused and underactive, 1.2 shows increased arousal with over-activity, and 1.3 depicts a hyperaroused, hyperactive Type 1.

Because arousal is generated both from within and without, shading the types in degrees of intensity produces a model that is both fixed and dynamic. It is both a picture of where you stand and where you might go. It depicts how we tend to be in "native mode" in response to the "default settings" in our brains, and how we may behave as we become more excited and engaged in response to stimulation.

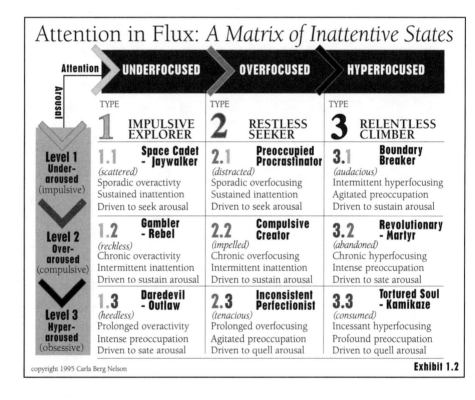

Attention in Flux: *A Matrix of Inattentive States*

Attention →	UNDERFOCUSED	OVERFOCUSED	HYPERFOCUSED
Arousal ↓	TYPE **1** IMPULSIVE EXPLORER	TYPE **2** RESTLESS SEEKER	TYPE **3** RELENTLESS CLIMBER
Level 1 Under-aroused (impulsive)	**1.1** Space Cadet - Jaywalker *(scattered)* Sporadic overactivty Sustained inattention Driven to seek arousal	**2.1** Preoccupied Procrastinator *(distracted)* Sporadic overfocusing Sustained inattention Driven to seek arousal	**3.1** Boundary Breaker *(audacious)* Intermittent hyperfocusing Agitated preoccupation Driven to sustain arousal
Level 2 Over-aroused (compulsive)	**1.2** Gambler - Rebel *(reckless)* Chronic overactivity Intermittent inattention Driven to sustain arousal	**2.2** Compulsive Creator *(impelled)* Chronic overfocusing Intermittent inattention Driven to sustain arousal	**3.2** Revolutionary - Martyr *(abandoned)* Chronic hyperfocusing Intense preoccupation Driven to sate arousal
Level 3 Hyper-aroused (obsessive)	**1.3** Daredevil - Outlaw *(heedless)* Prolonged overactivity Intense preoccupation Driven to sate arousal	**2.3** Inconsistent Perfectionist *(tenacious)* Prolonged overfocusing Agitated preoccupation Driven to quell arousal	**3.3** Tortured Soul - Kamikaze *(consumed)* Incessant hyperfocusing Profound preoccupation Driven to quell arousal

copyright 1995 Carla Berg Nelson   **Exhibit 1.2**

The matrix was created by plotting a scale of attention and arousal together. As you move down the side, you see the effects of increasing arousal, from Level 1 to Level 3. Moving across the top of the chart, from type to type, you see the effects of increasing attention. The more technical version describes these variations in clinical terms, while the version below gives each of the options a whimsical name to illustrate how they might behave.

50

From this matrix you can see why the Type 2 has an especially "bipolar" quality. The Type 2 is over-focused in native mode, but in his quest to sustain arousal he can move from under-engaged, inattentive preoccupation that resembles Type 1 under-focusing—to an over-aroused, overactive state of mind that resembles the hyper-focused Type 3, in effect, swinging between the poles of over- and under-attentiveness.

Type 3: Hyperfocus "Relentless Climber"

A different pole?: When I first heard Lynn Weiss lecture about her "Robin Williams" subtype I agreed the comic typified a kind of "mental hyperactivity" that belonged in the ADD spectrum. Then, I met a "Robin Williams" figure in the flesh and explored in depth how his process differed; just as vulnerable to over-focusing over-engagement and compulsivity as a Type 2 Restless Seeker, yet with distinct shades of impulsivity. It was also a mind full of wildly excited energy seeking an outlet that resembled the Impulsive Explorer. But, it was a group of its own.

Hypermental to the max: The rest of the Relentless Climber, or Type 3, band came into view when I read a piece in *Wired* magazine about Ted Nelson, father of "hypertext," the paradigm of information upon which the Internet rests, linking data by associative leaps instead of a step-by-step path of linear hierarchies. If Nelson coined the term which describes his technology, it may not be a coincidence the prefix is "hyper." Not only is he intensely hyperactive mentally, he's also been diagnosed ADD, the article said. The article painted a vivid picture of a mind reverberating so fast it could barely pause long enough to complete a whole sentence. The term "divine madness" took on a new meaning by the time I finished the article. The term "ADD" took on new meaning too.

Racing brain in overdrive: Ted Nelson seemed to personify every ADD quirk intensified: drivenness to the max, scatter to the extreme, and clutter at a level that makes the rest of us look like neat freaks; incredibly single-minded, yet flexible enough to leap large conceptual barriers in a flash. He didn't just invent hypertext, he lives it. Asked about his ADD, he called it an invention of the "regularity chauvinists" who like their logic linear and neat. He prefers to think of himself having a "hummingbird mind." Then I saw what was missing on my spectrum: Single-minded intensity so extreme, everyday reality starts to blur, a combination of over-focusing and over-arousal producing a collection of hyperfocusing sensitivities, a flying brain propelled by the fuel of obsession, winging so high it just might glimpse the whole globe at a glance. Another type altogether—and the true opposite pole.

Moving in time to the "beat" of your brain

My own experience gives a hint of what it's like to move through this matrix, shifting between different states of inattention over time. When I was young, chronically understimulated and too insecure to believe I could change it, I looked like a Type 2.1, a "Persistently Preoccupied Procrastinator." As my career took off, I found a source of gratifying stimulus to keep me engaged, becoming a Type 2.2, a "Compulsive Creator," where I've remained. Around intense projects in my work, I may shift again into a Type 2.3, the hyperengaged, but "Inconsistent Perfectionist." And some of the research I've done on these models showed me how it felt to become an obsessive Type 3 for awhile.

Now I can see why prior attempts to define ADD have been so conflict-ridden and confusing. It's not just biology, how we are wired at birth, nor only what we experience and how we respond. Like my matrix, our brains play both ways. Nature and nurture each perform functions that may remain fixed or may change. Neuroscience is showing us that how we react to our experience can actually alter our brains. New connections turn on and old ones switch off depending on which parts of our minds are exercised. So might the default settings in my head have shifted over time.

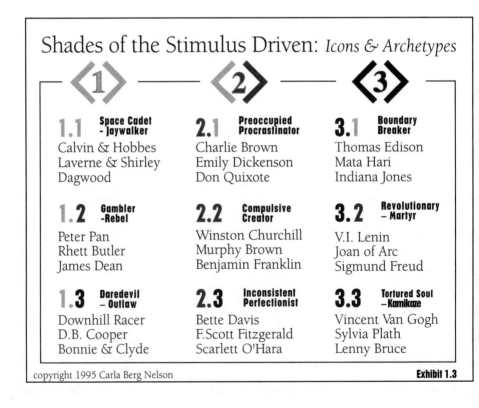

Shades of the Stimulus Driven: *Icons & Archetypes*

⟨1⟩

1.1 Space Cadet – Jaywalker
Calvin & Hobbes
Laverne & Shirley
Dagwood

1.2 Gambler -Rebel
Peter Pan
Rhett Butler
James Dean

1.3 Daredevil – Outlaw
Downhill Racer
D.B. Cooper
Bonnie & Clyde

⟨2⟩

2.1 Preoccupied Procrastinator
Charlie Brown
Emily Dickenson
Don Quixote

2.2 Compulsive Creator
Winston Churchill
Murphy Brown
Benjamin Franklin

2.3 Inconsistent Perfectionist
Bette Davis
F.Scott Fitzgerald
Scarlett O'Hara

⟨3⟩

3.1 Boundary Breaker
Thomas Edison
Mata Hari
Indiana Jones

3.2 Revolutionary – Martyr
V.I. Lenin
Joan of Arc
Sigmund Freud

3.3 Tortured Soul –Kamikaze
Vincent Van Gogh
Sylvia Plath
Lenny Bruce

copyright 1995 Carla Berg Nelson   **Exhibit 1.3**

But that's not to say I am any less ADD. That part of my wiring is too fundamental to totally alter. But by understanding how it operates, I have a much better shot at running it instead of having it run me.

Modeling ADD this way opens all sorts of doors and raises all sorts of questions. How to tell which type is which? How does one move this way instead of that? How might treatment strategies differ? And most importantly, how might we learn to listen to the rhythms of our minds, and dance in time to the beat of our brains?

We'll explore these and other questions in future papers.

Choosing Therapy and Medication

Introduction by Louis B. Cady, M.D.

THE POSSIBILITIES OF absolutely astounding improvement in the lives of children and adults with ADD/ADHD exists. So, too,does the possibility of side effects.

In this chapter, members of the ADD Forum debate the various pros and cons of medications. Carla Berg Nelson queries different doctors about ADD and presents a summary of their forthright comments. Tom Allen writes cogently about the possible benefits of biofeedback training in improving attention; therapist Richard Reither discusses how to find a competent therapist.

In medicine, one of the few Latin phrases that is still pounded into physicians is the nostrum: "Primum non nocere," which means "First, do no harm." In other words, the "cure" or "fix" should be better than the original problem.

In my experience, there are two fundamental errors in the optimum therapy for ADD/ADHD kids and adults: the first is to assume that medication is "going to make it all better" and that follow-up psychotherapy or talk therapy is merely the playground of the idle rich. The other extreme view holds that "pills" and

Dr. Louis B. Cady (74351,1275) is a psychiatrist in Evansville, IN who treats children, adolescents, and adults with ADD/ADHD. He did his residency in adult psychiatry at the Mayo Clinic in Rochester, MN. Dr. Cady's other interests include difficult-to-treat depression, eating disorders, and sleep disorders.

He is the medical director of the Disordered Eating Program at the Mulberry Center in Evansville, IN, as well as the medical director of the Sleep Diagnostic Center of Indiana. A prolific speaker and author, Cady will be releasing two books in 1996—one tentatively titled MASTERMIND: THE PSYCHIATRY OF WEALTH, SUCCESS, AND HAPPINESS, and another book, LEARNING AND LIVING: THE ABC'S OF LOVE FOR YOU AND YOUR CHILD.

that "zombifying, kid-poisoning, mind-controlling Ritalin" is only for "lazy parents/teachers who can't control their kids" and that you simply should be able to sit down and reason with the little darlings.

As the twentieth century draws to a close, one thing is startlingly clear. ADD and ADHD are brain disorders. You can no more "psychotherapize" ADD or ADHD away than you can lower a juvenile onset diabetic's blood sugar. Numerous studies support this assertion.

Unfortunately, no matter how good the biological "fix," problems linger in a child's (and adult's) self-esteem if he or she has been seriously compromised by ADD/ADHD. Home life may be a shambles and therapy is almost a must after the condition is under control. A new mindset is required.

Consider therapy for ADD as a "one-two" punch: medication for settling down the brain, then psychotherapy to help the patient readjust emotionally. Most people are understandably concerned about the following issues with medication:

☛ Will it work and be beneficial?

☛ Will it have unacceptable side effects?

☛ Will it actually make things worse?

These are reasonable considerations. In prescribing, wise physicians aim for "just right," an optimum balance between benefits and side effects. "Just right" means the target symptoms—inattention, wigglesomeness, hyperactivity, impulsiveness or aggression—are adequately treated without troublesome side effects. This is not difficult for an astute prescribing physician.

Internists, family practitioners, pediatricians, general psychiatrists, neurologists, and child psychiatrists all prescribe, but not all of them have the same amount of experience or the same familiarity with all the medication options. Unless you know "just right" is possible, you may accept something less. But it is possible to achieve if your doctor is flexible and you persist.

We all have different brain chemistry. Trials of different medications may be necessary. Dosage adjustments will be needed. Sometimes, two or even three or more medications are combined in difficult cases. But the goal is always be the same: control the symptoms; don't cause side effects.

Another common misconception is that somehow medications are treating the "symptoms" rather than the disorder itself. In my opinion, that is not true —at least, not if the medications are being appropriately prescribed. A reasonable dose of Ritalin, for example, which treats all of a child's impulsiveness, inattentiveness, and wigglesomeness, actually causes more norepinephrin to be released in the brain, "waking up" areas which are asleep at the switch. That, to me, is treating the disorder itself.

In Tom Allen's section on ADHD, "Biofeedback, and the Physiology of Arousal and Attention," he presents a very well-balanced view on the possible role of biofeedback in "treating" ADD/ADHD. He wisely points out that definitive studies are still forthcoming, and that "effective compensation" for mild difficulties in attention are probably the extent of the claims which can be made for this form of therapy. This form of therapy, just like medication, should also not be considered the end-all and be-all of therapy.

Richard Reither wraps up the chapter with a discussion of how to find that caring and competent therapist with some excellent advice. Finding one and paying for one are two different things, however. Psychoanalysts frequently advise patients to consider long-term therapy as a "capital expense," quite literally as an investment of their money in themselves. If the therapy eases family conflicts and helps a child get a better sense of himself or herself, it will have been worth every penny over the long-term.

Now get set to learn from some of the best, most caring, giving people you would ever want to meet as the ADD Forum folks talk therapy!

How Doctors May Differ About ADD

by Carla Berg Nelson, Sysop, ADD Forum, CompuServe

U NLESS YOU ARE A HEALTH PROFESSIONAL who hears a good deal of shop talk, you may not think about how common it is for doctors to differ. We layfolk tend to think of medicine as hard science, when it is really an art. We seek black and white answers, instead of seeing the shades of gray that doctors must decipher. And we may forget that clinicians themselves come from different schools at different times in different specialties, each with their own particular mix of professional experience and personal opinion.

This is why our forum staff so often advises members, "Learn all you can." To find a doctor who is a good fit, and to understand what you are told, you need a sense of how their perspectives may vary.

On the ADD Forum, we see physicians, psychologists and therapists talking shop in print every day. To illustrate the range of views we encounter online, we asked our "forum docs" to comment on issues they feel are critical to the understanding and treatment of ADD. You may wish to share some of their thoughts with your own physician.

Wastebasket or Umbrella?

Is the ADD diagnosis being over- or under-used? Some forum doctors are concerned that it is being used so broadly it could become a meaningless wastebasket category. Others see it as an umbrella for a collection of common symptoms that may arise from a number of causes. And more than a few also see ADD caught in the cross-fire of evolving knowledge and competing interests.

Where Nora Balderian, Los Angeles psychologist, feels the official clinical guidelines are often "useless," psychiatrist Louis Cady of Indiana sees a set of standards that work pretty well. Where neuroscientist Karl Jensen from North Carolina wonders if we are "substituting technical names" for what used to be seen as "normal variation," family practitioner Dr. Paul Elliott of Texas chafes at definitions he finds "unnecessarily restrictive."

Meanwhile, California psychiatrist Phil Kavenaugh is concerned that many of his colleagues overlook ADD when treating adults for addictions, compulsions and mood disorders, while Minnesota psychologist Robert Van Siclen worries equally about children who may be diagnosed ADD when they shouldn't be.

"All that I ask is that a debate about semantics not interfere with efforts to help children, teachers and families," says Stephen Katz, a New Jersey pediatrician, echoing what may be the true bottom line for many forum members.

Sysop Carla Nelson (74774,1756) is a journalist who frequently covers new developments in science and technology and one of the founding members of the ADD Forum.

Not sure where you stand? See how you feel after reading their reasons.

Written in sand, not stone

As Dr. Katz points out, the guidelines in the psychiatrist's DIAGNOSTIC AND STATISTICAL MANUAL (DSM) include a "Cautionary Statement" which says the book is intended to be "a consensus of current formulations of evolving knowledge." In other words, these diagnosing standards are not written in stone. They shift with the sands of time, as more becomes known.

Yet, as some forum members discover, clinicians may use the book as a Bible. This is a particular problem, Drs. Elliott and Kavenaugh suggest, when it comes to adults, as adult ADD is still not universally known (or accepted). Nora Balderian minces few words when she agrees: "Frankly, the DSM-IV is rather useless regarding the diagnosis in adults."

Dr. Katz has similar concerns on behalf of the youngsters he sees: "There are children and adolescents who do not meet all the criteria, but who benefit from the same techniques and therapies. All too often they are denied services because of inappropriately rigid adherence to DSM-IV criteria. This is a misuse of the DSM," he writes.

But child and adolescent specialist Dr. Cady feels the DSM-IV does do a good job of describing the different ways ADD can appear: "The current criteria neatly break ADD into four categories," he notes, listing them:

☞ Primarily inattentive type

☞ Hyperactive/Impulsive type

☞ Combined type

☞ Not otherwise specified

This makes it "fairly clear to differentiate the inattentive (dreamy, unfocused) type from the hyperactive/impulsive who is bouncing off the walls," he says. But, as he also points out, the psychiatric viewpoint is changing. "We are increasingly aware that not all disorders with the same 'symptoms' have the same biological underpinnings."

"Perhaps in the future," he muses, "we will break it down to 'norepinephrin deficit' and 'serotonin deficit' or 'combined deficit.' Or then again, there may be neurotransmitters involved which we haven't even discovered yet!"

"Obviously, if anybody knew the biological answers and had quick and easy tests, I would suggest we reclassify it on that basis. Since we don't have those tests (or even standards for them) yet, we can't. I suspect that the DSM will have to do until those discoveries are made," he concludes.

ADD and/or Something Else?

"It is not difficult to identify ADHD with all of the typical features. What requires knowledge, experience and judgment is to help [someone] who has subtle or less typical features of ADHD, or where it is part of a larger pattern or health problem," notes Dr. Katz.

Dr. Corydon Clark, a psychiatrist who practices in Nevada and California, finds ADD is rarely his sole diagnosis: "Normally, by mid- or late-adolescence, we see it complicated by one or more of a variety of related conditions: Anxiety Disorder, Depression or Dysthymia, OCD, Tourette's, Alcohol/Drug abuse, or episodic rage reactions which defy precise labeling."

"I think this is why the diagnosis so often gets confused," he suggests. "Making sure diagnosis and treatment covers the full range of ADD-related conditions may be the key to treatment success."

Phil Kavenaugh also sees frequent overlaps between ADD and other conditions and fears it results in missing the ADD altogether.

"Psychiatrists in my era learned . . . there was no ADD in adults," he notes. He himself shared that view for over 30 years, but "never was I more mistaken," he says.

Now he is concerned that many adults with ADD are "treated as if their depression, panic, obsessive-compulsive symptoms, eating disorders or addictions are their primary and only disorder." In particular, Dr. Kavenaugh has been struck by how many addicts improved after treatment for ADD. Years of seeing that pattern repeat convinced him "patients with addictions are not the morally weak people with Axis II 'character defects' I once thought."

"Alcohol and other drugs help them to quiet their 'scanning brains,'" he explains. "The medications I am prescribing for these patients, correctly diagnosed with ADD, help a great deal without all the stigma attached."

Paul Elliott shares this impression: "We have failed to recognize people with a history of substance abuse might be undiagnosed, self-medicating patients with ADD. I am now of the opinion that virtually any of the abusable substances will rather profoundly relieve the symptoms of ADD." But after treatment for ADD, "their interest in abusing is no longer present."

Dr. Elliott also feels that many of these combined, or "co-morbid," diagnoses are actually part of ADD, not separate. "ADD can produce or mimic many other disease processes," he notes, citing "depression, anxiety, panic disorder, personality disorder, phobias, obsessive/compulsive disorder (OCD), bipolar disorder, sleep disorders, and schizophrenia" as examples. As a result, he believes that if there is more than one psychiatric diagnosis, the patient should be "considered to have ADD until proven otherwise."

How to tell which is what?

"I personally tease out overlaps with a careful history," Louis Cady notes. "The diagnosis of ADD or ADHD can be made only after other possibilities are screened out. These possibilities include child abuse, pinworms, thyroid problems, and seizures."

"I always look for what came first. I do not assume everything that wiggles is ADHD, " he continues. Confusion is much less likely, Dr. Cady suggests, if a physician takes the following steps:

☛ Take a thorough clinical history

☛ Review patients' prior medical records

☛ Obtain a physical exam including blood count, electrolytes and thyroid function

☛ Screen the complete psychosocial situation at home

☛ Rule out sexual and physical abuse or trauma

☛ Examine the family tree

☛ Consider the sequence of events

This last point, Dr. Cady feels, is often missed. For example, was the child an impulsive wiggler long before he began to run wild? If so, it could be ADD together with a conduct disorder, or it could be the "pre-sociopathic compensatory behavior" of an ADD child with a negative sense of self who is angrily acting out his frustration and rage. In either case, "treating the underlying ADD may decrease the rage driving the conduct problem."

"Get the timeline straight! Don't confuse the effects with the cause," he warns his colleagues.

To Test or Not

If any one diagnostic issue has almost universal agreement among our forum docs, it is that diagnostic testing is optional. Every testing tool is subject to error since an ADDer may focus well in novel or stressful settings, which confuses the results of popular tests such as the CPT (continuous performance test). A thorough clinical history is the key, they tell us time and again, not a set of test scores.

Nonetheless, Paul Elliott notes, testing may be required to satisfy the physician as much as the patient or parent. "We are very reluctant to accept things which are not easily defined by laboratory or other 'objective' tests," he says of his peers. "We make changes slowly and methodically."

As a result, Dr. Elliott feels his colleagues are "as much a part of the problem of acknowledging ADD" as anyone else.

Louis Cady agrees that testing is optional. While he finds it "occasionally indicated in very confusing cases," he also feels "the best and the most reliable diagnosis is based on a good clinical history." Nora Balderian agrees "the patient's own history has been the most useful, especially in the context of early schooling, social, family and internal thinking patterns."

That is not to say testing is pointless. Dr. Balderian and others often use a CPT for confirming evidence. If time and money permit, an educational-psychological battery including the WISC (for children) or the WAIS (for adults) may also help detail particular processing obstacles that hamper a student in school. A large gap between the "verbal" and "performance" subparts of these tests also tends to confirm the presence of ADD. As Dr. Elliott notes, "a wide split between does not make the diagnosis, but it is highly suspicious."

The Dangers of Popularity

Sounding a note of caution, Robert Van Siclen is concerned that ADD is becoming too popular with some of his colleagues and their patients. "It is still the search for the magic pill that will make it easier to handle all children, fix all behavior problems," he writes. "It's cheaper than designing new educational environments, easier than confronting dysfunctional parents who don't set limits, much easier than accepting responsibility."

"There is a debate," he points out, "about whether AD/HD is one end of a 'normal curve' of attentional abilities or is somehow qualitatively different from normal variation in this trait."

At one end of the spectrum, Dr. Van Siclen is concerned that "the lower limits are being pushed" to include "increasing numbers of children who are simply misbehaving, or who are from stressed, unsupportive or dysfunctional families."

At the other end of the scale, he feels "increasing numbers of very troubled children" are being diagnosed ADD because it has become more "socially acceptable" than other diagnoses.

It troubles him to see parents who "describe very disturbing behavior and attribute it to AD/HD" for he fears it "deprives the child of the level of treatment the problem deserves."

What to treat first and how?

Paul Elliott says that when ADD is present it should almost always be treated as the primary condition. To illustrate, he discusses how his own approach to ADD with depression has evolved: "Like most physicians, I felt most comfortable dealing with something I understood . . . but I found that the depression seemed to respond less well and I never got back to dealing with the ADD."

Now, unless a patient is suicidal, he treats the ADD before he addresses the depression. "To my amazement," he notes, "it [has been] much more quickly beneficial and effective for the depression, as well."

Putting ADD at the head of the list may help other physical problems too, he says. In adults, "coronary artery disease and hypertension may also be more easily controlled, if ADD is addressed."

Some physicians may worry about using stimulant medication when other conditions are being treated, but "the psychostimulants are remarkably safe from the medical point of view," Dr. Elliott notes. With "caution and careful monitoring" they may be safely combined with other drugs.

ADD itself may also take a combined prescription, as Dr. Corydon Clark points out. In his experience, a single medication frequently proves to be "inadequate for effective management of the full range of symptoms."

One strategy we hear about often on the forum combines a psychostimulant, such as Dexedrine or Ritalin, with an "SSRI" antidepressant, such as Prozac, Paxil or Zoloft. Many of Phil Kavenaugh's patients have had "impressive results" from this two-pronged approach, he says, in particular, "patients who have gone in and out of depression for years, alcoholics and other addicts who frequently relapse, or those who have food, sexual or other behavioral addictions in addition to their emotional symptoms."

Dr. Kavenaugh has also observed that ADD patients often have an unusually speedy response to SSRI medications. While it usually takes weeks to see a change, many of his adult patients with ADD "responded to the very first dose." Forum members have reported similar reactions online. Despite doctor's predictions, their SSRI medications took effect within days. Dr. Kavenaugh feels it is likely they are experiencing an immediate effect on dopamine levels in the brain, a suspected factor in the biology of ADD.

Which med and when?

Elsewhere in his essay, Phil Kavenaugh notes, "it seems Ritalin often works better in children and young adults but Dexedrine is more (much more) effective in older adults." This observation has been echoed by many forum members, but a significant number also report Dexedrine has been more effective for their children too, particularly in its sustained release form.

Louis Cady has seen a range of response among his younger patients. Some ADD children, especially those with hyperactivity, seem to have "a clear deficit in neurotransmission of norepinephrin which is put right by the use of stimulant medications or some tricyclic antidepressants (which boost norepinephrin)," he explains. But sometimes he must also add "a serotonin-boosting drug (such as Prozac) to calm a child and cut down aggression." And a few cases have required using three drugs at once.

Paul Elliott adds another factor to this equation. He finds that standard doses of stimulants often need to be increased quite a bit before the optimum level is reached. "Several years ago it occurred to me we were undermedicating adults . . . I realized this because I am blessed with a practice of highly educated, trained observers as patients."

"Over time, I came to accept that higher doses, when tolerated and producing additional benefit, were appropriate." Larger doses, he found, were also helpful in some difficult cases of childhood ADD, but less often. None of his patients became chemically dependent on their medications. To the contrary, they often forgot to take them. This experience confirmed his impression that, "the psychostimulants were not truly habituating."

Which Kind of MD?

Finding the right diagnosis and treatment requires "determination, perseverance, and patience," as Dr. Elliott notes. Each patient must determine his or her own best course in consultation with a skilled M.D. But it isn't always obvious what kind of doctor to see. A psychiatrist? A neurologist? A family G.P.?

The bottom-line answer depends less on the specific specialty and more on specific experience with childhood or adult ADD. The more ADD they have seen and treated, the better aware they will be of its variations.

But even the most experienced don't always agree. Much of the controversy around ADD can be traced to "professional jealousies and turf warfare," Paul Elliott suggests. Some physicians may remain deliberately nearsighted about the implications of attention deficit because it challenges them to change the way they practice.

The psychiatrist of tomorrow will be less of a psychoanalyst and more of a pharmacologist, expert in the intricacies of medication and brain chemistry, he predicts. Some psychiatrists may resist this shift, but managed care will press all mental health practitioners into narrower niches.

Psychiatrists will become the experts in mental health medicine, including "polypharmacy," the balancing of multiple prescriptions. Psychologists will be the specialists in psychometric tests, such as the WISC, while therapists and counselors will be coaches for day-to-day coping skills. Few patients will seek (or be able to pay for) extended time on the analyst's couch any more.

But insofar as ADD is concerned, this may be just as well, Dr. Elliott feels, because ADD requires "more patient training and guidance than it does 'counseling' in the classical sense."

How much in a name?

Some skeptics still wonder if ADD is a "real" disorder. So many of the symptoms are behaviors we used to think of as "only" personality.

Part of that problem would go away with a different name, suggests Phil Kavenaugh. He prefers the less negative term "Scanning Brain Syndrome" to make it clear we are talking about "the way the brain and nervous system perceive the world," a condition which is "not a true disorder though it can become one." Through "intelligence, creativity or persistence, some ADDers overcome symptoms with "sheer force of will," he notes. But "they still have a scanning brain" and still may need treatment.

He is not alone in disliking the name. Dr. Mark Powell a family physician from Pennsylvania, writes: "I just can't bring myself to think of so many bright, articulate and engaging people as 'deficient' or 'disordered'." He fears the terms are so stigmatizing it deters people from seeking help. "While 'hyperactive' was neither accurate nor specific, it was a kinder term."

Neuroanatomist Karl Jensen PH.D., himself an adult with ADD, is concerned about more than the name. He wonders if our added understanding of brain biology has also been a mixed blessing. "As improvements in the magnifying glass of diagnosis uncover the complexities of the body and mind, syndromes and disorders are increasingly becoming parcellated. Ironically, in many cases it has become more difficult to clearly distinguish one condition from another—and even from 'normality' itself."

Robert Van Siclen thinks perhaps we are getting too fuzzy, not too precise. "If AD/HD is simply one end of the 'normal curve,' we have to be very careful to define the limits. At what level of inattention do we get concerned and [when] should we intervene? We have to keep the limits clear so we can keep our efforts focused on those who can really benefit from treatment."

Adapt our Environments (and Ourselves)?

"Since the ripe old age of 12, there was no doubt in my mind that there was a genetic basis for why I had always 'felt different.' But even then I knew it was not that simple—context or environment also had a critical role," Karl Jensen observes. These differences, he says, "become amplified" in work and school settings that do not permit diversity.

This tends "to deaden, rather than sharpen cognitive processes," he explains, and the shame and blame which goes along with it provokes defiance. The result is an "isolated and frustrated ADDer who has not been able to integrate social, emotional and cognitive cues." He hopes our added awareness of the biology of behavior will help us see the benefits of genetic diversity, and encourage us to be more accommodating toward our differences.

Meanwhile, "There is also the option of 'arranging ourselves,' " he points out. "I am convinced there are 'cognitive' and other skills that can be learned, and honed. Recognizing which skills are optimal is central to making full use of the wonderful advantages of 'the curious mind.'"

On that note, Paul Elliott sounds a similar chord. He agrees many ADD difficulties are intensified by the expectations of society. When we accept ADD "more realistically," he says, "these barriers will begin to fall." The "supposed weaknesses" will be recast to make "an excellent case for the strengths of the ADD brain."

In the interim, Dr. Elliott says, there will still be "a great bias" against accepting "the full and global nature of ADD." As an antidote, he impishly proposes a Machiavellian strategy:

"educate the masses of individuals with ADD and their families," he suggests. "Large numbers of people, appropriately informed, can then be unleashed like a swarm of educated lemmings on the professions. With this advancing wave, only two types of professionals will remain: those who understand and agree and those who are coming around to it."

The rest of his peers, he predicts, "will simply drown in the swarm."

Ritalin vs. Dexedrine

Wendy Hoechsetter queries forum members who have taken Ritalin and Dexedrine and professionals who have prescribed both. What differences did they experience?

Hi, everyone!

Has anyone out there taken both Ritalin and Dexedrine, or had a kid who was given both (at different times)? What, if any, differences did you experience?

What about you doctors who prescribe both? What has your experience been with the two meds in your practice?

—*Wendy Hoechsetter*

Wendy, I've given children Ritalin and Dexedrine at different times. It depends upon the side effects. Also, for a period of time, it was impossible to get Dexedrine; the company stopped making it for six months. Currently, I have no children on Dexedrine. Twenty years ago, I was working in a large child guidance clinic, seeing lots of ADHD children. I tried to see which drug would work better, couldn't really see any difference. The only reason to shift more to Ritalin was that the BNDD (Bureau of Narcotics and Dangerous Drugs), the current DEA, saw it as less dangerous if drug addicts got hold of it.

—*Bertram Warren,* M.D.

I'm asking because I'm about to switch to Dexedrine 5 mg spansules from Ritalin, mainly because I have such a difficult time remembering to take my midday dose that I've been unable to regularly get the dose I'm supposed to be on.

It's been impossible to accurately evaluate effectiveness because of this, although I've seen enough hints at positive effects the few times I *have* managed to get it all on board to make me think that a longer-acting preparation would do the trick for me.

Both doctors, and most of what I've read and heard elsewhere, seem to agree that the Ritalin-SR is *not* the way to go, though, because of the absorption issues. Anything I have to take more than BID [twice a day] has *always* been a major compliance problem for me—and all the understanding in the world of the importance, etc., hasn't made it any easier. So, I just need to work *with* that, not against it, and try to stick to QD [every day] or BID [twice a day] products (specifically a.m. and hs [hour of sleep, bedtime]) where possible.

I can sometimes manage for a week or so with antibiotics, for example, where I feel so lousy that every minute of the day is a constant reminder to take the next dose (grin), but the moment I no longer have that sort of built-in reminder—forget it.

The other reason I'm asking is because I haven't really read up yet on Dexedrine, let alone vs. Ritalin, and two doctors have told me two different things about how they compare. I, of course, understand the basics of this; I'm just not at all up on any of the subtleties. The guy who gave me the prescription said there was absolutely no difference in the side effect profile, while my psychiatrist seems to feel there is a *much* more pronounced problem with sleep, and with habituation, tolerance, addiction, etc. Obviously, I won't know for myself until I try it, but I'm just trying to get a little more feel for other people's personal experiences along these lines.

I finally found a pharmacy that has it, so I'm off to pick it up. I'm feeling very weird about the whole idea (but then again, I felt much the same way when I started the Ritalin, too). A part of me just really doesn't want to have anything to do with any of this.

—Wendy Hoechsetter

Wendy, by the time you see this you'll probably [be] off and running (oops-relaxing) on your new Dexedrine regimen (grin). I've used a good deal of both Ritalin and Dexedrine over a lot of years, and think that the Dexedrine spansule is more predictable than the Ritalin-SR, and, in my experience, more effective generally.

I haven't seen any side effects from the Dexedrine that are different from Ritalin in ADHD except that the Dexedrine lasts longer. I also haven't seen tolerance, nor psychological or physical addiction, in people using either for ADHD. Y'know, if there were such, or you were susceptible, the last thing you would worry about would be missing a dose.

I am eager to learn of your own observations and comparisons. But don't worry about the safety of the Dexedrine, in my opinion.

—David Trachtenberg, M.D.

David, thanks for the encouraging words. Y'know, no matter what I read and learn, no matter what my personal experiences, there's always still that little niggling thought that there's something "bad" about these meds. Just the social "stigma" I guess.

I was petrified when I started on the Ritalin, because I really didn't know what I would experience with it. I remember being unbelievably "wired" from Vivarin and Nodoz and so on, when I used them occasionally in college (*not* a pleasant sensation at all). I get a dreadful, jittery, shaky feeling whenever I have to take Proventil, and I was really afraid these meds would produce the same kind of thing. Fortunately, they haven't.

—Wendy Hoechsetter

ADHD, Biofeedback and the Physiology of Arousal and Attention

by Tom Allen

ORE THAN 30 YEARS AGO psychophysiologists became interested in the possibility that the mechanisms of attention and mental arousal might be malleable and capable of being trained. As early as 1962, a research psychologist, Dr. Thomas Mullholland, presented data that suggested attention and alertness could be brought under control through EEG biofeedback and self-regulation procedures, (Mullholland & Runnals, 1962).

Mullholland continued his research into the early 70's looking at the attentional shifting and orienting responses in children with relationship to the EEG and feedback procedures. His work was primarily experimental and not clinical in its orientation; but it laid the groundwork for much work that was to follow.

Just after World War II scientists, the military and the civilian aviation authorities became very concerned with the issue of vigilance and attention with regard to detection technology. It was discovered during the war that the detection efficiency of radar operators dropped off significantly after only 30 minutes of radar watching.

The issue of vigilance, attention and its maintenance took on specific and practical importance as the country's workforce became more reliant on detection-oriented technology for crucial tasks, like air traffic control and piloting sophisticated aircraft outfitted with an array of instruments and gauges. The potential for human error and the implications of reduced vigilance could be hazardous in a world reliant on high technology. (Mackworth, 1950)

At least one group of scientists was exploring the possibility that attention and vigilance could be enhanced by training people to reduce their amount of slow wave brain activity while performing a vigilance and attention task.

Using EEG biofeedback, Beatty and his colleagues were able to demonstrate convincingly that by training subjects to reduce the amount of slow wave Theta

Tom Allen is the director of Neurobehavioral Services at Neuropsychological Associates of Central Florida in Winter Park, Florida and one of the leading figures in the field of EEG biofeedback. He trained many of the therapists offering this specialty in the United States and Canada. He received his professional biofeedback training from The Georgetown University Family Center and The Menninger Clinic in Topeka, Kansas. He is currently a sysop on The Mind/Body Science Forum on CompuServe and is Vice President of Mind Media Labs, Inc., a software development and research firm.

Rhythm activity vigilance and attention performance would be improved dramatically (Beatty, et. al, 1974).

In the same study they were able to show that subjects who were trained to enhance their theta rhythm activity actually did more poorly on the attention performance task than they had originally when tested at the onset of the study prior to any training with EEG biofeedback. Theirs was a well-controlled study published in a leading scientific journal that demonstrated a convincing relationship between the slow theta rhythm and attention performance.

It also demonstrated that the mechanism of control of the theta rhythm could be brought under conscious control with proper feedback and training and that such training would improve vigilance and attention on an attention performance task. The ramifications of this study, and Beatty's subsequent studies, laid the scientific groundwork for the possibility that Attention Deficit Disorder could be treated effectively with EEG biofeedback procedures.

In 1976 Dr. Joel Lubar, of the University of Tennessee at Knoxville, published his first paper reporting his preliminary clinical findings following the treatment of a hyperactive child with EEG biofeedback (Lubar & Shouse, 1976).

Using a method designed to teach the child to suppress the slow theta rhythm and to enhance the faster sensorimotor rhythm Lubar was able to document a marked change in the child's behavior and functioning following treatment. Since that time Dr. Lubar has continued to produce research based on clinical case design that documents improvement in IQ, EEG measures and performance tests following the administration of 40-50 EEG biofeedback sessions to children with ADHD.

His work has been criticized by scientists and clinicians who object to his case report studies because they lack proper controls and scientific rigor. His reply to this criticism has been that the research is ongoing and will eventually lead to double-blind research trials in the future. However, a number of clinicians around the country have adopted Dr. Lubar's procedures and are reporting similar results.

In the past two years clinics have proliferated around the country that offer this treatment and it is estimated that approximately 400 – 500 physicians, psychologists and other practitioners are trained and offering this treatment at present. The question is, will it all pan out once the double-blind studies are done? In my opinion it is likely that it will; but the studies will also show that it is not quite as successful as the anecdotal reports suggest.

Some reports are touting an improvement figure of 80% or better and others are calling it a cure. I don't believe it. Dr. Lubar has never claimed it to be any more than an effective compensation and I will stick with that assessment myself.

From my own clinical experience it seems to be doing with ADHD children what it did for air traffic controllers in Beatty's studies. It improves their ability to focus and attend to something boring, something we could all stand to improve. It is like exercising a muscle. You exercise it and it gets stronger. This method is very much the same for attention. Beatty proved convincingly in highly controlled research studies that it could be done. Lubar applied the principle to ADHD children.

The application of EEG biofeedback is supported by findings Satterfield (1971) and others that demonstrate excessive slow wave activity and general underarousal to be present in a large number of ADHD children. (Dykman, et al., 1982; Satterfield et al. 1974; Zahn et al., 1975; Hastings and Barkley, 1978).

Also it has been suggested from other empirical studies of physiology in ADHD children that they are significantly disregulated in their autonomic nervous systems compared to normal children. (Cohen & Douglas, 1972; Conners, 1975; Zahn et al., 1975) This compels one to begin thinking about the possibility that the physiology may be a starting place for intervention through behavioral learning methods like biofeedback as an adjunct to medications and other therapies.

Without using EEG, Dr. Constantine Mangina has devised and researched a method of training the balance of right- and left-hand sweat response, technically known as bilateral electrodermal activity, to help hyperactive and learning disabled children to learn how to regulate and control their level of autonomic arousal.

His results in double-blind studies won him a Nobel Science Award for their rigor and their scientific merit. In a study that included 238 learning-disabled and hyperactive children he was able to show significant changes in performance on IQ and tests of perception following his treatment procedure. (Mangina & Mangina, 1992)

These kinds of findings outside of the EEG biofeedback arena, but within the realm of biofeedback in general, suggest there may be even more to the idea of psychophysiologic self-regulation training for the treatment of ADHD than meets the eye.

If the adoption by NASA of the method and technology gives any credence to Dr. Lubar's and previous researchers' work we should all take heed. Research scientist and psychologist Dr. Alan Pope at the NASA Langley Research Center along with Lockheed engineer Ed Bogart submitted a patent for an EEG feedback device to train pilots and children with attention deficit in attentional performance by shifting the threshold of feedback as attention performance and response increases in difficulty.

They call their new technology EAST for Expanded Attention Span Training System. It was developed initially to improve flight efficiency of NASA pilots. The work at NASA is a continuation of the Beatty and Mullholland studies from the 70's; but the application to Attention Deficit Disorder is a direct influence of Lubar's work. So things are moving forward. (Pope & Bogart, 1994)

Since both Mangina's and Lubar's methods involve the regulation of physiologic processes related to arousal, and the issue of disregulated arousal has come up consistently in the research history of ADHD, there just may be something to all the talk about EEG biofeedback. There is no doubt in my mind that Mangina's work is sound. He has produced the science and the double-blind studies to prove it. As for Lubar's work, the jury is still out; but the evidence is mounting for the defense of its validity as a treatment for ADHD.

Bibliography

Beatty, J., Greenberg, A. Deibler, W. P., & Ohanlon, W. F. (1974). *"Operant control of occipital theta rhythm affects performance in a radar monitoring task."* SCIENCE, 183, 871-873.

Cohen, N. J. & Douglas, V. I. (1972) *"Characteristics of the orienting response in hyperactive and normal children."* PSYCHOPHYSIOLOGY, 9: 238-245

Connors, C. K. (1975) *"Minimal brain dysfunction and psychopathology of children."* In A. Davis (Ed.), CHILD PERSONALITY AND PSYCHOPATHOLOGY: CURRENT TOPICS. (Vol. 2). Wiley, New York

Dykman R. A., Holcomb, P. J., Oglesby, D. M. and Ackerman, P. T. (1982) "Electrocortical frequencies in hyperactive, learning-disabled, mixed and normal children." BIOLOGICAL PSYCHIATRY, 17: 675-685.

Hastings, J. E. & Barkley, R. A. (1978). *"A review of psychophysiologic research with hyperactive children."* JOURNAL OF ABNORMAL CHILD PSYCHOLOGY, 6, 413-447

Lubar, J. O., Shouse, M. N. (1976) *"EEG and behavioral changes in a hyperactive child concurrent with training of the sensorimotor rhythm (SMR). A preliminary report."* BIOFEEDBACK & SELF REGULATION, 1, 293-306.

Mackworth, N. H. (1950). *"Researches of the measurement of human performance."* (Medical Research Council Special Report No. 268). London: H.M. Stationary Office.

Mangina, C. A. & Beuzeron-Mangina, J. H. (1992) *"Identification and standardization of bilateral electrodermal parameters of learning abilities and disabilities."* INTERNATIONAL JOURNAL OF PSYCHOPHYSIOLOGY, 12: 63-69

Mullholland, T., & Runnals, S. (1962) *"Evaluation of attention and alertness with a stimulus-brain feedback loop."* ELECTROENCEPHALOGRAPHY AND CLINICAL NEUROPHYSIOLOGY, 14, 847-852.

Pope, A. & Bogart, E. (1994) *"Expanded Attention Span Training System."* NASA Langley Research Center Patent Description.

Satterfield, J. H., & Dawson, M. E. (1971) *"Electrodermal Correlates of hyperactivity in children."* PSYCHOPHYSIOLOGY, 8: 191-197

Satterfield, J. H., Antonian, G., Brashears, G. C., Burleigh, A. C. and Dawson, M. E. (1974) *"Electrodermal studies of minimal brain dysfunction children."* In C. K. Connors (Ed.) CLINICAL USE OF STIMULANT DRUGS IN CHILDREN (No. 313) Amsterdam: Excerpta Medica International Congress Series.

Zahn, T. P., Abate, F. Little, B. C. and Wender, P. H. (1975) *"Minimal brain dysfunction, stimulant drugs and autonomic nervous system activity."* ARCHIVES GENERAL PSYCHIATRY, 32: 381-387.

THINK FAST! THE ADD EXPERIENCE

Seeking a Savvy Therapist
by Richard Reither, M.F.C.C.

On Finding a Therapist

Regarding the question about finding a therapist when there is no CH.A.D.D. group in the area: Another organization option would be the Learning Disabilities Association (LDA). If they are not available, I would start with any friends, church acquaintances, etc., who have an LD or ADHD child, and find out who they are working with and if they are happy.

Next, a local hospital or college may have a department with a team, or at least a psychologist who is knowledgeable about ADHD.

Next, go to the Yellow Pages. Ads for both psychologists and MFCCs [Marriage, Family & Child Counselor] are getting pretty descriptive nowadays on the services offered, and there may be a therapist who's listed as an ADHD specialist.

Qualifications

Call and talk directly with the therapist to find out about his or her license, training in ADHD-related issues, years in practice, number of cases they have and are treating with ADHD, etc.

If the person sounds good, make an appointment for an initial parent consultation, and then follow your "guts" as to whether this is someone you can work and feel comfortable with. Parents' intuition is generally correct.

Licensing

Regarding license, years in practice, number of cases, etc.: Optimally the therapist should be licensed in her/his state. This is usually the case for psychologists, although some states still don't have licensure for MFCCs or Social Workers. The license represents a protection to the consumer in that the therapist has gone through an extensive training period, testing and peer review before she/he can practice alone.

An added bonus is membership in a national organization such as the APA [American Psychological Association], AAMFC [American Association of Marriage & Family Therapist]) or NASW [National Association of Social Workers]. None of this of course assures quality, and that's where your "guts" come into

---

Richard Reither (76600,716) is a licensed Marriage, Family and Child Therapist in Fresno, CA. In private practice for the last ten years with a focus on the assessment and treatment of adults and children with learning and attention differences, he is a frequent guest lecturer on LD and ADHD subjects for school districts, organizations and the local CH.A.D.D. chapter.

play, but the chances are better that the person you are turning yourself and your child over to practices under structured and accepted guidelines.

Preparing for the Initial Visit

Before the initial consultation, it's a good idea to be equipped with questions for the therapist. That is where this forum (the libraries)and the growing number of books on the subject of ADHD for parents can come in handy. Questions usually deal with issues of etiology (where'd it come from), severity, medication, length of time anticipated in therapy, and type of therapy to be utilized. The therapist should be able to address all of these issues and more with ease, and her/his answers should essentially concur with what the current thinking is on ADHD (again, as found on this forum and in the current books on the market).

Therapist Expertise and Attitude

The therapist should have treated ADHD before (hopefully regularly) and be able to talk about support within the community (psychiatrists, pediatricians, ophthalmologists, audiologists and speech pathologists), all of whom may need to be called in as referral sources. I think an important common denominator with any of these professionals, in terms of whether you should work with them or not, is based on their attitude toward you the parent. This attitude should be one of care and respect, as opposed to condescension, or being "too busy" to really talk with you.

Therapeutic Techniques in Young Children

Regarding therapeutic techniques with very young children: This of course varies from therapist to therapist, but generally, for the very young child (birth to 3 or 4), it is often most beneficial for the parents to receive parent training in ADHD issues that they can then use with the child. When the child is seen by the therapist, often play therapy is used in order to help with expression of emotions, modeling appropriate behavior, building self esteem and working on impulse-control techniques. When there has been some form of early trauma involved, then of course it becomes more necessary for the child to be seen.

Therapy for Older Children

Finally, regarding therapy for children older than 4: It really involves many of the same things I mentioned before—but with increasing age, there can be increased talk-type therapy along with play therapy. Talk therapy alone usually is not as effective with an ADHD child because they need variety and motivating stimulation in order not to close down.

Big issues for the older children usually involve self-esteem, impulse control and social skills training. Often by 5 years old, the ADHD child's self es-

74

teem has already started to erode due to self-perceived differences. To children, different usually means "bad" or "less than," and that's where detrimental core beliefs get started.

With the help of the therapist the child can be treated with positive regard, and modeling of better social interactions can take place. Play therapy also allows the child to "vent" their pent up emotions in a "safe" place, thereby being able to deal with them with the accepting figure of the therapist.

When these children are accepted and treated with respect, it is exciting to watch them bloom. And bloom they will, since most ADHD children are very bright and creative.

ADD Through the Life-cycle

Introduction by Harlan Lampert, PH.D.
Clinical and Educational Psychologist Rockville, MD

THE FORUM HAS PRESENTED a unique opportunity for an exploration of the experiences and points of view of folks of all ages. From teens through grannies, from the student to the teacher, from the child to parent, the many roles that we live in our lives have had the spotlight over these past years.

The common thread that I have experienced is that we can best learn from our personal histories. As we grow, age, and move from role to role the struggle to understand our limitations and differences become an important means to help lead happier and more self-satisfied lives. We are constantly challenged to define and understand our experience. It is through this understanding, both from within and from the reactions of others, that our sense of competence and well-being can flourish.

A community embraces the diversity of experience. Experience can teach and hold and guide. This cyber-community has allowed the experiences of many to inform and support the struggles of those who have shared in the dialogues.

As a clinical psychologist, Harlan Lampert, PH.D. practices in both private and school-based settings. His work focuses on family and child-oriented issues especially those dealing with school related disabilities, clinical conditions, and family disruptions including divorce mediation and child custody evaluations. His practice includes assessment of ADHD, clinical, and learning problems; and therapies for children and adults. He is on the Professional Advisory Board of ChADD of Montgomery County, MD.

He was a teacher for 10 years in public and private schools. His students ranged from gifted to severely learning disabled. He also taught at the University of Maryland and at George Mason University in Virginia.

Attention Deficit Disorder in Children: Developmental, Parenting and Treatment Issues
by Pamela Darr Wright, LCSW

Introduction

Human growth and development, with the requisite learning of skills and mastery of cognitive and psychosocial tasks, unfolds in endlessly fascinating, complex patterns. If the child is to develop a healthy personality, then he must learn how to test reality, regulate impulses, stabilize moods, integrate feelings and actions, focus attention, and plan.

The DSM-III-R states that "In approximately half of the cases [of ADD], onset of the disorder is before age four." When an attentional problem is present, with the hallmark symptoms of distractibility, hyperactivity/restlessness, and/or impulsivity, the child's ability to master some or many of these tasks will be more difficult. Complicating the situation is the fact that many children with attentional problems also have other learning problems.

The parental role has always encompassed difficult periods when parents feel confused and worried about how well they are fulfilling their responsibilities. However, raising a child with Attention Deficit Disorder can be exceedingly frustrating, emotionally draining, and expensive. In many instances, the child's ADD-related problems cause ongoing problems in the parent-child relationship that can set the stage for an unhappy, guilt-ridden relationship between the child, parents (and siblings) that may persist, sometimes through life. The strain from raising these "difficult kids" takes a toll on many marriages, especially when parents differ in their approach to the child.

Complicating the family situation is the fact that Attention Deficit Disorder is often genetically transmitted from one generation to the next. Thus, we often find an ADD child being raised by an ADD parent who was never diagnosed and who has a very limited understanding of why their child is having problems (which may, incidentally, mirror problems that the parent himself experienced as a child).

The Infant: Developing Trust

During the first several months of life, the infant faces several critical developmental tasks, including learning how to regulate and calm himself and how to use the senses to learn about the world and the people in it. However, the most critical psycho-social task faced by the infant relates to the development of trust; the infant must learn that his needs will be reliably met by parents and caretakers. In developing trust, the infant also learns that he is dependent on parents and caretakers to meet all needs—for food, warmth, safety, comfort—for survival.

The ability to organize sensations and to feel tranquil may pose problems for babies who are later diagnosed as having attentional deficits. These babies are often described as "hyper-excitable," "colicky," "irritable," and "unsoothable" by their parents.

These infants are often very active, easily distracted, and over-reactive to stimuli. Their behavior might appear to be chaotic or unpredictable. They may also be extremely sensitive to sensations—visual, auditory or tactile. Parents' efforts to soothe these babies with words, songs, or stroking may be met with tensed muscles, arching backs, and loud crying.

Not surprisingly, parents often respond to a 'difficult' baby with confusion and alarm. The interrelationship between a nurturing parent and a child is critical. When parents have a child with whom they cannot cope, they usually assume it is their "fault"—that they are failing as parents. These feelings of failure can set the stage for problematic, guilt-laden, parent and child interactions that continue through life.

The Toddler: Tolerating Separation

The second psychosocial developmental stage faced by the young child is that of separation. The separation process occurs in gradual steps, from about nine months to three-and-a-half years. During this period, the child develops the ability to hold a mental image of the parent in his mind. He begins to explore and learn about his environment and tolerates longer periods of separation from his parents. As the child accomplishes the task of separating, a strong sense of autonomy and confidence develops.

The toddler is also beginning to connect feelings and behavior. He is learning to take the initiative to get his needs met. He is developing ideas and concepts, along with the awareness that objects have functions (i.e. cups are to drink from, refrigerators hold food). The youngster is beginning to accept limits, which in turn helps him learn what he can and cannot do. As a correlate, he needs to learn to tolerate frustration. Finally, he needs to learn how to recover from the stress of disappointments and adapt to changes in his environment.

These developmental tasks can present significant problems for children with attentional deficits. Typically, these youngsters have difficulty tolerating frustration and may be emotionally over-reactive. Parents describe them as "all-or-nothing" children who have difficulty calming themselves. They tend to "fall apart" easily, dissolving into tears of frustration when needs or wants are not met immediately.

The preschool child: individuation, identity and self-concept

"Who am I?" asks the preschool youngster, as he experiments with wildly different roles and identities. This child tends to be unpredictable, volatile, and charmingly affectionate—while also learning to be disarmingly adept at manipulating the environment and the significant others within it! Children between the ages of three and six have a well-earned reputation for learning how to "divide and conquer" to get their wants and needs met.

Not surprisingly, preschool youngsters often have great difficulty distinguishing between reality and fantasy. As they try on different identities (teacher, policeman, father, mother), their ability to think magically is an asset. Nothing is impossible when you are four or five!

As the child begins to develop a solid identity, his self-concept is also emerging. Each child's self-concept consists of images and beliefs about the self, including easily-verifiable facts:

"I am a girl. I have black hair."

And less-verifiable but strongly-held beliefs and images about the self:

"I am smart. I am good. I am lovable." Or the reverse, "I am dumb. I am bad. I am unlovable."

During the preschool years, the common behavioral signs exhibited by many children with attentional deficits—high activity levels, poor persistence, interpersonal/peer group problems, and difficulty in modulating behavior and impulses, often begin to create problems for the youngster. He may be fearful, confused, manipulative, or avoidant. Attention deficits and other learning disabilities are strong contributors to the emergence of overanxious disorders of childhood, including school phobias.

Since a diagnosis of Attention Deficit is usually not made until after the child has entered school, the atypical ways that these children react and respond during the first years of life are perplexing and distressing. Confused parents often send strong disapproving messages to the child that he can behave and stay under control if he tries hard enough. Concerned family members often criticize both child (for being bad) and parents (for being ineffective), creating even more stress between parents and child.

The Elementary School Child: Consolidation Stage

As the child shifts from preschool to elementary school, he consolidates the gains made during the previous stages (i.e., basic trust, separation, and indi-

THINK FAST! THE ADD EXPERIENCE

viduation). The major psycho-social tasks of childhood have been dealt with, freeing the latency-aged child to focus his energy on learning in school, in addition to developing and refining interpersonal relationships.

The school, as the vehicle for teaching academics and social skills, now occupies a central role in the child's life. Vast amounts of factual data must be learned. The child must learn how to read, write, do arithmetic, be a good friend, and be a good student. The elementary school child's task is to learn how to relate appropriately to adults (aside from parents) and children who are not siblings.

After entering the educational system, the child with attentional deficits will often begin to struggle and may lag behind his peers, academically and socially. Often, ADD youngsters have "social deficits" in that they have difficulty accurately interpreting and processing social information and cues. This "social deficit disorder," coupled with impulsivity, may lead to the development of socially unacceptable behaviors.

Paradoxically, many children and adults with Attention Deficit Disorder are also intensely sensitive to feedback from others. As the child becomes aware of his differences, is shunned or teased by peers, and criticized by teachers for being unable to remain in control, he begins to develop a negative self-image, low self-esteem, depression and anger. What parents and teachers, and other significant people tell the child about himself has a powerful impact on his developing self-concept. The child begins to view himself as he is viewed by others. Told repeatedly that "You could do better if you tried," he begins to feel that he is worthless because he can't always control his behavior." Sadly, these negative feelings about his self often persist through life.

How To Help

Attention Deficit Disorder is a neurobehavioral disorder that causes multiple problems for children. Typically, the child with ADD will experience difficulties in several areas of life, including learning, peer relationships, self-esteem, mood, behavior, and family relationships.

Medication helps to relieve many symptoms of distractibility and hyperactivity in about 75% of children. Most children are treated with psychostimulant medications (Ritalin, Cylert, Dexedrine). Others respond to a carefully titrated blend of antidepressant medication (the most commonly prescribed is imipramine), and/or psychostimulants. There are other medications which are used less frequently but also with good effect.

Therapy or counseling can also be useful in helping both the child and his family deal with ADD-related problems. If therapy is indicated, it is important to select a professional who is knowledgeable about ADD and its impact on family dynamics and relationships. Depending on the child's problems, therapy may include a variety of interventions, including social skills training, compliance training with parents, psychosocial education of parents and child, anger management training, cognitive therapy to improve self-esteem and mood, and family therapy with parents and siblings.

Finally, living with an ADD child can offer special charms and delights. These children can be very perceptive and sensitive to the plight of others. They are intensely curious, creative and inventive. Many are very affectionate. Most of their 'problems' arise from the fact that they process emotional and intellectual information somewhat differently from 'normal' children. Our culture places great value on conformity, especially in the training and education of children. If the child with ADD is raised and educated with an appreciation of his or her uniqueness and strengths, then that child can grow up to be a healthy, productive adult.

Guidelines for Parenting Attention Different Kids

by George Lynn, M.A., C.M.H.C.

A CHILD WITH ATTENTION DIFFERENCES literally sees the world differently than other kids. Though each child is unique, special parenting methods should be used to bring out these kids' strengths in intellect and creativity and to compensate for problems with short term memory, oppositional behavior, tics, and obsessive compulsive tendencies.

It is important to remember that Attention Different kids can be remarkably purposeful. Helping them achieve their intrinsic purposes is the best way to motivate them. For this reason it is essential to keep communications open so that you can determine what is currently important to your child in terms of goals, wants, and dreams. Once these are known, a data base exists for constructing a motivating context for him. Here are some guidelines:

1. Create positive alternative choices based on your child's purposes and encourage him to make a choice.

    Example: If you want him to finish a project, say "Would you like 10 minutes or 15 to finish your project?" or;

    If you want him to get his homework done, say "When would you like to complete your homework: after school or after dinner so that you can have your friend over?"

2. Use "I" statements, not "you" statements that move him toward positive outcomes.

    Do not say: "Don't talk to me in that tone of voice." Say: "I'll be glad to discuss this when respect is shown."

    Do not say: "Stop arguing with me." Say: "I'll be glad to discuss this as soon as the arguing stops."

    Do not say: "Pay attention" Say: "I'll start again as soon as I know that you are with me."

3. Keep your cool. Know your stress triggers and have another adult available to support you if possible. Attention Different kids react best to "matter-of-fact" communications. When you show anger, they will react quickly, in an oppositional manner. An ugly battle can result.

George Lynn, a mental health therapist who works with kids with the ADD and Tourette Syndrome diagnoses, is the father of two grown daughters and a bright 11-year-old child with Tourette's. He can be reached at PO Box 3363, Kirkland, WA 98083 (206) 454-1787 or CompuServe 73773,1454.

4. Make consequences specific to the problem and dole them out in small increments. If he refuses to eat dinner with the family, have him get his own dinner one night a week. If time out is required, make it for 3 or 5 minutes at a time, not a half hour or hour. Make consequences follow infractions close to real time. Short term memory problems make delayed consequences useless.

5. Don't get hooked into oppositional arguments. When you notice that you are arguing, state the desired outcome and disengage quickly. Let him have the last word. Allow him to cool off.

6. Keep rewards visible and immediate to desired action.

    Example: If you want him to control his behavior on the school bus, use a custom designed form that allows him to accumulate points toward a desired outcome when he behaves. Have him keep score each day. "Bus tickets" (behavior reports) or angry lectures do not work and can make the situation worse.

7. Reward for work completed. Do not punish for incomplete work.

    Example: If you want him to leave the house in time to get his bus, provide a jar of tokens by the front door that he gets to add to each time he gets out on time, or;

    If you want him to do his school work, set up a chip or point system that he adds to each day for work completed and redeems on weekly basis. Don't be afraid to use monetary rewards. Remember, the best motivators are rewards that help him achieve his purposes.

8. In problem situations use "reminder" language to overcome short term memory problems.

    Example: To get him to move out of contact when he is yelling or poking others say "When you can show me that you have control of your body by stopping your swearing and poking and get to your room, we can talk about what you want."

9. Don't push him past his capabilities. Keep homework assignments short. Allow use of keyboard for writing. Encourage use of the computer. Encourage him to write about his feelings. Have him keep a diary or journal.

10. Assist with sequencing and transitions and train him to do it himself. Attention Different kids hate to be surprised or rushed.

    Examples: If you want him in bed by 8:30 school nights, Remind him at 8:15 "You need to brush your teeth and be in bed in the next 15 minutes so that I can read to you." or;

    To help him learn to get his stuff together to get out the door in the morning, teach him a rhyme such as "Two, four, six, eight, get pack, lunch,

84

THINK FAST! THE ADD EXPERIENCE

homework, and wait. . ." Some Attention Different children have a keen ear for music and can carry a tune splendidly, or;

To help him do chores around the house, post a list of required steps on the fridge for him to follow.

11. Get on problems early. He may signal you that he is "heating up to a confrontation" by facial tensing, or acting angry or silly.

12. (Especially for Tourette children) Don't tell him not to have tics. You may be able to redirect some . . . . From pulling out hair, to gentle pulls or self message. From head banging, to snapping a rubber band on his wrist. Creativity is essential here.

13. Help him work through obsessions and compulsions (OCD) by making it O.K. to talk about them. These tend to get worse when the child is tired. Experiment with creative methods to ease the stress of these "mind tics." One child we know gets extremely bugged by people sitting near him with their elbows pointing at him. The parents' creative solution? Draping their elbows with Kleenex at appropriate times. Medication is available to help with OCD also. Consult your physician.

14. Physical exercise is a great way to let off the pressure that causes tics and hyperactivity. Team sports may be difficult for Attention Different kids so encourage solo exercise such as rope jumping, running for points, bicycling or exercycling.

15. Encourage pretend play, read to them, make up stories. Some Attention Different kids, especially Touretters, may not involve themselves much in pretend play. Helping them enjoy active play imagination can relax them and possibly contribute to long term healing. Bring out their natural, zany, sense of humor.

16. Encourage unstructured creativity and don't force a kid too quickly to define alternatives or implement solutions. A great strength of these kids is creativity, especially on the front end of the creative process; the asking of "what if" types of questions. Encourage mind play.

17. Most important, don't push yourself to be a perfect parent. Give yourself credit; yours is one of the most difficult, stressful, jobs in the world. We are all entitled to our share of mistakes. Take it one day at a time!

Yesterday's Child

by Janie Bowman

YESTERDAY'S CHILD WAS BORN in the 1800's. As a young boy, he was considered medically fragile. Every respiratory illness known to mankind in that age seemed to seize him. Even though Yesterday's Child spent many of his early years ill, this did not stop his insatiable curiosity and boyish escapades. TODAY's child would be described as "just being a boy."

YESTERDAY'S child often found himself in risky life and death situations. Around the age of five, this boy nearly drowned in a canal; then almost smothered as he sank into the depths of a grain elevator. TODAY's child would be described as "having no common sense."

YESTERDAY'S child was found asleep in the barn in a nest he had constructed, lying on top of the chicken and goose eggs he was trying to hatch. TODAY's child would be called "weird, eccentric." "Get off those eggs, you'll crack them!"

YESTERDAY'S child drove his parents to exhaustion by his persistent questioning of the world around him, determined to know the "whys," "what fors," and "what abouts" of his world. TODAY's child is searching for someone to ask.

YESTERDAY'S child, with no malice aforethought but only out of the intense curiosity of an inquisitive mind, set his father's barn on fire. For this he was publicly thrashed by his father, who tried to instill in him the serious consequences of his actions. TODAY's child would be called a "juvenile delinquent."

After only three months of formal education, YESTERDAY's child walked out of his school in a fit of rage. Running home, he could hear the thoughts of the schoolmaster echoing in his head: "stupid . . . stubborn . . . difficult." Thus, at the tender age of eight, YESTERDAY's child refused to return to school. The next day, YESTERDAY'S mother gave the schoolmaster a piece of her mind and withdrew the boy from school. From that day onward, she became YESTERDAY's teacher. TODAY's child would be called "a problem child, a bad boy, oppositional." And TODAY's mother would be told she was "highly excitable, and coddling her child." She would be encouraged by all the experts to force her child to return to school because "He'll outgrow it. He's got to learn to adjust."

YESTERDAY's child went swimming with a friend in a nearby creek. When the friend didn't surface for air, YESTERDAY's child waited for what seemed like forever. As darkness fell, in his own unique 5-year-old logic, YESTERDAY concluded that it was time to go home. As the town was trying to piece together the disappearance and drowning of his friend, he tried to explain how he waited for what seemed like forever. . . . TODAY's child would be treated for "Conduct Disorder" and undoubtedly find himself one step away from the juvenile justice system.

YESTERDAY just couldn't comprehend consequences; that much seems true. One day he attached wires to the tails of two cats and energetically rubbed their fur. This experiment in static electricity went astray when he was brutally clawed. One unsuspecting childhood friend suffered an upset stomach after YESTERDAY gave him some sort of powder just to see if the resulting gas it produced would send him flying. TODAY's child would be in long-term therapy for Attention Deficit Hyperactivity Disorder, Pervasive Development Disorder, or some other behavioral disorder.

YESTERDAY's mother complained constantly about the life-threatening condition of his bedroom. Fearing for the safety of her family and any others who ventured into the family home, YESTERDAY's mother moved his experiments into the cellar. YESTERDAY called it his laboratory and immersed himself in science, to the exclusion of what other "normal" kids were doing at his age. TODAY's child would be called "Schizoid," and TODAY's family would be labeled "dysfunctional." TODAY's child would be spending time in a court-ordered alternative school program, meeting with a psychiatrist twice a week for therapy, and be enrolled in a class to learn social skills.

At age 12, YESTERDAY's child insisted on going to work and began successfully earning his own wage. TODAY's child, at that age, would face a closed door to the world of mentorship in the workplace. TODAY's child would have to search beyond home and work for other avenues that accept and appreciate his abilities.

As you read about YESTERDAY's child, you are probably wondering how he could have survived and how he could have contributed to society in a positive way. Clearly, YESTERDAY had somebody who accepted his uniqueness, changed his environment to meet his needs, was not intimidated by his gifts, and tried sincerely to see the world through his eyes.

YESTERDAY's name is Thomas Alva Edison.

What is your child's name?

"What's ADD, You Say?"

by Matthew Kutz

ADD IS ME. The child of today, a child of triumph and a child of sorrow, a child of curiosity and knowledge. ADD is me! And I am ADD! Being in regular schools was an experience I will never forget. Most teachers when referring to ADD had no idea what they were talking about; they got everything wrong. They think you'll see and hear better if they sit you up front or sit you away in a corner. I am not blind, deaf, dumb, stupid nor a behavior problem. I am however attention deficit; my attention span doesn't last on any one subject very long unless I get totally consumed by a particular subject.

My special education teacher in fourth grade got angry because I corrected him about fruits and vegetables. He was explaining to the class that a tomato was a vegetable like a potato; but it is not, it is a fruit.

Being ADD is like being in a box and unable to get out. Punching your way out, the walls only turn to stone and the space gets smaller. My world begins to shrink.

Being ADD means you see things other people miss. When you see a peach you see a piece of fruit. I see the color, the texture, and the field where it grew.

Being ADD I'm not qualified to say how the brain functions but I am qualified to say how much it hurts when other people make fun of you. Sometimes it doesn't seem fair when they tease you and you want to bust their jaw but you walk away to keep from lowering yourself to their standards.

Being ADD is like being a hunter of today looking for new ways and new challenges to broaden my way. Being ADD doesn't mean life is over; it means it's just beginning. Being ADD means some things are more difficult for me to understand as my mind wants to investigate beyond what seems obvious to you.

Being ADD, when I read a book about marine life my mind allows me to travel with the fish and imagine life beneath the sea. Or I can read a book about astronomy and dance among the stars. I can do more than one thing at a time and do both well yet I can be stumped by some simple things.

I may not immediately comprehend that 3+4=7, but I may fully realize that n+26=51 and that the missing number is 25.

So when you meet me try to understand that what you are trying to teach me is totally boring if I've already learned it, or completely mystifies me if I

Matthew Kutz wrote this when he was a 13-year-old student enrolled in the Walnut Valley Unified Home Study Program in Walnut, California. This was originally published in the Spring 1993 edition of the Olympia Chapter, Learning Disabilities Association of Washington, Attention Deficit Newsletter and subsequently in other ADD newsletters nationwide.

haven't and have not caught on in a reasonable length of time. Be kind, patient and understanding; I will eventually learn it—then, I am promptly through with it and ready for a new challenge or my exploring mind will continue to hunt for a subject more absorbing than something I've already learned . . .

I cannot begin to tell you in a few short paragraphs what ADD is or isn't. I can only say it isn't hopelessness, despair, or regret. It is just a different way of being and it's just being me!"

Hunting Brains Engage in A Stimulus Quest

by Nina B.

DO YOU HAVE TO JUMP-START your brain for all sorts of tasks, from things as mundane as brushing your teeth to things as important as writing checks? And do you find, once turned on, that it almost takes an Act of Congress to get you to stop and do something else?

Have you always been chided for being either too fast or too slow? For always doing too much or too little? Have you always been a restless soul? Have you ever felt as if you were missing the gene for consistency?

If so, you have much in common with those who think of themselves as "Hunters."†

Unlike their more methodical, orderly "Farmer" counterparts, Hunters find it tortuous to function at a steady pace. It is as if the engine that powers their brains comes equipped from the factory with only two gears: full-speed ahead or full-stop.

Thus might a Hunter be a wandering dreamer or a human dynamo.

Different perceptions

I've spent three years speaking on-line with Hunters around the country. Many, including me, are parents of children with Attention Deficit Disorder, or ADD. Others are adults who've been diagnosed.

Thom Hartmann, author of ATTENTION DEFICIT DISORDER: A DIFFERENT PERCEPTION (Underwood-Miller, 1993) and founder of the ADD Forum on CompuServe, coined the Hunter concept. Many have since adopted it as a way to discuss their shared traits without clinical terms, as people differ about how to read the ADD label.

On one end, you have physicians such as Edward Hallowell and John Ratey who wrote DRIVEN TO DISTRACTION (Pantheon, 1994). They say it is not unlike being farsighted; that ADD is clearly just as deserving of aid and is no more a stigma, per se, than needing glasses to focus your eyes.

---

† For information about the Hunter/farmer premise, see "Are You a Hunter or a Farmer" by Thom Hartmann in Chapter 2 of this book.

Cast in that light, Steven Spielberg, Robin Williams, Thomas Edison and Winston Churchill have all been cited as examples of ADD-types.

On the other end, there are physicians such as the one who said on-line to a forum member "anyone who can write as well as you, is not ADD."

Funny, I thought. Another doctor once said the exactly the same to me. His point was that a well-functioning adult isn't "disordered" in the clinical sense of that word, attention issues or no.

But the doctor on-line had a different point.

He'd treated the more classical underattentive (and often hyperactive) type who has to jump-start his brain to turn on at all. The ADDer who can zoom in to excel if engaged, but zones out away from keen stimuli, had no place in his paradigm.

So could two clinicians say "Not ADD" in different ways, where a third and fourth might say, "Of course."?

Stimulus-seekers

Even more often than doctors debate, they come on-line to compare notes about the differences between ADD and other conditions such as depression.

As one who's always struggled to put the brakes on my roving mind and pace my attention more evenly, I know one very big clue: the issues begin in childhood and persist chronically, regardless of mood.

A depressed person may be persistently disengaged, but as feelings lift, the problems fade. A stimulus-driven ADD-type wrestles to resist wayward drives and urges even when he is feeling good.

There are many theories about what's happening. Some speak of cerebral chemistry involving serotonin and dopamine. Others wonder about over- and under-arousal in the reticular activating system. Some speculate about links to thyroid metabolism.

The causes aren't certain, and could be many, but it is known medication may help. Small doses of stimulants might provide the fuel needed to kick-start the engine or run it more smoothly. Without it, some folk "self-medicate" with nicotine, caffeine, or worse.

But even when prescriptions help, Hunters are still born to be Stimulus-seekers, still challenged to channel that "seeking" constructively.

Given how dynamic they can be if plugged in and turned on, helping Hunters discover, then build on, their strengths may be the key to everything else.

Intensity vs Intimacy

During the summer of 1994, forum members wrestled with the difference between intensity and intimacy in relationships. While there is no one answer to the question posed by psychologist Harlan Lampert, PH.D. of Maryland, their thoughtful insights are valuable.

Fm: *Harlan Lampert,* PH.D.
To: *All*

Hi y'all.

I've been lurking in these threads and want to throw out something for all to consider.

It's been my personal and professional experience that often people will mistake intensity, intense feeling, passion, and even obsession for intimacy.

Intimacy goes hand in hand with a certain level of trust and experience. Intensity mimics that as we get flooded with assumptions and projections about the other person.

Intimacy and intensity can coexist in relationships.

Any experience or observations or dispute with my assumptions and conceptualization of these ideas?

Fm: *Erik Magnuson*
To: *Harlan Lampert,* PH.D.

"Intensity vs. intimacy"—You *would* have to bring that up.

I had a period of intense infatuation with one woman and one night while drifting off to sleep, a voice in my head shouted "Intensity is not love!"

The definition of intimacy that I like best is: knowing that you will be heard. A problem with intense relationships is being so focused on passion (and sex) that being heard is not important—until things start coming apart.

Some of the most intimate relationships I've had have been very low key, but unfortunately lacking the passion that would lead them to something more.

I suspect that "intensity vs. intimacy" is as much a problem for "farmers" as it is for "hunters."

Fm: *Harlan Lampert,* PH.D.
To: *Erik Magnuson*

I like your notion of "knowing you'll be heard."

Question for you and all other men in this thread: How often do you experience that with other men? Why is it so hard?

Fm: *Erik Magnuson*
To: *Harlan Lampert, PH.D.*

Are you trying to get a great discussion started here? <triple grin!> (Looks like you're succeeding.)

Anyway, as to "knowing that I will be heard by other men," I experience that maybe a quarter of the time with men—and usually with the same men; i.e., I can count on a few men hearing me out and saying something that indicates they understood what I said in regard to emotional issues.

You asked: why is it so hard?

In part because I was repeatedly told as a child that boys don't cry (probably more often by women than men!) and also sensing the discomfort that a lot of other men had about their feelings. Also, a lot of literature showed the "ideal male" as being stoic.

Another reason was that I felt like an alien growing up (in part related to the previous paragraph) and didn't think *anyone* knew how I felt. One of the things that I like about this forum is finding people who've been through what I've been through or least make an attempt to understand.

Still another reason is the competiveness of men in a mixed group, especially a group of singles.

Any more questions? (grin)

Fm: *Rose Zagaja*
To: *Harlan Lampert, PH.D.*

Re: "intimacy and intensity can coexist in relationships."

I agree.

In my own mind's definition here, intimacy is about emotional (and sometimes physical) sharing in a relationship. I have many (emotionally) intimate relationships with forum members here. Then there are others that aren't intimate at all. Then there are the intimate relationships outside the cyber world. As risky as it can be at times, I really enjoy intimacy.

Intensity, on the other hand, is about the *strength* of the feelings (in my mind). My feelings are usually quite intense <strongly felt>.

Re: "Intensity mimics that as we get flooded with assumptions and projections about the other person."

Hmmm. Interesting point. Are you meaning that if we are intense, we may assume how the other person feels about us?? Then, maybe we get wrapped up in that intensity to the point of obsession??

IF that's the point, Doc (grin), then how does one distinguish whether they are feeling intense or intimate?

Fm: *Harlan Lampert, PH.D.*
To: *Rose Zagaja*

Now that I think about it, and respond to other messages in the thread, I'm getting clearer about this for myself.

It seems to me that intensity is more of an individual's experience, and intimacy is more of a shared experience. I guess I'm suggesting that there are two separate concepts of intensity that we are talking about. One is the *quantity* of feeling (as you describe in your message), the other is about a combination of the fantasy and the power that resides within the individual when the other person is not well known but is powerfully important.

And, no, it's probably not a continuum up to the point of obsession.

Fm: *Carlos Pedraza*
To: *Rose Zagaja*

I wanted to contribute my 2 cents worth. . .

Re: "IF that's the point, Doc (grin), then how does one distinguish whether they are feeling intense or intimate?"

My answer (tho I'm no doctor): Time. Time usually tells us whether the intensity of those first hours, days or weeks mature into the intimacy of lasting friendship.

I know we're talking semantics here, but to me "intensity" relates to the strength of emotion, while "intimacy" refers to the closeness friends are able to maintain over the long haul. Intimacy operates at the intellectual, emotional, and spiritual levels; sometimes on the physical, depending on the person.

Fm: *Dave deBronkart (Sysop)*
To: *Erik Magnuson*

I suddenly have an image of "intimacy" being the soul/mind equivalent of a snuggle/nestle. Like, when you're nestled with someone, if one of you moves to get more comfortable, the other stays snuggled, perhaps moving a bit in response to your move, staying comfortable while adjusting.

That would be in distinct contrast to a situation where your move makes the other person grunt and grumble in dissatisfaction.

Fm: *Erik Magnuson*
To: *Dave deBronkart (Sysop)*

Acceptance and companionship are a couple of necessities for intimacy (or was it that intimacy is necessary for companionship).

Acceptance is very important for intimacy. If I don't feel safe being who I am around someone, then I am *not* going to be intimate with that person. It

94

would seem that intimacy is taking the step of being who I really am and not putting on a mask. For ADD'ers, that means not trying to be "normal."

One of the definitions of intimacy is a warm friendship.

Anyway, I think I have a handle on what intimacy means, but the phrase that drives me up the wall is "emotionally unavailable."

Fm: *Louis J Hoechsetter, PH.D.*
To: *Harlan Lampert, PH.D.*

Until and if one is able to let go and completely trust the other, there surely will be waxing and waning. Until we accept the whole package there will be internal conflict relating to trusting the other with our emotional health.

I have been open and honest with people I did not trust to really hear me, knowing that they were the way they are and accepting them for what they were, unable to reciprocate a kind of trust of open honesty, but maintaining a shell of protection or even attack. My open honesty did not depend on the other person; sometimes I got hurt if I was unaware that they were the way they are. Unless I have a political consequence to pay, I am open and honest, at great cost sometimes, but that is me, and I do not want to operate from a stance of an actor on stage.

You will experience a sense of freedom if you just relax and be yourself with anyone and let them react as they will. Some have a problem with that. That is their problem, not yours. I think I have gained as many friends as I lost after I started just being myself. Problem is, there are sometimes unwanted consequences along with the freeing. If one is married and has kids and the system is thrown out of balance by your change, the system will split if the other party does not also relax and be him or herself. Consequences considered, a conscious choice is made; then it is no longer a conditioned response.

Fm: *Harlan Lampert, PH.D.*
To: *Louis J Hoechsetter, PH.D.*

The voice of experience. Thanks

Fm: *Susan Burgess (PR Sysop)*
To: *Dave deBronkart (Sysop)*

Notice how "having no fear to XXXX" is a repeating theme thru this discussion of intimacy?

The word "fear" is what I'm zeroing in on. Seems to be the basic emotion.

Then after the word fear or no-fear you list things like: trust, honesty, being yourself and so on.

Fm: *Dave deBronkart (Sysop)*
To: *Susan Burgess (PR Sysop)*

From time to time we mention, here, the ADD "heightened response" to one thing or another. I wonder if there's a heightened response to fear of one thing or another.

Or, maybe our ongoing introspection here just makes us more attuned to what goes on in our own minds, and that particular thing is the same in just about everyone's mind.

Fm: *Harlan Lampert, PH.D.*
To: *Dave deBronkart (Sysop)*

I think there's an experience of intimacy in a range of emotions, not just the snuggle/cuddle/comfortable type.

My experience of anger and conflict in my close relationships has taken on more and more of a quality of closeness even in the rage and pain, as I have gotten older and wiser (grin).

Mind you now, that I can be as blind as a bat when my fears of being shamed or humiliated show up. But at least I bounce back faster and faster.

Fm: *Carla Nelson (Sysop)*
To: *Dave deBronkart (Sysop)*

That Hunters would marry Farmers to help provide the structure they lack and deal with the things they can't stand to deal with, then find the Farmer becomes a full-time Judge and Jury (and perhaps Martyr), *is very* common I suspect <wry grin>.

Fm: *Dave deBronkart (Sysop)*
To: *Carla Nelson (Sysop)*

Re: Hunters marrying Farmers . . .

There's another angle to this that we discussed maybe a year ago— sometimes the steady/stable young spouse marries the wild and crazy one *because* the other is wild and crazy. That would be all well and good, but as time goes by, if the stable one says "He'll grow up and settle down," it can be quite a setup for disappointment.

And, the stable one can feel like there's a broken promise, which can leave the wild and crazy one saying "Huh??? Did I say I was gonna change?? I thought you LIKED me this way!"

Mind, all, I'm not saying anyone's right or wrong to want anything in particular. I am saying it's darned important for everyone to be *clear* about *what* they want, to avoid these crossed-expectation train wrecks.

Answers to questions about ADD: in conference with Dr. John Ratey

Forum members flocked to a Feb. 7, 1995 conference with Dr. John Ratey, coauthor with Dr. Ned Hallowell of the books DRIVEN TO DISTRACTION and ANSWERS TO DISTRACTION. ADD Forum Sysop Carla Nelson acted as emcee, presenting questions to Dr. Ratey that had been previously solicited from forum members. In this edited transcript, Dr. Ratey answers questions on everything from medicine to sex.

Carla (Host): Hello people and welcome!

Glad you could join us to hear John Ratey take forum questions. Before I introduce and start, let me make sure you all understand that we are only asking questions submitted in advance. So, please, all of you sit on your hands <grin>.

Now it's my pleasure to welcome John Ratey, M.D. of Boston, known to all of you I'm sure as coauthor of the wildly popular DRIVEN TO DISTRACTION and ANSWERS TO DISTRACTION, which just came out, written with his partner Ned Hallowell.

Welcome John!

John Ratey: Ah! Hi!

Carla (Host): Ready for me to start wading through this big stack of questions we have for you?

John Ratey: You bet!

Carla (Host): Here we go then with a question that gets asked here LOTS by both patients and their docs . . . and that is. . .

How do you distinguish ADD from clinical depression or bipolar?

John Ratey: Depression or bipolar illness is episodic and doesn't have a lifelong course. The whole point of ADD is that it's a brain *difference* that shows up early in life, and remains there. One can find symptoms going all the way back to the farthest reaches of memory, and this is one of the best ways to differentiate it from depression or bipolar, or any of the affective disorders.

Carla (Host): Thanks! Moving right along to a more everyday coping question: A forumite who is working on getting accommodations at work wants to know two things:

(1) Is a private office with a door an "unreasonable" accommodation? and. . .

(2) If not, what do you say to a boss who says, "Then everyone will want one."

John Ratey: It *is* a matter of office politics and being tactful in asking for any accommodations. However, if it can and will improve your productivity, then a valid argument can be made for this accommodation as well as other kinds.

Carla (Host): She will like hearing that I am sure (grin).

Next query is about psychotherapy . . . A forumite has been frustrated by physicians who insist they cannot Rx for Adult ADD unless the patient is also undergoing psychotherapy. She does not want therapy right now; has not found it helpful. "Must I?" she asks.

John Ratey: The whole issue of treating ADD in adults is, as you know, new. Some therapists have held on to the belief that psychotherapy and drug prescriptions must go hand in hand. This, however, as time shows the real facts, will be less and less the case. There is no literature, no studies yet, showing this; however, most therapists treating ADD in adults certainly do not see them in the typical weekly psychotherapy or anything close to that for the period that they're prescribing for.

Psychotherapy is not to be undersold, however. Often, there are many problems that go along with the ADD's life, and it's very useful, especially at the beginning, to sort out what is the brain's part and what is the psychological history, and psychotherapy's magic can help unravel, alert, and encourage people to change their psychological "traps."

Carla (Host): Could you speak a bit to what you mentioned in your books . . . about how psychotherapy needs to be set up differently for an ADDer?

John Ratey: First, we talk a lot about "coaching" as a primary tool in helping the ADD person get on track and stay on track. This is a different model, totally, than traditional psychotherapy. It's a much more active, intervening, encouraging therapy that doesn't encourage the development of transference, and in fact one interprets any transference-like issues or feelings for the therapist *immediately* to get them out of the room.

Coaching is a bit like hiring a nag (grin) that is friendly, humorous, but militantly vigilant. ADDers and their therapist will forget that they have the ADD. Everyone involved in an ADDer's life needs to be on alert that when things go WELL, they have to remind the system, or everyone, that they still have the ADD, and all the environmental engineering that has taken place has to be reinforced.

Carla (Host): Thanks! That was very helpful, changing gears to medication . . . A patient who found ADDerall most effective wants to know what other meds might work similarly and if any new drugs are in the pipeline?

John Ratey: The only new drugs in the pipeline are being developed for depression. Some of these will no doubt be used to treat ADD, either as an adjunct or even at times as a primary stimulant-like therapy.

For instance, Wellbutrin and now Effexor may have a place as a primary drug for treating the ADD. With the ADDerall removal, people will be searching for alternatives. Obviously, Dexedrine spansule, Desoxyn (which is an excellent drug and has probably the best long-acting preparation of all the stimulants) should be tried, also Desipramine in adults, either in low doses as I have always recommended, or in the more traditional high doses, might be considered.

As for ADDerall, the long-acting amphetamine is Dexedrine and Desoxyn.

Carla (Host): You lead right into two related questions I have here, which I will ask separately.

The first is regarding Wellbutrin and when/why it might be preferable to Ritalin?

John Ratey: Wellbutrin's effects will last throughout the day and the evening. One of the major problems with Ritalin is its short half-life. One of the major issues we try to treat in treating ADD is the ever-changing nature of the state of consciousness.

With any short-acting substance, like Ritalin, its own ebb and flow creates an uneven state of mind. Wellbutrin, when it works, creates a constant predictable state of consciousness. By consciousness, I mean attention—the inner environment where perception, association, and interpretation is done.

Carla (Host): Another patient asks what to do when you get bad [Ritalin] rebound with moods and depression, but antidepressants (including SSRIs) only seem to make it worse.

John Ratey: OK, lemme think about this . . . I often add a small dose of Desipramine, 10 – 30 mg/day, to people who have a rebound with Ritalin or Dexedrine. This *sometimes* works.

Also, one can switch entirely to Wellbutrin or Effexor, and explore whether or not this will bring about a more consistent and less choppy attention state.

And then, this points up a big issue: the therapist and the patient should constantly be on the hunt, looking for the right regimen— there is no cookbook, as most of you know—it is at best an inexact practice (let alone "science") at this point, so the hunt needs to continue.

Carla (Host): Thanks! . . . Moving on to a bit more humorous note, a woman writes, "My husband asked me to ask . . . why are ADDers so stubborn and picky?"

John Ratey: Huh! . . . The stubbornness can be thought of from many different angles, but one interesting one is that the ADD person has considered their position from many many different angles, and they truly believe that they have considered every alternative position out there, so once they land on an idea, an attitude, or finally make a decision, then they can be unmovable, with the belief, tho it may be false, and as I talk about in ANSWERS TO DISTRACTION, it may be a false intuition, or intuition gone awry, that leads them to holding onto a position that is completely laughable.

People with ADD can also think of themselves as being picky, again because they've done "thought experiments" on much of the world, and therefore feel that what they want *has* to be just right, just so.

Carla (Host): Moving along . . . Someone writes to ask for details about the NIMH study being done currently and what they hope to investigate. That and any other interesting research you can share.

John Ratey: There's a *lot* of research going on right now, trying to replicate the PET studies of Zametkin, attempting to validate Dr. Amen's SPECT studies, to see whether these hold *any* utility, and to study the changes that any medication such as Ritalin and Dexedrine have on our fancy brain scans.

With the new MRI machines that we have, we are getting better at seeing demonstrable differences in the brains of ADDers vs normals, in children, adults, and adolescents. In *Answers*, I spend a couple of pages talking of the actual differences we are *pretty* sure exist and can be seen in ADD brains.

Carla (Host): I particularly enjoyed your discussion of the neurobiology of ADD in *Answers*.

John Ratey: [Oh, good!(grin)]

Carla (Host): For forumites who haven't read it yet . . . could you give us a few hints and highlights?

John Ratey: First, one can think of the major problem of ADD as a sleepy cortex—that is, whatever the ADD type is, whether they always are dreaming, whether they shift from unfocused to hyperfocused, the problem is that the cortex, or the top part of the brain, is never functioning in a dependable way. Our medicines act to stimulate the upper regions of our cortexes, which then act as a brake on lower-brain functions. This is an important and key concept.

Also, we are finding specific differences in ADD brains. The corpus callosum is a bit smaller. (The corpus callosum is the "mind cable" that connects the right hemisphere and the left hemisphere.) This may eventually help us in sub-typing right-brainers and left-brainers in their type of ADD.

But it also suggests that the frequently heard complaint "I know what I want to say but can't find the words," or "I can see the image but I can't translate it into sequential logical language"—this may be part of the problem—the "mind cable." Also, there are some studies suggesting there's a difference in the caudate nucleus area of the brain. This area is responsible for shifting movements *and* attention. This seems to be under-active and underdeveloped in some of the studies.

Please bear in mind that these are HIGHly speculative, and I am just weaving them into *my* metaphors that make sense to me (and others (grin)).

Carla (Host): Well it could be speculative but it sure is fascinating! Thanks! People wonder about questions like that here often.

Moving along to the parenting side, a forumite wonders if there are some methods of discipline that are more appropriate/effective for an ADD preschooler than others.

John Raley: [pause while thinking] Consistency in discipline is the rule . . . maintaining and supporting the *limits* to the preschooler's behavior is really the key. That means getting *everybody* involved, to help shape the environment that the ADDer is moving in. (Any specific methods in question?)

Carla (Host): OK . . . before we leave the neuro scene, I just remembered I forgot (grin) . . . to ask you about your own upcoming book on neuro-biology issues?

John Raley: Now that you ask (grin) . . . it's out—*Neuropsychiatry of Personality Disorders* by Blackwell Science—it's a medical text, not a "popular" book, BUT, it's written and able to be understood by most intelligent people (e.g. most forum members).

Neuropsychiatry of addictions, frontal lobe problems, etc.—by the leading experts in their fields, are included, as well as a chapter on ADD.

Carla (Host): Great! That one goes on my list . . . Back to parenting . . . a parent of a fifth grader wants to know "how bad" a child's ADD should be before you try medication, i.e. what factors should guide the decision?

John Raley: When all non-medication measures have been attempted, when the teachers have been alerted, when tutoring has been offered, and the classroom behavior has been attempted to be altered as best it can, and STILL the child continues to be unstoppable, then medication should be considered.

Don't forget that BEFORE this point, the self-image problems that result from an out-of-control third- and fourth-grade experience will have already had an effect on the fifth grader, so the issue of medication is not one that should wait until the last ditch.

Kids get into a groove, habits, develop views of themselves very early. So decisions such as medication, which may be very useful, should be made with this fact well in mind.

Carla (Host): Thanks! Moving on to an ADDult concern . . . More than one forumite wonders about any tips for dealing with what you might call the Spouse In Denial Syndrome. aka . . . It's not my problem. (grin)

John Raley: Which is the denier—the ADD one or the ADDer's spouse?

Carla (Host): The non-ADDer.

John Raley: So the non-ADD spouse says, basically, "BS?"

Carla (Host): Right.

John Raley: Or just says "Don't ask ME to adjust?"

Carla (Host): Both!

John Raley: From the beginning, the appeal should go back to the initial
conditions of the marriage:
"Why did we get involved, anyway?"
"Isn't it worth anything? Isn't it worth a LOT?
"Shouldn't we try to make it better?"
The ADDer *has* to know and accept full responsibility for their
ADD, and really has to *ask*, almost beg, *implore* their spouse to help
them deal with their brain lapses. After all, these people got together
because they were in love, and likely the non-ADD spouse was
attracted to the zaniness of the ADDer. Appealing to first principles
is often the *only* way to unlock the angry non-ADD spouse.

We all know that the amount of pain that can be generated in a
marriage by ADD is huge, and there has to be the asking for forgive-
ness, if you will, of the ADDer from the spouse. But after that, they
both have to acknowledge the realities and each of their limits.

Carla (Host): Good answer! Thanks. Before I forget again (grin) let me stop and
ask how interested people can get your Neurobiology book . . .
from medical textbook houses? Or bookstores? Or?

John Raley: Call 1-800-215-1000 and ask for it.

Carla (Host): (grin) Okeydoke . . . More than one has asked . . . I guess because
docs differ . . . what are your feelings about Ritalin vacations on
weekends and holidays?

John Raley: My feelings in general about Ritalin, or any of the stimulants, or
any ADD medication, is that it's really up to the person. What works
for one person won't work for another. I have a number of patients
who ONLY take their Ritalin on weekends and holidays (!), because
their work demands are so intense that they only need a stimulant
on weekends!

Other patients find it useful to continue their medication on
weekends, and off days, because it allows them to function better
with their families, in leisure activities, sports, and allows them to
plan a bit more.

Otherwise, it's perfectly fine to stop the medicine if it doesn't have [a] bad effect. Being absolute about *anything* in using medicine with ADDers is a bad policy. It misses the point: the medicine is to help the brain function optimally, and really needs to be in the control of the patient. (WITH the doctor's participation.)

Carla (Host): Another med question . . . Is there a particular med strategy that might be more effective with ADD(U) which does not seem to be helped so much by stimulants.

John Raley: ADD(U)? You mean not hyperactive?

Carla (Host): Undifferentiated, I presume. That's the way the question was worded.

John Raley: That's what we discussed before, and in DRIVEN TO DISTRACTION—the antidepressants, exercise, meditation, biofeedback, more structuring . . . are sometimes the only things that work. If this person meant to imply that ADD without hyperactivity is less responsive to medicine, this goes against the collected wisdom and experience of other treaters, as well as my own experience—that is, ADD without H is very responsive to stimulant medication.

Carla (Host): Somebody asks about the genetic aspect, as her doctor said it is inherited,but she can't see any priors in her family and wonders if anything else might produce ADD?

John Raley: Sure: It may look like depression, addictions, anxiety disorders, criminality, eccentric . . . all these diagnoses and labels may be in the background, and they may be what we call "forme fruste" of the ADD that gets played out in this generation. This is the subject of another book that I'm working on which should be out next year.

Carla (Host): Another mom wonders if her child's ADD and his speech disorder are likely to be connected.

John Raley: Yes, very likely—we often see speech problems in ADD, because they result from the same neurobiological problem, that is, the "sleepy cortex."

Most speech problems have to do with not enough natural inhibition, which is the entire function of our highest cortex. SO, when the speech center is uninhibited, it comes out wrong. It comes out as stuttering, halting, mispronunciations . . . as the cortex works better, all speech functions improve. This is one of our major questions when looking at the longitudinal history of our patients—did they have speech problems as a child, which is indicative of this sleepier cortex?

Carla (Host): Back to meds again . . . Many ADDults report they still must deal with docs who won't prescribe stimulants for adults from fear of addiction or abuse. What can these patients cite for their docs besides "John and Ned say"? <smile>

John Ratey: In Answers to Distraction, in the Addiction chapter, I quote two very prestigious sources; Dr. Tom Detre and another doc, who have for years been saying that stimulants prescribed for ADD children, and when it was used in adults, was not addictive, and was unlikely to be abused.

This is certainly the case seen by *anyone* who treats ADD adults. This myth persists out there that Ritalin is a fun drug. Most people who have experienced taking Ritalin know that when you take too much, it feels *lousy*.

In fact, the drug culture sometimes takes Ritalin *and* Dexedrine with their hallucinogens, when what we know scientifically counters this belief—that is, it doesn't do that. But Ned and I have seen and treated over 3,000 ADDults and children and have yet to have a problem with abuse and/or addiction. The fact is, that if a good alliance is built and maintained that one doesn't need to worry about these problems.

The myth has been there for some time, since the "speed" culture of the 50s took hold. And like all traditions, it is very very difficult to change. The stimulants happen to be some of the cleanest drugs that we use in psychiatry—they have fewer side effects than most, they affect specific neurotransmitters, neurotransmitter *systems*, that is, and that's it—whereas most other drugs have *many* effects on the brain.

Carla (Host): Very good rebuttal! Thanks. . . . meds DO seem to top our list tonight, Somebody else wants to know of other polypharmaceutical combinations which have been found to be sometimes helpful besides combining SSRI and stimulants (or adding Desipramine as you mentioned)

John Ratey: The stimulant is the main drug used. Adjuncts that are particularly useful are a group called the beta-blockers—Propranolol or Inderal, and Corgard or nadolol. These are useful to help with temper tantrums, to help with somatic tension, tremors, tics, and general impulsiveness. Other drugs such as Clonidine have been used very successfully for many of the same complaints.

If mood instability is a prominent problem, and the SSRI's are not adequate, then Valproate or Tegretol can be very useful. One should avoid (except for occasional and very sporadic use) using the benzodiazepines like Valium, Ativan or Xanax. These drugs are now on every new doctor's spit list (grin) as we know that they reduce cognitive functions and deflect from the patient's quality of life.

To go on with the paradox of the fear of stimulants being addictive and abused, the benzodiazepines are still doled out fairly frequently and easily, and THESE are drugs well KNOWN to be abused and highly addictive, yet this tradition continues—even among the same doctors who fear Ritalin abuse!

The revolution with Prozac is really about the lack of side effects (Read: no depressing of cognitive function). This is why it has become a favorite household name so quickly: it does its business without making the person slower, duller-witted, less attentive, as many of the other medicines we've used have done.

Carla (Host): Thank you! I know I am not the only one enjoying the "Advanced ADD" discussion (grin) Moving along . . . A forumite says she particularly enjoyed the section in ANSWERS about ADD in prisons. Do you know if anyone is doing any ADD therapy in prisons?

John Ratey: Not yet, not to my knowledge. I'm going out to talk at the Men's Colony Prison at San Luis Obispo, CA about Aggression and ADD in March and I know that the prisoners and their jailers are interested in this.

Carla (Host): Speaking of your books again, some folks want to know if the "celebrity" ADDers you mentioned are acknowledged diagnoses . . . or more your musing. (grin)

John Ratey: People like Ross Perot, Clinton, and Bush are certainly not diagnosed, and looking at their presumed symptoms is something everyone likes to do, but it's certainly not diagnosis. I might add that Ned and I have been very careful not to diagnose like this, since diagnosis requires a full history. Do you have any names in mind?

Carla (Host): Dustin Hoffman was the particular one mentioned in the question.

John Ratey: Dustin Hoffman announced it on network TV, not *our* diagnosis. (grin) Mozart, on the other hand, we dug up and had a little talk with.(grin!)

Carla (Host): (laughing aloud!) On the subject of doctors again . . . I've been asked to ask you, by a frustrated patient, whether there are any plans in the works to offer some kind of certification for ADD specialists.

John Ratey: No, but we're talking *extensively* to psychiatrists and other physicians as we go around the country. There are some workshops that we've already been involved in and will continue to be doing to train people. I speak very often at medical school Grand Rounds, and now the request mainly is to talk about ADD and its diagnosis and treatment, especially in adults, and that was not the case, mostly, a few years ago.

For instance, today I was talking to the training director at NYU Medical School in psychiatry, who said that *everyone* is talking about our book DRIVEN TO NEW JERSEY. (double grin!) When he was Visiting Prof at Tufts, recently, he was very glad to hear that we now had the *answers* to New Jersey out. And, he wanted us to send a copy to Christie Whitman. (The gov. of NJ) <joke>

Carla (Host): Okay . . . moving back to couples stuff . . . A private note I received requested I inquire about the problem of ADDers drifting off (mentally) during sex.

John Ratey: Happens all the time. This is one of the major reasons why ADD women have trouble having orgasms: they lose their focus. Medicine that helps maintain their focus often helps them have orgasms for the first time in their lives.

Also, ADD *living* in the rapid pace, response-to-the-immediate world, can keep people from even *thinking* about sex. Let alone drifting off *during* it. So there are many problems that ADDers have, and like anything else, in attempting to rectify this problem, planning— assigning a time—and *practice* is heartily and forcefully recommended!

Carla (Host): Someone would like to hear some comments about the ADDers sense of time . . . re: NOW and NOT NOW.

John Ratey: Well, one can speculate forever about this, but "the time is now," as you said in your question, and that usually is *all* that it is for the ADD person. This leads to many, if not most, of the problems in living that ADD people have: since they're *so* much in the Now, they can't *plan*! They can't make goals, because the future isn't something they're really familiar with.

Carla (Host): Combining two questions . . . what about links to other conditions like Alzheimer's, Parkinson's, PDD and autism, any data (or speculation)?

John Raley: No reliable data, lots of speculation. Links between ADD and Alzheimer's is *hinted* at, but no data. We haven't been following ADD people longitudinally up until very recently, not long enough to look at that.

    The association with Parkinson's in the family history of ADD people is something that most neurologists pay attention to, but again there's no support in any data for this association.

    PDD and autism may be part of a spectrum that ADD is sometimes on.

Carla (Host): I was just passed another one, about a child suspended from school for uncontrollable giggles and teacher's failure to grant this could be connected to ADD. Comment?

John Raley: Of COURSE it can be connected to ADD!!!!! It's a problem with inhibition!! And if there's supporting evidence in other symptoms, it may be JUST the ADD!! Uncontrollable ANYTHING—moving—talking— daydreaming—fantasizing—that's what ADD's about! The lack of inhibition!

Carla (Host): Well this has been MOST informative! Thanks even more for all your time here tonight! We learned a great deal and it's always a pleasure when you come around. (grin)

John Raley: Wonderful to be with you! I look forward to coming back soon— this is always a VERY interesting crowd! Good questions!

Carla (Host): Delighted, too, that you and your wife hang out with us here now and then. (Yes, a very sharp group if I do say so myself <big grin>)

John Raley: Okay, thanks—off to check my mail!

Carla (Host): Best of luck. . . and look forward to doing this again!

"We Need a Wife!" — ADD in Women

Introduction by Morgan Adcock, Carla Nelson and Janie Bowman

UNTIL **ADD WITHOUT HYPERACTIVITY** became accepted as a separate clinical entity, it was thought that ADD was mostly a problem of restless young males. Now we know ADD persists throughout life, and that it affects large numbers of women as well as men. But study of the non-hyperactive form of ADD is still fairly new, and study of ADD in females, even newer. Thus, science has only just begun to address how ADD might have an impact upon developing womanhood, PMS, pregnancy, lactation, and menopause, or mental health and emotional well-being, not to mention relationships.

Until more clinical data is compiled, women with ADD are largely dependent upon the information they exchange with each other. As a medium for exchange, the ADD Forum on CompuServe is a valuable resource.

ADD poses a number of particular challenges for women, not the least of which is the way in which they are at odds with traditional cultural norms. The domestic duties for which women still feel largely responsible require the sort of patient, methodical persistence ADDers find incredibly difficult, if not painful, because the chores aren't very stimulating.

Yet, the women are the ones who are still expected to perform most familial tasks.

In true forum partnership-style, this introduction was written in a round robin exchange among Sysops Morgan Adcock (74777,3462), Janie Bowman (72662,3716) and Carla Nelson (74774,1756). While Morgan and Carla are blessed with the "hunter trait" (ADD) Janie is a so-called "farmer" (non-ADD woman) who enjoys working with creative ADDers.

More than one ADD couple has joked, but only partly in jest, "We need a wife!"

Organizing; planning; keeping family members on task and on schedule; housekeeping; teaching children social and study skills; paying attention to details and being attuned to community values are society's expectations of women—yet, they are the most difficult expectations for ADDers to fulfill.

So it is that the tasks they are most often expected to do may be the ones for which they are the least suited. The result? Guilt may be the most common side effect of ADD in women.

Now that it has become much more common for women to work outside the home, ADD women are able to find more of the stimulation they crave. But in the workplace other obstacles await. The professions most suited to ADDers are often those that are most male-dominated.

Even when women find their ways into these work areas, they still confront a double standard of sorts; they are still expected to act in "womanly," non-ADD ways. The abruptness, independence, drive, and pragmatism so often esteemed, or at least tolerated in men, are so often devalued or criticized in women.

Females with ADD have been struggling to rein their wandering minds throughout their lifespan—from the spacey, dreamlike nemesis of childhood to the expectations of parenthood; from the, "Act like a lady, PUH-LEEEZE!" hyperactivity of earlier years to the active ADDult mind which constantly scans the environment seeking stimulation.

Now, within the intimate distance provided by online communications, women across the country and around the world are finding each other, sharing their experiences and their knowledge and offering mutual aid and comfort. What's more, they're having an incredibly good time doing it!

Thus are ADD women learning to look beyond the psychostigma of past definitions and redefine themselves and their lives—together.

WOMEN, PMS, AND ADD/ADHD
by Louis B. Cady, M.D.

When discussing ADD in women, a great deal of time is spent on the subject of the relationship of serotonin, PMS, and ADD/ADHD. Numerous psychiatric studies have been performed which relate a postulated deficit of central serotonin to premenstrual syndrome, or "premenstrual dysphoric disorder."

In order to avoid stigmatizing women, however, it should be clearly kept in mind that most women simply do not suffer from "PMS"—at least, not to a significant degree. Most every woman has cramping, bloating, and some feelings of fatigue and tiredness—men would too if they hemorrhaged every month! On the other hand, only some 2 – 5% of women have severe problems with PMS, and probably one third of women have mild to moderate symptoms.

Serotonin and PMS

A number of studies have correlated lowered states of serotonin with PMS. Here is some of the evidence:

☛ Treatment with serotonin-boosting drugs stabilizes PMS and attentuates or extinguishes a number of the symptoms. The most recent report of significant benefit was published by Steiner in the *New England Journal of Medicine*, in June, 1995, and dealt with the use of Prozac. This was widely quoted by the media, and appeared in/on both *USA Today* as well as CNN.

☛ Eating carbohydrates, sweets, and crunchy snacks (usually carbohydrates) is something that some women CRAVE premenstrually. Interestingly enough, these high carbohydrate foods provide the building blocks for the brain to produce more serotonin; hence, this is a self-medication approach (with food) which seems to be operating.* (see footnote on next page)

☛ This is similar to a finding in one study of treatment-seeking adult cocaine abusers (298 patients), showing fully one-third of them were diagnosable as having ADHD as children. Their average age of onset of use was younger, they used more cocaine, and they used it more frequently. These unfortunate children who were not diagnosed and treated were essentially "look-

---

Dr. Louis B. Cady is a psychiatrist in Evansville, Indiana who treats children, adolescents, and adults with ADD/ADHD. He did his residency in adult psychiatry at the Mayo Clinic in Rochester, MN. Dr. Cady's other interests include difficult-to-treat depression, eating disorders, and sleep disorders. He is the Medical Director of the Disordered Eating Program at the Mulberry Center in Evansville, IN, as well as the Medical Director of the Sleep Diagnostic Center of Indiana. A prolific speaker and author, Cady will be releasing two books in 1996—one tentatively titled MASTERMIND: THE PSYCHIATRY OF WEALTH, SUCCESS, AND HAPPINESS, and another book, LEARNING AND LIVING THE ABC'S OF LOVE FOR YOU AND YOUR CHILD. He can be reached on CompuServe at 74351,1275.

ing for Mr. Good-Drug" and they found that using cocaine—a stimulant—gave them what they needed. Some of my adult patients who abused stimulants and cocaine report that it had a wonderful calming effect for them. Hence, the drive to try to find a food, drug, or substance which will make us feel better and make up for natural chemical deficits seems to be quite high!

☞ Irritability, rage attacks and impulsiveness, and a general ability to maintain control of emotions can all be related to low serotonin. Interestingly, previous studies of people who killed themselves by extremely violent means (hanging, gunshot wound, or jumping from a tall building) were all found to have low breakdown-products from serotonin in their spinal fluid (which basically allows a direct measurement of the amount of serotonin in the brain). One study of violent and impulsive alcoholic offenders found that the impulsive and violent offenders, but not all of the comparison control group alcoholics, had a comparatively lower amount of serotonin in the brain. Ragefulness, inability to maintain control, and impulsive "popping off" or "exploding" can all be found in women with severe PMS.

☞ Finally, the coincidence of a number of the symptoms of PMS with those for depression is remarkable. In both disorders, appetite changes, sad mood, irritability, concentration problems, suicidal thoughts, sleep problems, and energy changes can all take place. When women get recurrently suicidally depressed pre-menstrually each month, they often comment, "Why is this happening to me? I have nothing to be upset or depressed about!" Treatment with a serotonin-boosting SSRI** may quickly eliminate the cycling mood disorder of premenstrual dysphoria in women.

It is fairly well established that curing what is presumed to be a low amount of central serotonin in depression correlates with some patients getting better. Thus, if you can stabilize depression with serotonin boosting drugs, and there are crossover symptoms of depression in a PMS syndrome, it seems logical that serotonin boosting-drugs would be helpful in treating it as well. And, of course, they are!

---

* It should be noted that phosphoenolpyruvate, the next to the last breakdown product in the process of glycolysis (which is the process of burning up simple and complex sugars which the body takes in from carbohydrates, e.g., Fritos. Nachos, Doritos, etc.) is combined with another chemical to launch into the metabolic pathway to create tryptophan. Having enough tryptophan around is the rate limiting step (or "bottleneck") for the production of serotonin. Hence, it's reasonable to assume that by loading up on carbohydrates, driving the glycolysis pathway, and making more phosphoenolpyruvate, the body is essentially loading up on the raw materials WAY DOWN THE PIPELINE in order to be ready to make plenty of tryptophan and, ultimately, serotonin.

　　Main sources of tryptophan include the "animal proteins" including meat and dairy products (milk and eggs). This also includes ice cream, which is why it may be a favorite binge food.

** Selective Serotonin Reuptake Inhibitor

THINK FAST! THE ADD EXPERIENCE

PMS & ADD/ADHD

Couple PMS with ADD/ADHD and one has an explosive combination. ADHD + PMS is probably the combination which is most incendiary, as ADHD patients, by definition, typically have problems moderating impulses (or "stifling themselves", as Archie Bunker used to say). Purely ADD women may simply be overwhelmed because they "can't get it all done" because of concentration and organization problems, leading to stress (which can deplete serotonin, as well as norepinephrin in the brain).

Now there is a dual problem: the decreased serotonin makes them more impulsive; the lower norepinephrin can actually make it even MORE difficult to concentrate, "pay attention", and stay organized. Hence, the woman is locked into a vicious circle where she can't get out on the other end until her menstrual cycle returns to more stable levels of estrogen and progesterone, her serotonin starts coming back up, and her stress decreases also. Even then, she may be in such a tailspin from one cycle that she never gets back to "normal" before the next one!

In reviewing the relationship between PMS and ADD, let me offer these opinions:

Yes, PMS can certainly worsen the irritability and impulsiveness of ADHD, and it can probably exacerbate a woman's frustration level with her lack of organization and accomplishment if she suffers from pure ADD.

Similarly, ADHD can exacerbate PMS, because the impulsiveness of ADHD (which can partially or exclusively be explained, in some cases, by a norepinephrin deficit) can end up being superimposed upon the impulsiveness and tendency to rage and aggression, which is worsened by the lack or serotonin.

Self Advocacy: Working with Schools

Introduction by Peter W. D. Wright, Attorney at Law

Educating Children with Attention Differences

Children with attention differences are difficult to educate. They are impulsive, distractible, and often very bright and creative. Quick to spot injustices and quick to tell adults about them, they persevere and procrastinate and have enormous difficulty becoming organized and staying on task.

They may have fine motor and sequencing and visual perceptual problems. Their written language skills may be atrocious. Along with auditory processing and memory problems, they may have difficulty sitting still, paying attention, and conforming to the demands of the large traditional classroom.

Even though they are plagued by frustration and impatience about their own shortcomings, they may also have great empathy for others.

We must succeed at our job of educating these children who are square pegs who don't fit neatly into round holes. Remediation and appropriate accommodations are vital to assure success in life and in school. And we must keep their self-esteem intact by sincerely praising them for their true accomplishments, which are many but not necessarily "mainstream."

As an adult with learning disabilities and ADD, I appreciate the struggle ADD children often experience in school. I remember my fifth-grade teacher stumping the entire class about the capitol of New York State—it was not New

Mr. Wright (75116,364) is a Special education attorney who successfully represented Shannon Carter in the landmark U.S. Supreme Court case "Florence County School District Four v. Shannon Carter." He can be reached at Courthouse Commons, 4104 East Parham Road, Richmond, VA 23228-2734, Office (804) 755-3000, Voice Mail (804) 257-0857.

York City. Knowing that it was Albany and finally summoning up enough nerve to speak up, I volunteered that I had the answer. Nervous and tongue tied, I blurted out "Alabama!" The teacher ridiculed me in front of the class and later to the other teachers in the lunchroom.

On the other hand, we often find teachers struggling to teach ADD children without benefit of extra help or knowledge about ADD. What can we do when a teacher says, "Help! I have three ADD students in my class!"

The school experiences of ADD children, their parents and the teachers who educate them are not unique. The issues are global; only the names and dates change.

What is unique, however, is the willingness of people to share their experiences in an open forum. While struggles, accommodations and experiences were once hidden from public view, parents are talking with one another and sharing their children's individual education plans with others worldwide. Teachers are discovering new and innovative ways to work with ADD students while disclosing their concerns over parental denial and the lack of resources. Students are learning self-advocacy skills and are not ashamed to share their true feelings with other children and adults.

People with ADD often have painful recollections. However, these experiences can also be powerful motivators toward future success. Understanding ADD and special education rights and working hand-in-hand with schools is the first course of action toward securing our children's success.

We are raising a new generation of children who aren't intimidated or ashamed by the "ADD" label. Having ADD can be turned from a disability into a gift of enduring creativity and uniqueness of thought. If harnessed and developed, having ADD can lead to incredible accomplishments and an enriched quality of life for all.

School Problems—Advice?

When your child has problems in school what do you do? Call an attorney? Let the child work it out? Intercede? Jump into advocacy issues? Talk to friends? There is a range of remedies to try.

Sixth grader Mark Davis turned to ADD Forum members for advice when he didn't know how to handle a serious problem in school.

"What do you do when something happens that doesn't seem fair?" he asked.

Adults and other students responded with suggestions, support, and experiences of their own.

To: *All*

This message is almost totally in Mark's words.

My son Mark, who is in 6th grade, has a dilemma in school and he'd like me to ask all of you if you have any ideas for him that could help him out—he wants to know what he can do.

Mark frequently comes home from school angry, usually about his teacher's aide, "Mr. B." For example, this happened today:

The teacher had to go home sick, and after lunch and recess, they did their afternoon work, even though it was time for English. In the middle of afternoon work, Mark asked Mr. B., "What happened to English?" Mr. B. pointed to Mark's English book, which was part of afternoon work.

Mark said that that was part of afternoon work and asked again, "What happened to English?" They went back and forth a few times in this vein. And then, in between that, a classmate said, "Yeah, what *did* happen to English?"

So both kids got lots of extra English work, which Mark says wasn't even English work.

Mark was nearly done with his extra work and his regular work, when Mr. B. asked him what he wanted to do when he was done. Mark said he wanted to work on the computer and Mr. B. said, "Okay."

Then, when Mark actually finished his work, Mr. B. insisted he had to go to the gym rather than use the computer. Mark told Mr. B. that he thought this was not fair, since Mr. B. had asked him what he wanted to do, and had agreed.

Mark told Mr. B. he was a tease and that if Mark were younger he would have broken out in tears at this. Then, Mr. B. said that, "People change their minds," and sent Mark to timeout instead of going to the gym for the rest of the afternoon.

And, on top of that, when Mark was doing his work the kids were very mean to him, but he controlled himself for the whole time.

What can Mark do to improve his situation at school? He tries very hard but hasn't found anything he can do that will make this get better. He doesn't want to be in a power struggle with Mr. B., but Mr. B. seems to want to be in a power struggle with Mark.

—*Elisa Davis (Sysop) for son Mark Davis*

Elisa, Please tell Mark that I'm proud of him for staying cool today!

A wonderfully useful technique for totally disarming, and sometimes winning over people who seem to have decided to make one's life miserable, is to be very, very nice to them. No matter how unpleasant the person is, you always respond as if they're being nice and be super nice to them. Always greet the person in a nice way and if possible, find something nice to say . . . such as, "That's a really nice shirt you're wearing today," or "Thanks for (insert something appropriate), I appreciate you doing that." After a while, they start feeling kind of silly . . . and find they can't help but be, at the least, halfway decent toward you. Sometimes, they even end up liking you a whole lot and becoming a friend. (I won over a hostile principal, and actually ended up being friends with her, this way.)

—*Elna Hensley /Staff*

Mark, I am telling my Mom what to write because I cannot talk and type. I have problems too. Mrs. R. C., my resource room teacher, tells me to do one thing. Mrs. C, her aide, tells me to do something different.

The other kids in the room with me do not try. They call me names and knock my papers on the floor. I want to go to college and work with things in space. They don't want to do anything but play.

Mom and I talked about what to do. We said I could talk with my resource room teacher. We said I could talk with my counselor. Do you have a counselor at school? Mrs. F., she helps me not to be mad. She has her job to help kids like me. Maybe your people like Mrs. F. can help you make things better.

I guess I do not know how to help you. I hope you have someone like Mrs. F. at your school.

—*Dennis D. Griswold, Jr.*

This is to Mark and Dennis:

I am 35 years old, but your messages made me feel such strong feelings that I wanted to respond to you. You are both great guys for being mature, brave, and confident enough to share your stories.

I vividly remember living through situations like yours, and it still makes me feel very hurt and angry. I realize now that most of the kids and the adults who are so unkind or unfair, are truly the weak ones in the situation.

Keep talking to your folks, even if the situations seem embarrassing. Falling into the trap of hating the other people is so easy, but instead try, if you can (I know it is really hard) to blow them off and focus on developing your own strengths, and pursuing your own personal best. Find things you like to do, and places to use your talents.

—*Rob Robertson*

I am 11 and in the 6th grade. I have a very annoying teacher, Mrs. "C." I knew I'd have organization problems this year, as always, so I took precautionary steps. I went and bought a notebook with a calendar, daily planner, and the six folders I'd need. And when I got to school, she said that I couldn't use them. Then I went and bought a smaller, business type folder that would only hold my six folders, Because she'd said that the problem was size. But I couldn't use that either, because of some strange reason I still don't understand.

Then there's the late assignments. I understand that it is my fault that I miss assignments. I also understand that I am supposed to complete them and turn them in. But I don't understand what type of magic she expects me to use to do the work sheets after they're gone. I mean, she won't give me another copy of any assignments that are late when I lose them. I have to tell my dad to call her first!

Also, she threatens me. I go to an advanced math course at the junior high every day. Sometimes she'll tell me I can't go if I don't have my desk clean, or some abstract assignment turned in. And sometimes she threatens extra special events. Like recently, she said I couldn't go to the field trip that we were taking if I didn't complete the homework assignment(s) that I owed.

It just seems that, unless I have a substitute, I come home angry each night. I'm scared to do things wrong, or rather, not the way she wants it done. I'm scared to talk to her, I'm scared of her. I guess the fact that she's nearly 7 feet tall doesn't help any. I often feel as if I'm going to die after she yells at me, and sometimes I wish I did. I realize now that I've spent about an hour at the keyboard, doing nothing but list bad things about my teacher, and that I could spend five more if I wanted to. I guess it just feels good to tell somebody about it.

—*Mike George*

Mike, can I make a suggestion? You articulated your concerns about your teacher very, very well here, I can see it took a lot of effort. Maybe you could print out your own message and bring it in to your counselor at school. Mark did that with his first message in this discussion, and he actually got people to make changes at school!

I bet Mrs. C. doesn't even know how upsetting some of her actions are to you. She probably doesn't want to make you get upset, she just wants you to get your homework done and not bother her. Easy for her to ask, not so easy for you to accomplish! (grin) A mediator might be able to help the two of you [feel] more comfortable.

—*Elisa Davis (Sysop)*

I am 11 and in 6th grade. Before school started Mom took me into school. That way I could see the building and maybe not get lost. I met the principal and counselor. They gave my Mom a list of what I would need. Mom and I went out and buy everything on the list. I got eight single subject notebooks, ruler, black ink pens, and #2 pencils. I had my tape recorder and calculator too. I'm supposed to use the tape recorder because I can't write fast or good. The principal said it was fine cause I have a thing called a IEP that says I can use the tape recorder.

The first day of school I handed the tape recorder to my first teacher like the principal said I was to. She gave it back to me and yelled. She told me if she saw it again she would take it and even my Mom could not get it back. I put it in my backpack. They gave me a locker and would not let me try the numbers so I could use it.

In English class the teacher asked me some questions. I have problems talking. I stutter. I couldn't answer her. She asked all the kids in the class if I had a problem with my speech. She said "does this kid have a speech problem or what." They all laughed at me.

In science class the teacher said if I didn't have a red ink pen, a black ink pen and a folder and a single subject notebook, and my books covered with grocery bags I would get detention. He picked up my notebook [trapper keeper] and banged it on my desk and said it was no good. He said he didn't want to see that kind of book.

In study skills class we had to write some stuff on paper. I cannot write or read cursive writing. She ripped up my paper and told me to grow up that I would pay detention if I did not write in cursive. I could not talk to her when she asked me for an answer. She said I had to write in cursive a paper saying that I would not print anymore 50 times and turn it in tomorrow.

When I got home I cried. I did not want to go back. My Mom was upset too cause my IEP says different. She went into school and fixed things.

Then I went to the learning center for English, Reading and Math. The old English teacher sent in a paper saying I was skipping classes. The assistant principal took me out of a class and yelled at me and said I would have to pay in-house detention because I skipped class. I had not I was in the learning center. I could not answer the principal because of how I talk.

My Mom went into school again and took care of things.

I hate how some teachers treat me. I am not stupid. I try real hard and I don't know why they all can't see that. My social studies and science teacher now see that. I get mad at the school.

I want to know why some of these people at school won't see that I am working hard and I am smart. I know lots of things that a lot of kids do not. They say things to me that make me want to cry but I know I can't. I hate school. I hate those people. I think they are stupid. I know I can't hit them. Mom says I should make my being mad make me try as hard as I can to prove to them I am smarter than they are. I don't know if I can do that.

—*Dennis D. Griswold, Jr.*

Hi, I am Greg Nelson, 13, 8th grade and have been in your situation many times. Because I don't get good grades people assume that I am not as smart as I am and I don't have many ways to prove they are wrong. On all the tests I take from doctors I score high but none of the kids know that. If I tell them they probably wouldn't believe me anyway because I don't get good grades. But I am better at one skill than any other teacher or student in the school. I am a computer whiz because I have grown up around them all my life. This alone will pretty much ensure me a decent future. I know it is hard but where there is a will there is a way.

Sincerely . . .Greg

p.s. I don't write in cursive either.

I read Dennis's message this morning. It made me remember a lot about how things were when my daughter was in sixth grade. That was one of the hardest years in school for her, because she has ADD but we didn't know it yet.

Sarah is now in 12th grade and she is going to a wonderful college next year. She has *terrible* cursive handwriting and her printing isn't so great, either! (grin) But she gets to do most of her work on the computer keyboard, so that isn't a problem anymore. In fact, in college they won't *let* people turn in work in cursive!!!

You are a brave kid [Dennis], and very grown-up about what you have had to deal with in school. You have learned a lot about how to be in unfair situations without losing your cool. Many adults don't know as much about this as you do!

Dennis, you won't be in sixth grade forever. You will get older and do something great with your life, and forget all about the sixth-grade teachers who didn't do what they were supposed to do to help you.

—*Pam Jacobs [Staff]*

Hiding Reality in Class

Parents often sense that their child is having difficulty at school, and become confused when teachers or school staff say, "Your child's not having any problems. Everything's fine!" We join the discussion in progress as forum members and educators examine the reasons for what appears to be a "conspiracy of silence."

Pam, you wrote to me saying:

"Good luck reviewing what went wrong at Nico's school. I know exactly what you and Elisa are talking about re: the conspiracy of silence. I have gone into classrooms and asked how Sarah was doing socially and been told everything seemed fine, when all that meant was that she wasn't disruptive. Sigh. What do you think it is that keeps teachers from reporting their observations in cases like this? That someone will expect them to "fix" something they don't know how to fix—or what?"

This is the very question I have been struggling with in our situation.

It could be that the teachers either have or are told to have low expectations, that they are told to create a success or to avoid a failure, or that as you say, they don't know what to do to remediate.

I hope that some of our teacher members will jump into this discussion about why teachers sometimes aren't honest with parents about a classroom situation.

—*Linda Rawson (Sysop)*

Linda, I wish I knew . . . I don't know about the low expectations. I don't think that's it, though . . . at least it wasn't in our case.

We got plenty of complaints about the academic arena—work not turned in, etc., but few concerns voiced about social adjustment. I have to guess that these teachers felt that parents could handle being told about academic issues, but not social ones, because social behavior seems to go more to the heart of "who" the child is, and I think they see that as unchangeable. But I may be attributing too much to the teachers I have in mind.

—*Pam Jacobs [Staff]*

Hi, if you don't mind that I make some comments, I have been hearing and reading that many, many parents are not satisfied with the teaching their children are receiving. I am a teacher and naturally since I'm perfect I never get into anything like that (grin) but I do have a few things that have come into mind here.

First, about social adjustment/behavior. Most teacher-training institutions that I've become familiar with don't train teachers in that area at all. I got a teaching credential for "severely-handicapped" from Cal State LA and I was extremely, extremely lucky to get a lot of help with behavioral and social issues, but teachers who were pursuing Learning Handicapped or other credentials received no training in those areas unless they took extra courses to get the training. I have seen this occur in other places also.

Secondly, for my particular specialty, there is really no set curriculum. I was lucky to get some pointers in how to modify curriculum but when I got into my first classroom all I found were tons and tons of worksheets. Some districts have thick books of guidelines which specify "life skills", etc. but it's not like a regular ed. class with textbooks. Most of my students can't read, or if they read they don't comprehend. And each one is on a vastly different level. So it's constantly modify, create, modify again.

And what about the social issues, the behaviors? What do you write home to a parent when their child has been trying to eat gum off the underside of the lunch tables?

I learned, unfortunately, early on, that as a teacher, most of the time (hope I'm not offending anyone here) that it all ends up being "*my fault*." So many parents will blame the teachers and think that somehow we can do everything all by ourselves. So the parent calls the administrator and complains about the negative information. The administrator then pressures the teacher about it. Therefore, teachers are very reluctant to give parents the "reality" you were asking for.

Finally, I don't get a good sense from parents what they really want. I send home parent questionnaires and the information I get back is often very scanty. Parents seem to mistrust teachers, maybe for good reason (grin), but it doesn't help us out at all.

Also, you must remember that teachers operate under administrations and the agenda of a district may be different than that of a teacher but we have to keep our jobs! Sometimes we can't advocate like we would wish to. Especially when this might mean the school would have to spend some more money!!

Paying the rent imposes a large burden also. You would be absolutely amazed at how word gets around that a certain teacher is not being politically correct. One has to be extremely careful. I have been out at the end of a limb with most of the limb sawed off many a time because I value my ethics more than I value my job. I have had some big troubles because of it. But there really is a line which even I will not cross because if I got a reputation for making trouble I couldn't get a job anywhere. Because I know that, as an excellent teacher, I can affect the lives of my students better when employed and not being 100 percent of an advocate than I could if I wasn't a teacher at all. I chose this path.

Sometimes you keep your mouth shut, bite your tongue and then try to find a different administration, a different school. The people with real power are the parents because you can call for a fair hearing (in California that's what it's called), get a lawyer, etc.

—Edna

As a former parent of an ADHD son and currently a psychologist in a school system, I think teachers may not give reality to parents because they fear it will hurt too much. Many teachers don't know how to tell a parent "bad news" and prefer to avoid the discussion. Your point about low expectations is well taken, but I would like to think it is more an issue of sensitivity. Perhaps a parent should tell the teacher (up front) that they can handle reality and want honesty. It may help.

—Linda Halperin

Thanks very much for your perspective, which is very valuable.

What would you suggest a parent do to convince a teacher that the parent truly wants the "bad news"?

I can understand that a teacher could have had some very bad experiences when parents thought they wanted to hear it, but didn't really.

—Linda Rawson (Sysop)

I have met with many parents in the 29 years of being an educator in many capacities. I have observed that school personnel respond best to parents who are informed, have done their homework and "do it with class." By that I mean, be calm, honest about your own expectations and understanding of the problem, compliment the teacher for their efforts—even if you think it could be better, (threatening behavior only exacerbates the problems), ask what you could do to help at home, let the teacher know you have no hidden agenda, and if all else fails, let the school know that you know your rights (in a gentle way) and will seek an administrator to discuss the problem. Hope this helps.

—Linda Halperin

Your message is a great help to all the parents in this forum who are trying to work out their children's programs with the schools. You certainly have seen a lot of parents in 29 years!

I agree with you and have read other messages on the forum saying that being pleasant and not being confrontational is the best approach. Evidently, school personnel are so used to dealing with outraged, bitter parents that it surprises them very pleasantly not to meet with this attitude.

Have you encountered the administrator who is very conciliatory and agrees with the parents, but then takes no action? How would you suggest handling that situation, in line with these recommendations?

—*Linda Rawson (Sysop)*

In regard to the resistive administrator who is conciliatory, but doesn't follow through, . . . I think the parents have to keep working on him/her to wear him/her down. Making appointments where parents bring in articles, books, tapes, etc. can be helpful. Be persistent—let him/her know you're not going away until something is implemented. Start a *strong parent group*. Ask what he/she is doing to train staff and if he/she isn't doing anything, offer to bring in a workshop, or give one yourself. There are packaged slide presentations from CH.A.D.D. and videos for teachers to view.

Administrators need to get budgets passed. They don't want adversity. Again, I tell people to do their homework and "do it with class." I have seen it work wonders. The parents who are most successful are those who can remain calm and objective—BUT covertly deadly. The parent who has been most successful in my district has started a parent group, a Saturday morning program for the kids and many other valued programs. She is called a sleeping giant who is respected by teachers, administrators and parents.

—*Linda Halperin*

One comment about "honest communication." Think of some really bizarre situation and then try to write a non-offensive, politically correct description of it to a parent that may already have sued the school district four times. Instead of a thesaurus, we need a dictionary of politically correct euphemisms (grin!). Sometimes by the time we finish formulating a way to say things we end up laughing hysterically.

One of my favorites is a recent comment someone else wrote about a chronic liar. The formulation went, "doesn't just confine herself to the truth."

Maybe this is how bad communication begins? Hope you got a laugh out of that one.

I really agree with you that we are there for the students, and that's why we have to make sure we stay there and don't wind up flipping burgers somewhere!

Hope these comments help someone somewhere and that I have not offended anyone. Thanks for reading.

—*Edna*

EMERGENCY! CRISIS! HELP!

What to do when that moment strikes: you and the school district are completely at odds. They're wrong, you are sure of it, and you reach for the phone to call an attorney. What happens?

Well-known attorney Peter W. D. Wright shares his instructions to parents in an excerpt from THE PARENT/ADVOCATE: FIRST STEPS.

Wright successfully represented Shannon Carter before The United States Supreme Court in the landmark decision entitled: Florence County School District Four v. Shannon Carter. A unanimous decision was issued on November 9, 1993, just 34 days after oral argument.

A copy of Wright's fascinating personal story of his preparation for facing the Supreme Court Justices is in the ADD Forum Legal and Advocacy library under the name of WRIGHT.TXT. A short summary of the Carter case appears in this section.

The Parent/Advocate: First Steps
A Special Education Attorney's Response
To the Parent's Initial Frantic Telephone Call.

The parent's initial call to the special education attorney is almost always precipitated by an emergency situation at school. The crisis may be that the public school has stated that:

☞ The new triennial evaluations have disclosed that the true problem is not an educational issue. They may even say that your child is not motivated; or

☞ They have realized that your child's true problem is not a learning disability but that your child is emotionally disturbed and needs to have the placement and program changed; or

☞ According to the "experts" your child's real problems are caused by your dysfunctional family, which may be composed of a single parent or a couple with marital problems; or

☞ They are going to continue with the same special education services and program that your child has been receiving for the past several years because your child is "really making progress" even though you have recognized that your child still can barely read and has significant written language problems; or

---

The Shannon Carter Case

In the mid-eighties, Shannon Carter was a functionally illiterate,high school student with an above-average IQ who was evaluated by her school district and told that she was a slow learner, lazy and unmotivated. A private evaluation revealed learning disabilities and Attention Deficit Disorder.

The school district offered Shannon three hours a week of special education instead of the recommended self-contained classroom. This meant that Shannon would have a half-year of education gain after a year of education and would fall further and further behind. Shannon's parents declined. Instead, they enrolled her in Trident Academy, a private school specializing in learning disabilities. Shannon graduated from Trident with her class and on grade level.

Shannon's parents requested to be reimbursed for their daughter's tuition and after a series of hearings and appeals, "Florence County School District Four v. Shannon Carter" went before the U.S. Supreme Court. The Carters were represented by attorney Peter W.D. Wright, and on November 9, 1993, thirty-four days after oral argument, the U.S. Supreme Court ruled in favor of Shannon Carter in a landmark Special education decision affirming that Shannon's education at Trident was not only appropriate, but that it must also be free.

☛ They have decided to discontinue special education services because your child is not benefiting from the program and doesn't really need it anyway.

In such situations, the usual immediate response by the parent is self-destructive. Parents often experience anger toward the child, each other, and toward the school officials. They feel guilty, confused, frustrated, helpless, fearful, and remorseful. From their perspective, as parents who have relied upon the assertions and recommendations of "expert" school officials for years and now realize that their child has regressed and is worse off than before, they feel betrayed by the school system.

Amid such emotional turmoil, quick action is tantamount to shooting wildly from the hip and expending all of your ammunition before the opposition has fired a single shot. When they do open fire, you will find yourself exposed and vulnerable, and your child will suffer.

As parents, it is your job to slow the action down, regroup, hold your fire, analyze the battleground, determine the weapons that will be used, and locate the high ground. Only then can you plot your strategy so that you can take the hill and prevail without firing a single shot or taking any casualties.

Preparation for Litigation

This approach to special education advocacy, relying heavily on the use of tactics and strategy, is not unique to special education issues.

There is absolutely no justification for treating special education cases less seriously than any other type of civil litigation. The dollars available for intensive special education remedial services are finite. Special education litigation, as is the case with most litigation, is about money and access to costly limited resources.

Special education litigation and due process hearings are usually far more difficult than most other types of litigation.

Long-Range Preparation

So, an emergency or crisis has hit. What do you do? For the next day or two, do nothing. Read and re-read the literature you have received from me. Then you need to focus on long-range planning and short-term solutions.

At this point you may want to jump to the section on Short-Term Relief. DON'T! It is important that you read this article completely in sequence. Before we discuss short-term relief, you need to learn how to become your child's best advocate. Take your time; don't be impulsive. It is too easy to obtain temporary, short-term relief and actually unknowingly exacerbate the situation and damage your child.

You must begin to embark on a course of self-study to learn all that you can about the law, about your child's learning style and the best way for your child to be educated—to read, write and do arithmetic.

To learn how to best help your child, you must join, for at least one year, a number of the national organizations related to special education.

I recommend that parents join the following organizations who can provide a wealth of literature and information that is useful to parents and children with all kinds of handicaps, not just learning disabilities and ADD.

☞ The Learning Disabilities Association of America
4156 Library Road
Pittsburgh, PA 15234
(412) 341-1515

☞ The Orton Dyslexia Society
8600 LaSalle Road, Suite 32
Chester Building
Baltimore, MD 21286
(410) 296-0232.

☛ CH.A.D.D. (Children and Adults with ADD)
499 NW 70th Ave., Suite 308
Plantation, FL 33317
(305) 587-3700

☛ The National Foundation for Learning Disabilities
381 Park Avenue South, Suite 1420
New York, NY 10016.
(212) 545-7510

As you begin to become educated about disabilities, handicaps, legal rights, and educational remediation techniques, you will find that membership in multiple organizations will be especially helpful.

You need to read:

☛ NO EASY ANSWERS and SUCCEEDING AGAINST THE ODDS by Sally Smith

☛ THE MISUNDERSTOOD CHILD by Larry Silver, M.D. (the revised edition)

☛ SOMETHING'S WRONG WITH MY CHILD by Richardson, Brutten and Mangel.

☛ ATTENTION DEFICIT DISORDER IN ADULTS by Lynn Weiss, PH.D.

☛ ATTENTION DEFICIT DISORDER: A DIFFERENT PERCEPTION (Subtitle "A Hunter in a Farmer's World") by Thom Hartmann

☛ DRIVEN TO DISTRACTION by Edward M. Hallowell, M.D. and John J. Ratey, M.D.

I recommend that you purchase UNDERSTANDING LEARNING DISABILITIES: A PARENT GUIDE AND WORKBOOK from The Learning Disabilities Council, P.O. Box 8451, Richmond, VA 23226. Telephone: (804) 748-5012. Cost: $21.70 postpaid. Their extensive information about special education is helpful for parents of all children with all handicapping characteristics.

If you have a computer and a modem, you will be able to access a tremendous number of resources. My wife, Pamela Darr Wright, and I are active on CompuServe and have uploaded a number of articles into the libraries in the ADD Forum, and the Disabilities and Education Forum.

By joining several organizations you will receive information that is in the local, state, and (most important), national newsletters of each organization. This information will place you on the cutting edge of any new educational, scientific and legal developments in this field. The cost of membership will be repaid hundreds of times over to the benefit of your child's future.

You must read about and understand the law. You should be familiar with the November 9, 1993 U. S. Supreme Court's Florence County School District Four v. Shannon Carter case and its "default" theory. Your nearby law school may subscribe to a publication entitled INDIVIDUALS WITH DISABILITIES EDUCA-

TION LAW REPORTER (IDELR) published by LRP Publications in Horsham, Pennsylvania. The "topical index" in IDELR will provide you with many cases similar to your issue.

You need to understand how to write an Individual Educational Program (IEP) and be familiar with Appendix C of the Special Education Regulations regarding goals and objectives in IEPs. NICHCY, the National Information Center for Children and Youth with Disabilities, has information available on IEPs and Appendix C free of charge. Call 1-800-695-0285.

You need to read YOUR CHILD'S IEP: PRACTICAL AND LEGAL GUIDANCE FOR PARENTS written by Pamela Darr Wright. It is available in the Legal and Advocacy Library of the ADD Forum of CompuServe or directly from us.

Additionally, you will need to understand tests and measurements, the bell curve, standard scores and percentile ranks.

You will want to call your State's Department of Special Education and obtain all literature, brochures, and material they have in regard to Special Education, IEPs and Section 504 Rehabilitation Act requirements.

You will also want information from your State's Protection and Advocacy Office and other state and local advocacy groups that provide information to parents.

In summary, you will need to become an expert in the global nature of your child's abilities, disabilities (i.e., the facts of the case), the law, IEPs, and understand tests and measurements.

Long-Term Planning

Thus, your first steps are to call the organizations mentioned above and request membership material and a listing of publications that they have available for sale.

Second, call your state and local departments of education and the protection and advocacy agencies and request information that they may have.

Third, request a complete copy of your child's entire cumulative and confidential file from your child's public school, the central administrative office where the special education department is located, and from all other public and private sector agencies and individuals that may have any information on your child.

Long-Term Planning and Preparation of a Home-Based School File

I recommend that the parent organize all evaluations, IEPs, reports and other documents in a loose-leaf three ring notebook in chronological order. Do not sort by IEP, evaluations, letters, etc. Placing materials in chronological order provides a better history and is also an easier method of organization.

The date of each document should be lightly written in pencil on the front page of each document in the lower right hand corner as follows: 11/9/93. Do not relinquish your copies to anyone, ever! Instead, make photocopies available. Since you will often need to make copies of the documents, do not mark your master copies with yellow highlighters, red pens or even write on them.

Separately, make an additional list, in chronological order, of the dates, names and scores of all individualized and standardized tests ever administered to your child. With your loose-leaf three ring notebook, now known as "The File" and your test history list in hand, have the private sector educational diagnostician or psychologist explain the significance of the scores using percentile ranks.

The above file should only include information related to your child. In a separate file you will want to organize the educational and legal information that you receive from local and national advocacy agencies.

Taking these steps as a part of your long-range planning will get you pointed in the right direction so that future situations are neither crises nor emergencies. Future incidents which are similar to the current situation (which led to your contacting an attorney) can be artfully turned by the skilled, educated parent into an opportunity to acquire even better services for your child.

To do so requires knowledge, tactics, strategy and skilled advocacy, without placing your emotions in front of you for the world to see and attack. Your emotions must be placed behind you, into the knapsack on your back, and be used as the motivating, driving force that keeps you advancing, step by step, toward that high ground.

Short-Term Relief

Now, let's look at short-term temporary solutions, i.e., Band-Aids. It is important to place your child's self-esteem at the top of the list. The child must know you love and care for him, even though some of his behaviors may be unacceptable.

You will probably need to consult with a private sector educational diagnostician, psychologist, psychiatrist or clinical social worker, to reduce the present stress. Often, additional private sector testing is necessary to develop baseline data to learn what is going on and why.

You will also need to depolarize the emotions between yourselves and the school if they have gotten out of hand, which is the usual case by the time a parent calls an attorney. This does not mean acquiescence to their position or assertions. It means removing the emotional element, even if the school officials are fanning the flames.

Videotapes and audio tapes are available from a number of the organizations previously noted. Parents and child can often have immediate relief after viewing many of the tapes and jointly starting on a course of self-study.

It is also important to understand that what appears to some as a disability, may, in fact, have a corresponding powerful ability that goes hand in hand with the "disability." For example, the ADD distractible child can also "hyperfocus" in a manner far more intense than other children. (See ATTENTION DEFICIT DISORDER: A DIFFERENT PERCEPTION by Thom Hartmann) These children learn differently and need to be taught differently, but they may not necessarily need to be "disabled" or "handicapped" except for legal purposes and entitlement to services.

KNOWLEDGE equals EMPOWERMENT equals SUCCESS!

In essence, the purpose of short-term relief, as in many medical matters, is to relieve the painful impact of the present, severe symptoms and begin a diagnostic study of the cause. You can then embark upon long-term treatment to cure the problem and reduce the probability of its reoccurrence.

By becoming knowledgeable about IEPs, the law and how to artfully advocate, you will turn the tide of your child's battered self-esteem while you defuse the fighting within your family and among your family, your child and the school district. By becoming an expert in disability, educational and remediation techniques, you become your child's expert advocate as you start that march toward the high ground. You're no longer powerless but are now able to face any crisis with knowledge and empowerment.

101 Ways To Help Children With ADD Learn: Tips from Successful Teachers

Introduction by Douglas Levin

URING THE U.S. CONGRESS' CONSIDERATION of the 1990 Amendments to the education of the Handicapped Act, Congress came to recognize that for most school personnel information about ADD was not readily accessible, and what was accessible was confusing and often contradictory. Consequently, Congress asked the Office of Special Education Programs (OSEP), Office of Special Education and Rehabilitative Services (OSERS), in the U.S. Department of Education, to solicit public comment about the education of children and youth with ADD, and to establish research centers to synthesize and communicate state-of-the-art knowledge about the education of children with ADD to those who needed it most—school personnel, parents, and other medical and health care practitioners.

As directed by the U.S. Congress, OSEP funded five research centers to collect, synthesize, and analyze existing research and practice knowledge on the education of children and youth with ADD. As a result of the centers' synthesis activities, OSEP was able to identify gaps in the knowledge base and target them for future investments. For example, OSEP funded researchers to conduct addi-

Douglas Levin, Research Analyst, Chesapeake Institute, 1000 Thomas Jefferson St., NW, Suite 400, Washington, DC 20007 (202) 944-5375. Internet:dLevin@air-dc.org

tional studies on effective educational practices and the context that supports those practices for children and youth with ADD, because the synthesis activities revealed that there was a lack of information on those topics. Furthermore, OSEP is collaborating with the National Institute of Mental Health (NIMH) on a five-year six-site study on interventions for children with ADD.

OSEP also contracted with Chesapeake Institute to undertake a variety of communication activities to enhance the quality, usability, and impact on practice of the research they funded. To achieve this aim, OSEP facilitated meaningful, substantive, and lasting exchanges of information across agencies, centers, associations, and other entities representing stakeholders in the education of children and youth with ADD. These activities included:

☞ Convening a national forum on the educational needs of children with ADD that brought together parents of children with ADD and other stakeholders from the fields of education, mental health, and medicine;

☞ Conducting focus groups to guide the development of a series of consumer-oriented research-based products to address the information needs of parents, educators, and health professionals;

☞ Fostering linkages with national education and parent associations and teacher unions to communicate the information products through their on-going publication and professional development activities;

☞ Holding a press event that attracted national attention to the U.S. Department of Education's work to educate children with ADD as well as to those who have supported the Department in its work, including Senator William Frist (R-TN), Senator Tom Harkin (D-IA), and Senator James M. Jeffords (R-VT);

☞ Releasing a highly accessible information kit for educators and parents on the education of children with ADD that includes as its centerpiece two videos—"Facing the Challenges of ADD" and "One Child in Every Classroom" —which takes viewers into the homes, classrooms, and lives of children and families living with ADD.

Organizations OSEP collaborated with include Children and Adults with Attention Deficit Disorder, the National Education Association, the American Federation of Teachers, the National Association of Elementary School Principals, the - National Attention Deficit Disorder Association, the National Association of School Psychologists, the National Association of State Directors of Special Education, the National Information Center for Children and Youth with Disabilities, the National Congress of Parents and Teachers, the Learning Disabilities Association of America, The Council for Exceptional Children, the Beach Center on Families and Disabilities, and the National Institute of Mental Health.

Materials from the Department of Education Information Kit are available from the ERIC Clearinghouse on Disabilities and Gifted Education, 1-800-328-0272, as well as in electronic format through the ADD Forum (GO ADD) on Compuserve, 1-800-524-3388, and on the PROGRAM.EVAL bulletin board on SpecialNet, 1-800-927-3000.

101 Ways To Help Children With ADD Learn: Tips from Successful Teachers

RESEARCH SHOWS THERE ARE an estimated 3 to 5 percent of school-age children with Attention Deficit Disorder. In response to the needs expressed by teachers for teaching strategies that work with these children, the U.S. Department of Education has supported research in classrooms to determine successful teaching techniques employed by elementary school teachers to keep children focused and on task. The following tips, for experienced and inexperienced elementary school teachers alike, are tried and true methods for reaching children with ADD.

Children with ADD typically have problems with inattention, impulsiveness, and hyperactivity. They often have difficulty paying attention in class and seem to shift aimlessly from one unfinished activity to another. These children generally appear restless, fidgeting constantly in their seats, playing with pencils or other objects, or disturbing nearby students. Many children with ADD also have difficulty following their teachers' instructions or forming friendships with other children in the class.

Like other children with disabilities, children with ADD learn best when their teachers understand their special needs and individualize their educational program to meet these needs.

101 WAYS TO HELP CHILDREN WITH ADD LEARN is a how-to guide with instructional practices you can use to help children with ADD in your class. The practices themselves should be part of an educational program based around three key components—classroom accommodations, behavior management, and individualized academic instruction.

To make this book as valuable a resource as possible, you should consider these steps in developing an effective educational program for your students with ADD:

Published By Division of Innovation and Development, Office of Special Education Programs, Office of Special Education and Rehabilitative Services, U.S. Department of Education.

This document was developed by the Chesapeake Institute, Washington, D.C., with The Widmeyer Group, Washington, D.C., as part of contract #HS92017001 from the Office of Special Education Programs, Office of Special Education and Rehabilitative Services, United States Department of Education. The points of view expressed in this publication are those of the authors and do not necessarily reflect the position or policy of the U.S. Department of Education. We encourage the reproduction and distribution of this publication.

- *Evaluate the Child's Individual Needs.* Assess the unique educational needs of a child with ADD in your class. Working with a multi-disciplinary team, consider both academic and behavioral needs, using formal diagnostic assessments and informal classroom observations.

- *Select Appropriate Instructional Practices.* Determine which instructional practices will meet the academic and behavioral needs you have identified for the child. Select practices that fit the content, are age appropriate, and gain the cooperation of the child.

- *Integrate Appropriate Practices Within an Individualized Program.* Combine the practices you have selected into an individualized educational program. Plan how to integrate the educational activities provided to other children in your class with those selected for the child with ADD.

Because no two children with ADD are alike, no single educational program, practice, or setting will be best for all children.

ADD: What Teachers Should Know, which is also in the information kit, describes ways in which effective teachers have individualized educational programs for children with ADD in their classes. Illustrated with real-life stories of effective educational practices for 12 children with ADD, these ideas can guide you in determining how best to design and implement an effective program for children with ADD in your class.

Academic Instruction

Children with ADD often have difficulty learning and achieving academically in school. Effective teachers constantly monitor the child and adapt and individualize academic instruction.

General Instructional Principles

Effective teachers help prepare their students to learn when they introduce, conduct, and conclude each academic lesson. These principles of effective instruction, which reflect what we know about how to educate all children in the class, will especially help a child with ADD to stay focused on his assigned tasks as he transitions from one lesson to another throughout the school day.

Students with ADD benefit from clear statements about their teacher's expectations at the beginning of the lesson. Consider these strategies.

1. *Review Previous Lessons.* Review information about previous lesson on this topic. For example, remind children that yesterday's lesson focused on learning how to regroup in subtraction. Review several problems before describing the current lesson.

2. *Set Learning Expectations.* State what students are expected to learn during the lesson. For example, explain to students that a language arts lesson will involve reading a story about Paul Bunyan and identifying new vocabulary words in the story.

3. *Set Behavioral Expectations.* Describe how students are expected to behave during the lesson. For example, tell children that they may talk quietly to their neighbors as they work on a seatwork assignment or raise their hands to get your attention.

4. *State Needed Materials.* Identify all materials that the child will need during the lesson. For example, specify that children need their journals and pencils for journal writing or their crayons, scissors, and colored paper for an art project; rather than leaving children to figure out on their own the materials required for a lesson.

5. *Explain Additional Resources.* Tell students how to obtain help in mastering the lesson. For example, remind the children to refer to a particular page in the text book to get help in completing a worksheet.

When conducting an academic lesson, effective teachers use some of the following strategies.

6. *Use Audio-visual Materials.* Use a variety of audio-visual materials to present academic lessons. For example, use an overhead projector to demonstrate how to solve an addition problem requiring regrouping. The students can work on the problem at their desks, while you manipulate counters on the projector screen.

7. *Check Student Performance.* Question individual students about their mastery of the lesson. For example, you can ask a student doing seatwork to demonstrate how he or she arrived at the answer to a problem or ask individual students to state, in their own words, how the main character felt at the end of the story.

8. *Ask Probing Questions.* Probe for the correct answer before calling on another student and allow children sufficient time to work out the answer to a question. Count at least 15 seconds before giving the answer and ask follow-up questions that give the child an opportunity to demonstrate what he or she knows.

9. *Perform On-going Student Evaluation.* Identify students who need additional assistance. Watch for signs of lack of comprehension, such as day-dreaming or visual or verbal indications of frustration. Provide these children with extra explanation or ask another student to serve as a peer tutor for the lesson.

10. *Help Students Self-Correct Their Own Mistakes.* Describe how students can identify and correct their own mistakes. For example, remind students that they should check their calculations in mathematics problems and reiterate how they can do that; remind students of particularly difficult spelling rules and how students can watch out for "easy-to-make" errors.

11. *Focus Dawdling Students.* Remind students who dawdle to keep working and redirect these students to focus on their assigned task. For example, you can provide follow-up directions or assign learning partners. These practices can be directed at individual children or at the entire class.

12. *Lower Noise Level.* Monitor the noise level in the classroom and provide corrective feedback, as needed. If the noise level exceeds the level appropriate for the type of lesson, remind all students—or individual students—about the behavior rules stated at the beginning of the lesson.

Students with ADD often have difficulty refocusing their attention as they end one academic lesson and move on to the next lesson. Effective teachers help their students prepare for these transitions when concluding a lesson.

13. *Provide Advance Warnings.* Provide advance warning that a lesson is about to end. Announce five or ten minutes prior to the end of the lesson (particularly for seatwork and group projects) how much time remains. You may also want to tell students at the beginning of the lesson how much time they will have to complete it.

14. *Check Assignments.* Check completed assignments for at least some students. Review with some students what they have learned during the lessons, to get a sense of how ready the class was for the lesson and how to plan the next lesson.

15. *Preview the Next Lesson.* Instruct students how to begin preparing for the next lesson. For example, inform children that they need to put away their textbooks and come to the front of the room for a large group spelling lesson.

Individualized Instructional Practices

Effective teachers individualize their instructional practices based on the needs of their students in different academic subjects. Students have different ways of getting information, not all of which involve traditional reading and listening. Individualized lessons in language arts, mathematics, and organizational skills benefit not only children with ADD, but also other children who have diverse learning needs.

Language Arts Reading Comprehension

To help children with ADD who are poor readers improve their reading comprehension skills, try the following instructional practices:

16. *Silent Reading Time.* Establish a fixed time each day for silent reading (e.g., DEAR: Drop Everything And Read).

17. *Follow -Along Reading.* Ask the child to read a story silently while listening to other students or the teacher read the story out loud to the entire class.

18. *Partner Reading Activities.* Pair the child with ADD with another student partner who is a strong reader. The partners take turns reading orally and listening to each other.

19. *Storyboards.* Ask the child to make storyboards that illustrate the sequence of main events in a story.

20. *Storytelling.* Schedule "storytelling" sessions where the child can retell a story he or she has read recently.

21. *Play-acting.* Schedule "play-acting" sessions where the child can role play different characters in a favorite story.

22. *Word Bank.* Keep a word bank or dictionary of new or "hard-to-read" sight vocabulary words.

23. *Board Games for Reading Comprehension.* Play board games that provide practice with target reading comprehension skills or sight vocabulary words.

24. *Computer Games for Reading Comprehension.* Schedule computer time for the child to have "drill-and-practice" with sight vocabulary words.

Phonics and Grammar

To help children with ADD master phonics and grammar rules, the following are effective:

25. *Mnemonics for Phonics and Grammar.* Teach the child mnemonics that provide reminders about hard-to-learn grammatical rules such as (a) correct punctuation, (b) irregular verb tenses, and (c) correct capitalization.

26. *Word Families.* Teach the child to recognize and read word families that illustrate particular phonetic concepts (e.g., "ph" sounds).

27. *"Everyday" Examples of Grammar Rules.* Take advantage of naturally occurring events to teach grammar rules skills in the context of everyday life. For example, ask a boy and a girl who are reading a story together questions about the proper use of male and female pronouns.

28. *Board Games for Phonics and Grammar.* Play board games that practice phonetically irregular words.

29. *Computer Games for Phonics and Grammar.* Use a computer to provide opportunities to have "drill-and-practice" with phonics or grammar lessons.

30. *Structured Programs for Phonics and Grammar.* Teach phonics and grammar skills through a structured program such as Sandy Rief's "Simply Phonics" program.

Writing Assignments

In composing stories or other writing assignments, children with ADD benefit from the following practices:

31. *Standards for Writing Assignments.* Identify and teach the child classroom-wide standards for acceptable written work.

32. *Recognizing Parts of a Story.* Teach the student how to describe the major parts of a story (e.g., plot, main characters, setting, conflict, and resolution).

33. *Post Office.* Establish a "post office" in the classroom and provide students with opportunities to write, mail, and receive letters to and from their classmates and teacher.

34. *Visualizing Compositions.* Ask the child to close his or her eyes and visualize a paragraph that the teacher reads aloud. Another variation of this technique is to ask a student to describe a recent event while the other students have their eyes closed.

35. *Proofreading Compositions.* Require that the child proofread his or her work before turning in written assignments. Provide the child with a list of items to check when proofreading his or her own work.

Spelling

To help children with ADD who are poor spellers master their spelling lessons, the following have been found to be helpful:

36. *Teaching Frequently Used Spelling Words.* Assign spelling words that the child routinely uses in his or her speech each day.

37. *Creating a Dictionary of Misspelled Words.* Ask the child to keep a personal dictionary of frequently misspelled words.

38. *Using Partner Spelling Activities.* Pair the child with another student. Ask the partners to quiz each other about how to spell new words. Encourage both students to guess the correct spelling.

39. *Working with Manipulatives.* Use cut out letters or other manipulatives to spell out hard-to-learn words.

40. *Using Color-Coded Letters.* Color code different letters in "hard-to-spell" words (e.g., receipt).

41. *Using Movement Activities.* Combine movement activities with spelling lessons (e.g., jump rope while spelling words out loud).

42. *Using "Everyday" Examples of Hard-to-Spell Words.* Take advantage of naturally occurring events to teach difficult spelling words in context. For example, ask a child eating a cheese sandwich to spell "sandwich."

Handwriting

Students with ADD who have difficulty with manuscript or cursive writing benefit from these instructional practices.

43. *Individual Chalkboards.* Ask the child to practice copying and erasing the target words on a small, individual chalkboard. Two children can be paired to practice their target words together.

44. *Quiet Places for Handwriting.* Provide the child with a special "quiet place" (e.g., on a table outside the classroom) to complete his or her handwriting assignments.

45. *Spacing Words on a Page.* Teach the child to use his or her finger to measure how much space to leave between each word in a written assignment.

46. *Special Writing Paper.* Ask the child to use special paper with vertical lines to learn to space letters and words on a page.

47. *Tape Recorders.* Ask the student to dictate writing assignments into a tape recorder.

48. *Dictating Writing Assignments.* Have the teacher or another student write down a story told by a child with ADD.

49. *Structured Programs for Handwriting.* Teach handwriting skills through a structured program such as Jan Olson's "Handwriting Without Tears" program.

Mathematics

There are several individualized instructional practices that can help children with ADD improve their basic computation skills. The following are just a few:

50. *Recognizing Patterns in Mathematics.* Teach the student to recognize patterns when adding, subtracting, multiplying, or dividing whole numbers.

51. *Partner Mathematics Activities.* Pair a child with ADD with another student and provide opportunities for the partners to quiz each other about basic computation skills.

52. *Mnemonics for Basic Computation.* Teach the child mnemonics that describe basic steps in computing whole numbers. For example, "Don't Miss Susie's Boat" can be used to help the student recall the basic steps in long division (i.e., divide, multiply, subtract, and bring down).

53. *"Real Life" Examples of Money Skills.* Provide the child with naturally occurring, "real life" opportunities to practice target money skills. For example, ask the child to calculate his or her change when paying for lunch in the school cafeteria.

54. *Color Coding Arithmetic Symbols.* Color code basic arithmetic symbols such as +, −, and = to provide visual cues for children when they are computing whole numbers.

55. *Using Calculators To Check Basic Computation.* Ask the child to use a calculator to check his addition, subtraction, multiplication, or division.

56. *Board Games for Basic Computation.* Ask the child to play board games to practice adding, subtracting, multiplying, and dividing whole numbers.

57. *Computer Games for Basic Computation.* Schedule computer time for the child for "drill-and-practice" with basic computation facts.

58. *Structured Programs for Basic Computation.* Teach basic computation skills through a structured program such as Innovative Learning Concepts' "Touch Math" program.

Solving Word Problems

To help children with ADD improve their skill in solving word problems in mathematics, try the following.

59. *Rereading the Problem.* Teach the child to read a word problem two times before beginning to compute the answer.

60. *Using Clue Words.* Teach the child "clue words" that identify which operation to use when solving word problems. For example, words such as "sum," "total," or "all together" may indicate an addition operation.

61. *Mnemonics for Word Problems.* Teach students mnemonics that help remind them of basic questions to ask in solving word problems (e.g., what is the question asked in the problem, what information do you have to figure out the answer, and what operation should you use to compute the answer).

62. *"Real Life" Examples of Word Problems.* Ask the student to create and solve word problems that provide practice with specific target operations such as addition, subtraction, multiplication, or division. These problems can be based on recent, "real life" events in the children's lives.

63. *Using Calculators to Check Word Problems.* Ask the student to use a calculator to check his or her answers to assigned word problems.

Special Materials

Some children with ADD benefit from using special materials to help them complete their mathematics assignments.

64. *Number Lines.* Provide a number line for the child to use when computing whole numbers.

65. *Manipulatives.* Use manipulatives to help students gain basic computation skills such as counting poker chips when adding single-digit numbers.

66. *Graph Paper.* Ask the child to use graph paper to help organize columns when adding, subtracting, multiplying, or dividing whole numbers.

Organizational Skills

Many students with ADD are easily distracted and have difficulty focusing their attention on assigned tasks. However, there are several practices that can help children with ADD improve their organization of homework and other daily assignments.

67. *Assignment Notebook.* Provide the child with an assignment notebook to help organize homework and other seatwork.

68. *Color-Coded Folders.* Provide the child with color-coded folders to help organize assignments for different academic subjects (e.g., reading, mathematics, social science, and science).

69. *Homework Partners.* Assign the child a partner to help record homework and other seatwork in the proper folders and assignment notebook.

70. *Cleaning Out Desks and Book Bags.* Ask the child to periodically sort through and clean out his or her desk, book bag, and other special places where written assignments are stored.

Finishing on Time

Children with ADD who have difficulty finishing their assignments on time can also benefit from individualized instruction that helps them improve their time management skills.

71. *Using a Wristwatch.* Teach the child how to read and use a wristwatch to manage his or her time when completing assigned work.

72. *Using a Calendar.* Teach the child how to read and use a calendar to schedule his or her assignments.

144

73. *Practicing Sequencing Activities.* Provide the child with supervised opportunities to break down a long assignment into a sequence of short, interrelated activities.

74. *Creating a Daily Activity Schedule.* Tape a schedule of planned daily activities to the child's desk.

Study Skills

75. *Using Venn Diagrams.* Teach a child with ADD how to use Venn diagrams to help illustrate and organize key concepts in reading, mathematics, or other academic subjects.

76. *Note-Taking Skills.* Teach a child with ADD how to take notes when organizing key academic concepts that he or she has learned with a program such as Anita Archer's "Skills for School Success."

77. *Developing a Checklist of Frequent Mistakes.* Provide the child with a checklist of mistakes that he or she frequently makes in written assignments (e.g., punctuation or capitalization errors), mathematics (e.g., addition or subtraction errors), or other academic subjects. Teach the child how to use this list when proofreading his or her work at home and school.

78. *Using a Checklist of Homework Supplies.* Provide the child with a checklist that identifies categories of items needed for homework assignments (e.g., books, pencils, and homework assignment sheets).

79. *Preparing Uncluttered Workspace.* Teach a child with ADD how to prepare an uncluttered workspace to complete his assignments. For example, instruct the child to clear away unnecessary books or other materials before beginning a seatwork assignment.

80. *Monitoring Homework Assignments.* Keep track of how well your students with ADD complete their assigned homework. Discuss and resolve with them and their parents any problems in completing these assignments. For example, evaluate the difficulty of the assignments and how long the children spend on their homework each night.

Behavior Management

Children with ADD often are impulsive and hyperactive. Effective teachers use behavior management techniques to help these children learn how to control their behavior.

Verbal Reinforcement

Students with ADD benefit from frequent reinforcement of appropriate behavior and correction of inappropriate behavior. Verbal reinforcement takes on the form of praise and reprimands. In addition, it is sometimes helpful to selectively ignore inappropriate behavior.

81. *Verbal Praise.* Simple phrases such as "good job" encourage a child to act appropriately. Praise children frequently, and look for a behavior to praise before—not after—a child is off task.

82. *Verbal Reprimands.* Do not hesitate to request that a child change his or her behavior. The most effective reprimands are brief and directed at the child's behavior—not at the child.

83. *Selective Ignoring of Inappropriate Behavior.* Carefully evaluate whether to intervene when a child misbehaves. In some instances, it is helpful to ignore the child's inappropriate behavior, particularly if a child is misbehaving to get your attention.

Behavioral Management

Effective teachers also use behavioral prompts with their students with ADD, as well as with other students in the class. These prompts help remind students about your expectations for their learning and behavior in the classroom.

84. *Visual Cues.* Establish simple, non-intrusive visual cues to remind the child to remain on task. For example, you can point at the child while looking him or her in the eye, or hold out your hand, palm down, near the child.

85. *Proximity Control.* When talking to a child, move to where the child is standing or sitting. Your physical proximity to the child will help the child to focus and pay attention to what you are saying.

Counseling

In some instances, children with ADD need counseling to learn how to manage their own behavior.

86. *Classroom Interviews.* Discuss how to resolve social conflicts with classroom interviews. Conduct impromptu counseling sessions with one student or a small group of students in the classroom where the conflict arises. In this setting, ask two children who are arguing about a game to discuss how to settle their differences. Encourage the children to resolve their problem by talking to each other, while you quietly monitor their interactions during the interview.

87. *Social Skills Classes.* Teach children with ADD appropriate social skills using a structured pull-out class. For example, you can ask the children to role

play and model different solutions to common social problems. It is critical to provide for the generalization of these skills, including structured opportunities for the children to use the social skills they learn.

Managing Own Behavior

For some children with ADD, behavioral contracts, tangible rewards, or token economy systems are helpful in teaching them how to manage their own behavior. Because students' individual needs are different, it is important for teachers to evaluate whether these practices are appropriate for their classrooms.

88. *Behavioral Contract*. Identify specific academic or behavioral goals for the child with ADD. Work together with the child to cooperatively identify appropriate goals such as completing homework assignments on time and obeying safety rules on the school playground. Take the time to ensure that the child agrees that his or her goals are important to master.

89. *Tangible Rewards*. Use tangible rewards to reinforce appropriate behavior. These rewards can include (a) stickers such as "happy faces" or sports team emblems or (b) privileges, such as extra time on the computer or lunch with the teacher. In some cases, you may be able to enlist the support of parents in rewarding the children at home.

90. *Token Economy System*. Use token economy systems to motivate a child to achieve a goal identified in a behavioral contract. For example, a child can earn points for each homework assignment completed on time. In some cases, students also lose points for each homework assignment not completed on time. After earning a specified number of points, the student receives a tangible reward such as extra time on a computer or a "free period" on Friday afternoon.

Classroom Accommodations

Many children with ADD benefit from accommodations that reduce distractions in the classroom environment. These accommodations, which include modifications within both the physical environment and learning environment of the classroom, help some children with ADD stay on task and learn.

Accommodations of the physical environment include determining where a child with ADD will sit in the classroom. There are two main types of special seat assignments.

91. *Seat Near the Teacher*. Assign a child a seat near your desk or the front of the room. This seat assignment provides opportunities for you to monitor and reinforce the child's on-task behavior.

92. *Seat Near a Student Role Model.* Assign a child a seat near a student role model. This seat arrangement provides opportunities for children to work cooperatively and learn from their peers in the class.

Effective teachers also use different environmental prompts to make accommodations within the physical environment of the classroom.

93. *Hand Gestures.* Use hand signals to communicate privately with a child with ADD. For example, ask the child to raise his or her hand every time you ask a question. A closed fist can signal that the child knows the answer; an open palm can signal that he or she does not know the answer. You would call on the child to answer only when he or she makes a fist.

94. *Egg Timers.* Note for the children the time at which the lesson is starting and the time at which it will conclude. Set a timer to indicate to children how much time remains in the lesson and place it at the front of the classroom; the children can check the timer to see how much time remains. Interim prompts can be used as well. For instance, children can monitor their own progress during a 30-minute lesson if the timer is set for 10 minutes three times.

95. *Classroom Lights.* Turning the classroom lights "on and off" prompts children that the noise level in the room is too high and they should be quiet. This practice can also be used to signal that it is time to begin preparing for the next lesson.

96. *Music.* Play music on a tape recorder or chords on a piano to prompt children that they are too noisy. In addition, playing different types of music on a tape recorder communicates to children what level of activity is appropriate for a particular lesson. For example, play quiet classical music for quiet seat activities and jazz for active group activities.

Effective teachers make accommodations in the learning environment by guiding children with ADD with follow-up directions.

97. *Follow-Up Oral Directions.* After giving directions to the class as a whole, provide additional, oral directions for a child with ADD. For example, ask the child if he or she understood the directions, and repeat the directions together.

98. *Follow-up Written Directions.* Provide follow-up directions in writing. For example, write the page number for an assignment on the blackboard. You can remind the child to look at the blackboard if he or she forgets the assignment.

Effective teachers also use special instructional tools to modify the classroom learning environment and accommodate the special needs of their students with ADD.

99. *Highlighting Key Words*. Highlight key words in the instructions on worksheets to help the child with ADD focus on the directions. You can prepare the worksheet before the lesson begins or underline key words as you and the child read the directions together.

100. *Using Pointers*. Teach the child to use a pointer to help visually track written words on a page. For example, provide the child with a bookmark to help him or her follow along when students are taking turns reading aloud.

101. *Adapting Worksheets*. Teach a child how to adapt instructional worksheets. For example, help a child fold his or her reading worksheet to reveal only one question at a time. The child can also use a blank piece of paper to cover the other questions on the page.

Living Successfully With ADD

Introduction by Dr. John R. Shumate and Janie Bowman

LIVING SUCCESSFULLY WITH ADD often means taking a personal inventory of those areas that are causing the most concern—and then doing something about it. Thousands of messages posted on the ADD Forum over the past three years show that four key issues stand front and center: clutter and organization; memorization skills; creative careers; and tying all of these together satisfactorily.

People in the "Think Fast!" lane are attracted to clutter because "I might need it someday!" But, just what do you do with all that clutter on your desk . . . and in your mind?

The quest for creative freedom may mean choosing a profession that sparks your creativity and dampens the tedious, "boring" paperwork. The message threads, "Ten Best . . ." and "Ten Worst Jobs for ADDers" are spontaneous reflections (only an ADDer is capable of the anomaly "spontaneous reflection") to the often rhetorical question "What do you want to be when you grow up?"

Do you feel like you're the only person in the world who can't find your keys? Acquiring good memory skills for the simplest of things is a critical survival skill. Forgetting your significant other's name when you're all set to introduce her to your Great Aunt Amelia can be rather . . . er, embarrassing.

Taking the puzzles of ADD and piecing together the picture that's "you" is a varied and unique experience. Finding the tools and skills can be tedious, so

Dr. John R. Shumate (71644,3107) is a pastor and professor of theology in Southern California. He has a very supportive (non-ADD) wife, Sandi, and two terrific daughters: Kristi, who is ADD, and Bethany. John and Kristi's motto is: "If ADD were easy, everyone would have it. So thank God—you must be special." Janie Bowman (72662,3716) is the non-ADD parent of two ADD children and a free-lance writer.

Creative Decluttering: Removing clutter is hard and dangerous work. Someone on my staff came by yesterday and said, "You need to be more organized. Have a place for everything and put everything in its place."

So, I stuffed a fax machine up his nose.

What I Need Is a book on organization written by my mother. My mother's filing system was to put the object needing attention on top of something else and forget about it. We didn't have a house cleaner—we had a team of anthropologists from U.C.L.A. They came once a week and committed archeology in every room. When they finished, we called someone with a backhoe to take care of the rest.

—Dr. John R. Shumate

having a "coach" may be one solution—someone who can explore organization skills with you, remind you about appointments and help establish life and career goals.

What works for your best friend, boss, or neighbor may not necessarily help you. Whining isn't winning. Living successfully with ADD means that you'll need very different strategies (and a sense of humor) for the very hard and dangerous work ahead.

Confronting Your Clutter
by Carolyn A. Koehnline, M.A.

YOU KNOW WHAT CLUTTER IS. It's that unsorted pile of junk mail, bills, and "things that might be important" that is spilling off the coffee table. It's those miscellaneous items that got shoved into the hall closet the last time your Aunt Minnie visited. It could be paper, fabric, hardware, electronic equipment, boxes, or plastic containers. It could be piled up, spread out, or stuffed into grocery bags. If it's hanging around, getting in your way, not quite in your life and not quite out of it, it's clutter.

It's not surprising that a lot of people with ADD have clutter problems. Most Americans are at least a little overwhelmed by the sheer volume of "stuff" flowing into the average home. Staying on top of it requires some tolerance for dealing with mundane tasks, an acceptance of the necessity of putting things away, and some ability to prioritize and make decisions; not the most common traits for people with ADD. Add a dose of perfectionism or rebelliousness, and clutter can be even more daunting.

On the one hand, who cares? What's the big deal? So you have some extra stuff floating around your house. It's not like having cancer or being addicted to heroin. It's a funny problem. On the other hand, clutter, in it's own insidious way, manages to keep a lot of people from fully doing what's most important to them. It distracts us, makes us lose things, and makes us late. It depresses and shames us. It complicates our already overwhelmingly complex lives, and keeps us from having simple, beautiful environments in which to live and work.

But deciding you want to de-clutter your life and actually managing to do it are two very different things. When you sit down with the good intention to clear that coffee table, at least a dozen things will occur to you that are far more urgent, or at least more interesting. If you do manage to clear it off, it's bound to be full two days later. And when you finally get around to tackling the hall closet, you know from past experience you'll end up with a couch heaped with coats because halfway through something will come up. So why bother?

It's worth bothering because your living and working environments directly affect the quality of your life. But if you're going to attempt to de-clutter, it's important to set yourself up for success instead of reinforcing past failures. The following is a set of guidelines to help you do just that.

Copyright © 1994 by Carolyn A. Koehnline, M.A.

Carolyn A. Koehnline, M.A. is a state certified mental health counselor with a private practice in Bellingham, WA She also teaches classes and workshops on "Confronting Clutter" and offers consultations to individuals and couples. She can be reached at (360) 676-8717.

1. *Do it for the right reasons.* If you start to de-clutter because you think you "should" or because someone else is shaming you into it, sooner or later your rebellious side will sabotage the plan. Better to inspire yourself. How will your life be easier? What will you be able to do that you can't do now? How will you use the time, space and energy that become available?

2. *Be specific about what you'd like to change.* It's not enough to say "I want to deal with my clutter." What room? Which part? How do you want it to look when you're finished? If your requests of yourself are too vague, they'll be too easy to forget.

3. *Focus on one step at a time.* Choose one area. Decide when you'll work on it and for how long, and schedule it on your calendar. Decide what tools you'll need. Boxes? Labels? Markers? Sticky-notes? I also like to use a timer and make a deal with myself not to get caught up in another project until after it rings. Don't focus on how much there is to do. Remember the ant who moves an entire anthill one grain of sand at a time.

4. *Create systems and make real homes for things.* Appointment books, calendars, notebooks, to-do lists and active files can help you keep track of daily activities. Having *real* places for unpaid bills and invitations to events will make it far more likely you'll actually find them again. You may want to consult a professional organizer, visit a store with organizing supplies, or check out books for ideas on creating orderly spaces and systems. MESSIE NO MORE by Sandra Felton, NOT FOR PACKRATS ONLY by Don Aslett, TAMING THE PAPER TIGER by Barbara Hemphill, and HOW TO CONQUER CLUTTER by Stephanie Culp are all helpful.

5. *Slowly build your tolerance for spaciousness.* One of the reasons that coffee table fills up again so quickly is simply that you're used to seeing it that way. When you walk by that nice clean surface your brain registers it as "empty" and therefore, "a good place to put things." You will need to slowly teach yourself that empty spaces have spaciousness, which you need in your life, and that they don't necessarily have to be filled with things.

6. *Get support.* Two of the hardest things about confronting your clutter are the isolation and the lack of structure. Basically, you are your own boss, and that makes it doubly easy to get distracted. A buddy can make all the difference when you are facing work that is physically, mentally, and emotionally challenging. He or she can help you take your goals more seriously and break them down into bite-sized pieces, encourage you, help problem-solve, and notice and delight in accomplishments, no matter what their size. But be careful to choose someone who is compassionate, able to focus, and respectful.

7. *Be kind to yourself.* Because confronting your clutter means dealing with things you've been avoiding, it unfortunately provides endless opportunities for beating yourself up. Don't give in to that temptation. Speak to yourself in gentle and encouraging words.

Remember, confronting your clutter is not about getting rid of everything. Nor is it about hanging onto everything and getting it all neatly organized. Dealing with your clutter is a way of acknowledging that as a human being you must make choices about how you will use time, energy, space, and other precious resources. Consciously letting go of the things that you don't truly want or need opens up the possibility of creating real places in your home and your life for those things that are most life-giving and meaningful to you.

Memorization Techniques
For Non-Linear Minds
by Robert E. Frazier

OR ME, THE TASK OF MEMORIZING DETAIL has always been a chore. Yet, it seems that much of the education we receive involves a *lot* of such activity. We take history classes, and memorize lots of names, dates, and places that have no meaning whatsoever to us, regurgitate them onto a test, and hope our score is above a "C" when we complete the semester. Yet, there is absolutely *no* meaning to the information, and it is quickly lost and "re-taught" to us, over and over, if only to reinforce this "by rote" memorization technique in our minds.

Yet, for the ADD mind, which many believe operates in a "non-linear" fashion, this type of "by rote" memorization is not only appalling, but represents a detestable activity which is best avoided at all costs, including bad grades, disciplinary problems, and so on. But, this seems to me to be the *only* method presented to us during our grade school lives, and we are expected to have mastered it by the time we reach high school and college.

Unfortunately, in my opinion, it works well *only* for linear minds. Repetition just isn't in the diet of a non-linear thinker, who constantly searches for the "new" and "interesting" among the "background" of "ordinary."

All of the memory experts I know of agree on one thing: the human brain remembers through *association*. By my own observations, there seem to be certain pathways along which memories are stored. My field of expertise is in computers and information science. As such, I have an affinity toward an analogy (and not an incorrect one) between the human brain and a computer. Computers cannot think, but they *can* remember very, very well.

Yet, even with computers, remembering where something has been placed is a typical problem as their storage capacity increases. Those of us who have large hard drives cluttered with thousands of files know exactly what I'm talking about. So, with the computer comes an organizing method that tries to define a "group" or "sub-group" of files, so that they can be more quickly identified through something that is common to them, and more easily understood, and more easily located. In the case of the computer, it is a named directory or sub-

Copyright © 1995 by Robert E. Frazier

Robert Frazier, part owner of a software development and consulting firm, was taught to read phonetically by his parents at age 4. He "flunked" kindergarten due to poor "socialization," and though never formally diagnosed, much of the information he's read indicates he probably would have been diagnosed as having ADHD. He can be reached at CompuServe 70172,177.

directory. The name is important to us, since it represents what we are looking for, and not where the data is. And, we use that name, along a *pathway*, to finally locate our file.

The human brain is similar. The different directories might be labeled "sight," "hearing," "smell," "taste," "touch," "fear," "pain," "love," "hate," "pleasure," "humor," and so on, based on the experience that is associated with the item to be remembered. The brain stores all of its information chemically. One hypothesis suggests that the memory is re-triggered by firing the neurons "attached" to it in a similar pattern to that of the memory itself (like a computer address), thus causing the person "remembering" to re-experience the sensations stored as a "memory."

So, if we consider how computers store information (number addresses) we can also attempt to create an easily recognized address for our brain to use to "store" data as well. This technique is referred to as "association" and has been successfully employed for years by several memory experts. I refer to these "addresses" of information as "pathways" by which we can retrieve information from our own brains. To initiate the pathway, we need to have a starting point that's easily remembered by itself, and once invoked, the pathway is followed directly to the information we are trying to remember.

Example: Suppose your wife or husband or parent called you on the phone and asked you to pick up some items at the store. You didn't have a pen or paper with you, and you needed to remember the list quickly. It is a list of several items, none of which are related to one another in any common purpose. You must memorize them as quickly as possible . . .

Here is the list:

1. Bananas

2. Brillo pads

3. Pork chops

4. A carving knife

5. Butter

6. Dog food

7. Canned peas

8. Beans

9. Flashlight batteries

These are typical items you find in any grocery store, with no real relationship to one another. And, you must remember them in a hurry, and remember them accurately. So, how do you do it? Well, one associative technique you can use is to visualize each item acting on a different part of your body, in a manner that causes a strong emotional response. Since you are walking to the store (in this example, we'll say you are walking) then we will begin with the feet and work up. So, you might memorize the list like so:

1. Bananas—imagine you are wearing bananas instead of shoes, and people are laughing at you.

2. Brillo Pads—you are wearing Brillo Pads on your knee caps, like knee pads, while scrubbing a floor. (That's pretty funny, if you think about it.)

3. Pork chops—your legs are *now* oversized pork chops, complete with plastic wrap and a tag (at $1.89 a pound—how much are your legs worth??)

4. A carving knife—imagine a carving knife stabbed into your navel. *ouch!*

5. Butter—there is *butter* smeared all over your chest!

6. Dog food—the dog is licking the butter on your chest! (*Down* Fido!)

7. Canned peas—You are wearing a necklace about your neck, made entirely of peas, with little cans for charms.

8. Beans—you have beans stuffed in your nose. Or, in your ears, if you prefer (there's a song called "Beans in my ears" as I recall . . .).

9. Flashlight batteries—Your hair is "rolled up" in curlers, except that the curlers are flashlight batteries.

OK—now, *without* peeking, let's see how much you remember:
    You are walking to the store, so start with your feet ...

1. Feet = ?

2. Knees = ?

3. Legs/Thighs = ?

4. Abdomen/Navel = ?

5. Chest = ?

6. Chest (again) = ? (related to the one above)

7. Neck = ?

8. Head/Face/Nose/Ears = ?

9. Hair = ?

You can grade this one yourself.

Okay, you say, I understand that this works for things like *grocery lists*, but I have a bunch of *numbers* I have to remember, including dates, and places that I've never *been* to, and people's names I've never *heard* of. So, how do I remember *these*? Well, the truth is, you remember *everything* you experience—absolutely *everything*.

The only problem is that you merely forgot where you "put" the information. It's not lost, but you need to find some "key" that you can use to retrieve it. And, since the information is stored in *multiple* locations, if you reliably associate the information with multiple "pathways" you are much more likely to retrieve it. So, when studying it is *very* helpful to employ as many of your five senses as possible, and if you reflect on the information, or draw conclusions from it, you are that much more likely to recall it later on.

Some people memorize well by *doing*. A typical activity that may help in this area could involve some level of "rote," but hopefully in a manner that does not allow you to lose interest.

For example: Let's suppose you had to remember a series of dates within a given year, for various battles fought in the Civil War, and you had to relate each date to the place where the battle was fought. Well, one way to memorize this would be to create a large calendar. Then, using small cards with the battles on them, arrange them according to their date (possibly just the month and first digit of the date to begin with).

Then, shuffle them up again, and repeat the task. Since each repetition involves several skills, and is "different enough" each time through, it will not quickly become "boring" (like writing something down 50 times to memorize it). Also, if you repeat the name of each battle and the date while placing it down, you end up creating an additional "pathway" in which the information is stored.

So, using this technique, you store the information by experience in doing a task using sight, speech, hearing as well as any cognitive activity that might be going on as you try to correctly place the various "battle cards" "without peeking."

At some point in time, though, you may need to memorize something that is totally abstract, without any obvious relationship to anything else. But, there is a good example of how to do this that is often used by biology students. This is the method of "mnemonics", or making a word/phrase out of the initials of what we want to memorize.

In biology class I learned the order of the various biological classifications by memorizing the phrase: "Kings Play Chess On Fine Grain Sand," representing "Kingdom," "Phylum," "Class," "Order," "Family," "Genus," and "Species," which I still remember, even 30 years later. Obviously this method works. And, similar to this method is a "visual mnemonic" used by electrical engineers, known as the "right hand rule" and the "left hand rule". When the hand is placed in the correct position, the thumb represents "Motion", the 1st finger on the hand "Field", and the middle finger "Current". When I was in the Navy I was taught that this could be remembered by "Mary's Fuzzy Cat". Well, similar.

Those of us who have musical inclination may wish to make up songs, or rhythmic "raps" to memorize something. We all know how well those TV commercial jingles stick in our heads. If you don't believe me, just try filling in the blank on these items below:

"You deserve a break today, so get up and get away, to . . ."; ". . . tastes good like a cigarette should" (for those old enough to remember); "Plop, plop, fizz, fizz, oh what a relief it is" (product is: . . .).

Fortunately, advertisers don't use such jingles nearly as often as they used to, so my examples are a bit dated. Still, the technique works well, and can be used for remembering various things. In fact, the effort you make in creating the song (which is best kept to the tune of something you already know, so you can recall it easily) reinforces the memorization process even more. Therefore, it is best to make up your own songs and not "borrow" anyone else's unless you are out of choices for the moment.

Whatever means of memorizing information you choose to use for yourself, you must involve something that you are already good at, or else you will spend an inordinate amount of time perfecting your "method" while at the same time you may fail to learn how to memorize effectively.

Repeated success is an imprint part of "learning how to learn," and not just "doing better next time." So, start with something you know, and build on it. The techniques I outlined above may not work for you, but the principles behind them will. After all, our brains work pretty much the same way, in general, and we need to have some sort of easily retrieved "pathway" by which we can access information in our minds.

ADD Coaching— Questions & Answers

by Nancy Ratey, Ed.M. and Susan Sussman, M.Ed.

What is ADD Coaching?

ADD Coaching is a process in which a coach works with an individual with ADD on any or all of the following:

- Planning and setting goals

- Building organizational strategies, time management skills, and prioritizing skills

- Developing strategies to maintain focus and concentration

- Helping to create and maintain a medication titration log

- Creating structure, support and encouragement

- Providing a safe space to work on social skills

- Effectively managing ADD in the workplace

Is Coaching the Same as Psychotherapy?

No! Coaching is different from psychotherapy. Psychotherapy is generally long-term and deals with intra- and inter-personal issues. Coaching acknowledges these issues but is more interactive. The ADD coach strives to help individuals learn new behaviors and strategies which enable him to overcome areas of difficulty. The coach helps to break tasks down into manageable sized pieces, helps to translate thoughts into actions, and can act as a pillar of support and encouragement.

How does coaching work?

The client and the coach work as a team, identifying areas of difficulty and agreeing on strategies to use to begin the process of overcoming these difficulties. The client agrees to become accountable for her time and actions, and the coach agrees to hold the client accountable. The coach is flexible and can work

For more information, contact Nancy Ratey, ED.M. (74472,62) and Susan Sussman, M.ED. (75471,3101), co-founders, The National Coaching Network, Box 353, Lafayette Hill, PA 19444. The phone and fax number is 610-825-4505. Currently, NCN is only making collect return calls. The National Coaching Network is developing a database of coaches nationwide and provides training, administrative information, and support for ADD individuals and ADD coaches. A newsletter, "Coaching Matters" is published quarterly and is available by subscription.

with the client in person; by telephone, fax or an online service; in an office; at the client's home; or at the client's work site. The coach is amenable to working alone or in a team with the client's psychotherapist, physician, and/or work-site personnel.

Individuals with ADD are often aware that they must design their environment so they will be productive and have the proper reminders built in. Using people like supervisors and spouses as coaches often generates feelings of inadequacy and frustration due to the nature of these relationships. The coach is an emotionally neutral person in the life of an individual with ADD. The strong feelings that may be attached to a spouse or supervisor are absent in the coaching relationship. Thus the coach can offer suggestions and reminders, provide structure and boundaries and be perceived by the client as helpful and supportive. Coaching can be the client's way of designing an environment that meets his own unique needs.

How does coaching help an individual with ADD?

Working in particular skill areas such as time management and organization are often a client's primary concern. However, for the individual with ADD, symptoms can become more frequent and/or severe during times of stress and fatigue.

Paying attention to life-style issues in coaching helps individuals learn to promote their own well-being. In addition to working in particular skill areas, the ADD coach supports clients in examining life-style issues and making changes. Areas such as diet, sleep habits, exercise programs, and other aspects of self-nurturing are examined. Recommendations are made to foster health and balance in these important aspects of daily life.

Coaches also help clients with feelings of being overwhelmed. When they are supersaturated by stimuli, some individuals with ADD tend to "shut down." Coaches help people learn to select target areas to concentrate on—leaving everything else outside the area of focus for that moment.

Where did the concept of coaching come from?

Coaches and the concept of coaching have been around for a long time. We are all familiar with sports coaches, music teachers, mentors, and role models. Coaching takes place in all aspects of life - in supportive relationships with family members, in business and industry, in extracurricular activities, in tutoring of all kinds.

Individuals with ADD often know what changes they want to make in their lives, but don't always know how to make those changes. And most importantly, they can get distracted from their goals. The coach can be instrumental in starting an ongoing process of defining long-range goals and short-term objectives, and in keeping the individual on the defined path once it becomes clear. Many athletes and musicians rely on the knowledge and experience of a coach to help them set and achieve goals and make steady progress. Many individuals with ADD also use a coach to help them assess their strengths and weaknesses, learn how to compensate for weaknesses, and develop personal styles that draw on their strengths.

How long does coaching last and what is the cost?

There are as many answers to this question as there are coaches and clients. Depending on a client's needs, a coaching relationship may last from a few weeks to several months, to an ongoing professional relationship. An average client might expect to spend at least several months in a coaching relationship. The cost for ADD coaching depends on various factors, including geographical region and the qualifications of the coach.

Ten Worst Jobs for ADDers?

Want to guess what the 10 worst jobs for ADDers could be? Match your answers against these from forum members!

To: *All*

What are your opinions on the 10 worst jobs for ADDers?

I started thinking about this while watching a court reporter recently. No way I could pay attention that way!

—*Linda Rawson (Sysop)*

Linda,

You sure about that??

Think about it this way. There are a bunch of people usually scurrying about in the courtroom. Add to that the arguments, objections, and sidebars (I've been watching too much OJ! (grin!)). To make it more enticing, you are part of unfolding a mystery. With every witness you may have this sense of "Ohhhhhhh."

Court reporters are able to "watch" everything happening while they are keyboarding. You'd be amazed how you can automatically input stuff without really focusing. I do it all the time (grin!).

I've been a note-taker (shorthand) in quite a few situations where I've been very interested in the goings-on. I quite enjoyed it, particularly when doing so during a lawyer/client interview. I found it fascinating.

I guess the only problem would be the length of time you have to be sitting down. But, Judge Ito's Court Reporter is "up" rather often with those ever-popular sidebars (grin!).

—*Rose Zagaja/Staff*

Re: Court reporters are able to "watch" everything happening while they are keyboarding.

That would be the precise problem I would have: getting too absorbed in what was going on and losing interest and attention to the keyboarding!

You have to pay attention to a lot going on very fast in that situation, process it all very carefully and get it down carefully, too.

Re: I guess the only problem would be the length of time you have to be sitting down. But, Judge Ito's Court Reporter is "up" rather often with those ever-popular sidebars (grin!).

(Laughing) Maybe the lawyers all have ADHD!

—*Linda Rawson (Sysop)*

Linda, according to the session I attended at the ADDA CO, housewife is one of them!

—*Deb Land*

Deb,

Really? 'Housewife' is one of the 10 worst jobs 4 ADDers?

You wouldn't be speaking from *personal experience*, now, would you? (And, you're not married to your house, I'm sure).

—*Bob Frazier*

Bob, that's what they said at the conference I just attended!

Re: You wouldn't be speaking from *personal experience*, now, would you?

Nope, never been a housewife. My husband and I have always worked outside of our home, and taken equal responsibility for work "in" our home. (So, OK, he's a "bit" more responsible than I am!(grin!))

Re: (And, you're not married to your house, I'm sure).

Nope, not me! But I know of some people that appear to be!

—*Deb Land*

Linda,

Among the 10 Worst Jobs for ADDers:

Accounting/tax preparation. Ugh.

—*Jim Foster*

Linda, how about *this* list:

1) Maintenance mechanic (maintenance only, no troubleshooting)

2) Assembly line worker

3) File clerk (filing all day, nothing else)

4) Accountant

5) Farmer (of course!)

6) U.S. patent office clerk,

7) Human Resources department staff member.

8) Anything that involves "paperwork"

That's all I can think of for now—if I get other ideas I'll add them. I'll check to see what others think, too. It might be quite interesting.

—*Bob Frazier*

Bob, I have worked as both a farmer and as a file clerk. I agree about the file clerk, but farming was a very stimulating, absorbing thing to do, believe it or not.

—*Linda Rawson (Sysop)*

Linda, the only job I was ever fired from was one in which I was "reorganized" into a situation for which there was no creativity at all, and I was given little training and little help. And, it had nothing to do with computers.

—*Bob Frazier*

Bob, given what you say about that job, in some ways it must have been a relief to be fired. It sounds like torture to me, too.

—*Linda Rawson (Sysop)*

Linda, how about school bus driver?

Live mannequin?

Or . . . Buckingham Palace Guard?

—*B. J. Yahr*

Just to butt in . . . [My] hubby is ADD and works nights at a grocery store. He does very well. During the day.. he also works part time with me . . . we drive school buses!!! He is the most well-liked driver in our fleet (125 drivers) the kids and parents adore him because he is so "overachieving." (Laughing)

—*Lorri D. McColgan*

Ten Best Jobs for ADDers?

Completing a list of 10 worst jobs for people with ADD, the group turned its collective attention to the best jobs for ADDers.

To: *Thom Hartmann (Sysop)*

I have, with much interest and empathy, followed the thread concerning the *worst* jobs for ADDers. I find myself in a *worst* job at the present time and, as I am considering a change, I thought that it would be of help to myself and perhaps others to examine jobs and careers with respect to the obvious extra-abilities that we often possess.

Sooo . . . What are the *best* jobs or careers for those profoundly affected by ADD?

—Sandy

FWIW, Sandy, I wrote a book about this, called FOCUS YOUR ENERGY (available or orderable from any bookstore). Don't want to sound like I'm flogging my own books (I'm really not), but the book takes about 100 pages to go into it all, and that's far more room than we have here in a message. (grin)

In general, though, jobs with lots of variety, short-term projects, and lots of adrenaline work well for ADDers.

—Thom Hartmann (Sysop)

Thanks for your reply. I have read both "Hunters/Farmers" (ATTENTION DEFICIT DISORDER: A DIFFERENT PERCEPTION), the first book I read after diagnosis 5 months ago, and FOCUS YOUR ENERGY. Incidentally, I found them both quite perceptive and informative and I go so far as to give a copy of "H/F" to friends not or newly acquainted with ADD and want to know a little more. Your 'new' perspective seems to be a little less threatening than some of the more *technical* literature.

I have had a number of jobs and/or businesses over the past 30+/- working years and have, as you suggest, found the ones with much variety/stimulus the most enjoyable and sustainable. I seem to be the consummate 'hunter' and even now am continuing the hunt for *survival*. ADD seems to enforce our most primal instincts (at the expense of most everything else).

Again, thank you for your reply and for your books. They have been most helpful to this Hunter.

—Sandy

I think that teaching is a great job for ADDers. The constant traffic of the classroom keeps one's stimulation level high, and the only drawback is the frustration of waiting to grade papers until midnight when they are due. I have solved this with OHIO (Only Handle It Once) with great success. Think about it.

—*Marlin E. Bynum*

Re: I think that teaching is a great job for ADDers.

Try adult training—the difference is:

Just a couple of days at a time—no time to get bored. Each group is new—with specific requirements Hyperfocus is a major asset—keeping track of each student is a great skill to have.

I've gone back to computer training, as a home-based business, 4 years ago. I've focused on one specific topic and market my workshops throughout the West Coast. When I'm *on* (in class), I'm very focused on the students and do a really great job (high marks from students!). Between workshops, I have time to come down from the high of being *on* to market, learn, and do all kinds of other fun, and distracting, things. I have administrative and bookkeeping support (both of which I find very boooooring).

—*Jim Porzak*

IMBO (In my bombastic opinion), any job that requires creativity, fast thinking, quick adaptation to unexpected conditions, troubleshooting, etc. lends itself to being filled by an ADD'er/nonlinear thinker.

—*Bob Frazier*

Any examples come to mind in the corporate/business arena? I'm looking right now. I have a splendid opportunity to create my own position in this rapidly growing family company.

—*G. Gregory Dunn*

A) Engineer or researcher (any field)

B) Troubleshooting/repair technician (any field)

C) Department 'troubleshooter' (the one who always finds the causes for all of those nitpicky issues that nobody ever has time to deal with but constantly make life hard)

D) Marketing department, doing market research or establishing new markets for existing or new products.

E) Financial analyst, doing cost accounting for the purpose of reducing overall process costs, and any related "troubleshooting" activity associated with it.

Basically, any kind of job that changes unexpectedly every day, or requires some kind of creativity, troubleshooting skills, etc. lends itself to an ADD-like mind.

My opinion, of course.

—*Bob Frazier*

About your question: "Any examples come to mind in the corporate/business arena?"

Pardon my jumping in, but I think it also depends on whether you're an introvert or extrovert on the Myers-Briggs scale. If you're an extrovert (you draw energy from interacting with people), you might do well in a sales or customer support position. If you're an introvert, however (you need to be alone to replenish your energy stores, and you find interacting with people draining), then you might do better with product development or shipping. You might check out the book WHAT COLOR IS YOUR PARACHUTE? by Richard Nelson Bolles.

Whatever you do, try to pair up with a "farmer" type secretary or assistant, who is content to work *with* you and not ambitiously looking ahead to the next job (or yours!).

—*Kathy FS*

Neurobehavioral Syndromes with Features of ADD

Introduction by Dale E. Hammerschmidt, M.D., F.A.C.P.
Associate Professor of Medicine, University of Minnesota

ONE OF THE EVER-PRESENT PROBLEMS in dealing with neurobehavioral disorders is that we understand them only approximately. In most cases, we know very little about the genetics, biochemistry and neurophysiology of the disorders. So we diagnose them as "syndromes" . . . loosely lumped-together collections of signs and symptoms that form patterns and give us some useful information about prognosis and likely response to drugs and other therapies. If we think that Johnny and Suzie really have the same exact syndrome, just because both of them meet the diagnostic criteria for ADD, we're probably fooling ourselves.

There are quite a few other neurobehavioral syndromes which have features of ADD, which may initially be diagnosed as ADD, or which respond to the same sort of interventions as one might use for ADD. There are, on the other hand, also many people with ADD who have features of other neurobehavioral disorders as well—tics, compulsions, rages, panics, defiance to name a few. In

---

Dale E. Hammerschmidt, M.D., F.A.C.P., is an Associate Professor of Medicine and Senior Editor, Journal of Laboratory and Clinical Medicine *at the University of Minnesota. He is a sysop on the ADD Forum on CompuServe. He can be reached at UMHC, University of Minnesota, Box 480, 500 Southeast Harvard Street, Minneapolis, Minnesota 55455.*

many cases, you can argue long and hard (and inconclusively) about just what might be the "best" or "most correct" or "most appropriate" diagnosis to give a child.

Perhaps the best single example is the tic disorder Tourette Syndrome. In some studies, as many as 75% of TS kids have signs of ADD, and as many as 35% actually meet the diagnostic criteria. The ADD features are often present long before tics are recognized; when tics appear, it becomes a semantic issue whether you now call the child "ADD *and* TS" or "TS with prominent ADD features." The drugs used to treat ADD may make tics worse in as many as 30 percent of people with tic disorders . . . so a pretty common scenario is:

ADD Diagnosis → Ritalin therapy → Worsening tics → New diagnosis of TS.

Similar overlap syndromes are seen between ADD and Obsessive-Compulsive Disorder, Pervasive Developmental Disorder, Autism-spectrum disorders, Explosive Rage Disorder, Oppositional-Defiant Disorder and even Bipolar Disorder. There are probably risk genes in common among all of these syndromes.

Because the borders among these disorders are so blurry, the ADD Forum has often included discussion of the kindred neurobehavioral disorders—enough so that it was useful to create a forum section for them.

Tourette Syndrome Primer
by Dale E. Hammerschmidt , M.D., F.A.C.P.

What Is Tourette Syndrome?

Described by French neurologist Georges Gilles de la Tourette more than a century ago, Tourette Syndrome (TS) is a sometimes-dramatic disorder that is uncommon enough that most people aren't aware of it. It has bizarre enough symptoms that patients are often thought to be crazy or to be possessed by demons. It seems to be inherited as a dominant trait, which means that an affected parent has a very high likelihood of having affected children. It's a bit more likely to be fully manifest (and diagnosed) in boys; only about two-thirds of girls carrying the gene have diagnosable TS but many of the other third have enough compulsions to be diagnosed as having obsessive-compulsive disorder (OCD).

The diagnostic hallmarks of the disease are tics. The diagnosis is made when a child has both motor and vocal tics, which start in childhood and persist for more than a year.

Tics are more-or-less involuntary behaviors; that is, they can often be suppressed temporarily, but it's difficult. They may be very simple or very complex; the complex ones can be hard to recognize as tics until after some of the less dramatic ones have appeared.

Common *motor* tics are grimaces, eye blinking, shrugging, head jerking, spitting, nose rubbing, leg tapping, funny steps when walking.

Common *vocal* tics are throat clearing, grunting, sniffing, coughing, repeating words, even barking or cursing.

There are several sub-varieties of tics. A *pure motor* tic may go on with the patient not even aware of it. A *sensory/motor* tic is one in which the patient feels a distinct need to carry out the action. Some authorities feel that most TS tics are *sensory/motor*, to the point that other movement disorders should be considered if all a patient's tics are pure motor tics.

There are some *verbal* tics (vocal tics that involve words) that are rather common in TS and rather uncommon in the rest of the universe, so are worth mentioning specifically. Coprolalia (the word means s**t-talk) is uncontrollable outbursts of profanity or obscenity. Echolalia is the compulsive repetition of words or sounds made by others. Echopraxia is for mimicking actions). Palilalia is the repetition of one's own words, often sounding as though the person is trying to take a running start to finish a sentence.

For more information, contact the Tourette Syndrome Association, a national information, Advocacy and research support organization with many state and local chapters; 42-40 Bell Boulevard, Bayside, New York 11361-2861; (718) 224-2999. ($35 a year suggested dues, but no one is turned away)

Neurobehavioral Syndromes with Features of ADD

The complexity of the tics ranges from a simple twitch to a very complicated behavior . . . simply put, there's really a continuum between tics and compulsions, and it's kind of hard to draw the line between the two.

That makes it less surprising, perhaps, that many TS patients and many siblings of TS patients have lots of compulsions—sometimes enough to meet the diagnostic criteria for obsessive-compulsive disorder (OCD).

Many TS kids also have features of ADHD (Attention Deficit/Hyperactivity Disorder), and may meet the criteria for diagnosis of that problem. It's not known whether this is a real linkage of two disorders or not—it may just mean that having one will make the other a lot more likely to be diagnosed if it's also present. Ritalin, which is used to treat ADHD, makes tics worse in about 30–40% of people with tics who get it. So a fairly common scenario is that a kid may be diagnosed to have probable or definite ADHD; Ritalin is prescribed; tics become obvious; diagnosis is refined/advanced to TS.

Many TS kids also have features of Pervasive Developmental Disorder (PDD) of the Asperger type. (Again, as in ADD/TS, it's not yet clear if this is a real biological and genetic link.) This is hard to describe succinctly, though at a TS Support Group meeting I once heard it described as "all the social/behavioral problems common in TS, but without the tics." When Asperger described the syndrome in 1942, he called it "autistic psychopathy," but the kids are not as autistic (inwardly oriented) as the ones we now describe with the term "(Kanner's) Autism." You can think of them as having almost a dyslexia-like problem in learning to recognize social cues, which leads to social retardation which can be quite severe, even if the child is very bright.

This leads to a huge number of school adjustment problems and the like; these are often not handled well, because school officials are often unfamiliar enough with the disorder that they haven't a clue how to deal with it. Often, they will interpret the child's intelligence as evidence that he "knows better" than to do all these things, then will punish the child for tics or for behavioral problems that are neurologic in origin. Even a teacher who is well informed about neurobehavioral disorders may have a difficult time managing such children, and they sometimes must be taught in circumstances short of full mainstreaming.

Tics tend to get worse about the time of puberty, and tend to get less severe in later life. But there's striking patient-to-patient, day-to-day and month-to-month variation. Anxiety may make the tics worse, and concentration on a task may suppress them.

TS seems to be caused by abnormalities in the metabolism of a brain messenger chemical called *dopamine*. There are abnormal levels of this chemical in some brain areas in TS patients, and many of the helpful drugs are things that influence how the brain metabolizes dopamine.

There's also a suggestion that some of the kids with the more severe PDD symptoms may have a second, related defect which has a different effect on dopamine. The genes for TS and PDD have not yet been found, so many of the details are still a bit speculative.

There are drugs which help control tics, so that the majority of TS patients can function reasonably well. The ones with PDD features may need to reach adulthood to have enough social maturity to function well, and a few of them prove incapable of independent living. Haloperidol (brand name **Haldol**™) is the "textbook" front-line drug; it works quite well, but sometimes leads to too much sedation, a bit of a flat affect, or a funny syndrome of school avoidance.

In doses higher than those used in TS, it can cause some more serious neurologic side effects (such as a movement problem called "tardive dyskinesia")— it's not certain that this is ever a problem in TS, but it's a theoretical concern that leads some people to use haloperidol less enthusiastically.

Tardive dyskinesia is a movement disorder that can include tremors, tics or writhing. It looks a bit like Parkinson's disease, and is sometimes called "drug-induced Parkinsonism."

On of the problems in studying whether Haldol can cause it in the low doses used for TS is that it can have some symptomatic overlap with TS. Lip smacking, for example, is common in TD and also common in TS.

Pimozide (**Orap**™) is the "textbook" second-line TS-specific drug, and is used in patients who do poorly on Haldol.

Clonidine™ is a blood pressure medication that also influences dopamine balance, and seems to help many patients with fewer side effects (it's sedating at first, but most folks grow tolerant of this effect). It is rapidly becoming many physicians' drug of first choice, because it seems likely to be extremely safe in the long term. Its action doesn't last long, so there may be a "roller-coaster" effect: tic control may be excellent and sedation may be troublesome in the first hour or so; tic control may worsen and sedation may lessen as the drug wears off. There's a skin patch form, which helps even out the effect. Because it is a drug to lower blood pressure, some folks find that it makes it hard for them to stand up fast without getting woozy.

Mellaril™ and other sedative/tranquilizer drugs may be helpful for anxiety and the "hyper" state that some TS patients have, and thus may be especially helpful in school integration problems. They are less potent as anti-tic medications, though.

Prozac™ (fluoxetine) may help compulsions and associated depressive symptoms, as may other antidepressants which are in the group known as "SSRIs" (Selective Serotonin Re-uptake Inhibitors). Others among the many in this group are clomipramine (**Anafranil**™); **Paxil, Zoloft.**

Is it ADD or Autism?

by Louis Cady, M.D.

ONE OF THE SIGNIFICANT THEMES of the following thread is, "How do you tell the difference between autism and ADD/ADHD"? Like the forum members who tackle this issue, I too can pretty well spot it "when it walks in the door."

Although the description of "social and language delay" in autism is technically correct, it is more useful for the uninitiated to compare the way ADD/ADHD kids, as well as autistic ones, interact with others. The "social delay" can actually be reflected in some fairly bizarre behavior, pervaded by a sort of indifference to emotional connectedness between the autistic child and his or her parents, siblings, and family acquaintances.

ADHD children, particularly if they have a severe case (and are not currently being treated with adequate amounts and types of medication) can certainly rage and throw temper fits if they get their will crossed, but usually the adult or parent can tell what it is that set the child into such a foul mood (even if it seems relatively minor). Further, there is almost always some emotional bonding between the child and his or her parents (even though it can be strained with severe ADHD!).

In autism, on the other hand, frequently it is *impossible* to figure out what sent the child into a tailspin—maybe it was a squeaky door, or rough linens on the bed. Or, once the culprit is figured out, a mature, normal adult (or even child) can't possibly understand how *that* little thing could have upset a child so, as the connection seems totally illogical and irrational.

Not getting to go to the ice cream store with the family on a planned outing, however, can put an ADHD child into a tizzy. Even though parents may not agree that one should get that upset about it, they can at least empathize that the ADHD child is simply getting frustrated about not getting his way. This is understandable. Pitching a hissy fit because you're not allowed to sit in the middle of the floor and spin a wheel around for six hours at a time, however, is more difficult to empathize with!

Furthermore, autistic children can seem "cold," unconcerned with the feelings of others, totally self-preoccupied, and incapable of giving and receiving

Dr. Louis B. Cady is a psychiatrist in Evansville, Indiana who treats children, adolescents, and adults with ADD/ADHD. His other interests include difficult-to-treat depression, eating disorders, and sleep disorders. He is the Medical Director of the Disordered Eating Program at the Mulberry Center in Evansville, IN, as well as the Medical Director of the Sleep Diagnostic Center of Indiana. A prolific speaker and author, Cady will be releasing two books in 1996—one tentatively titled, "MASTERMIND: THE PSYCHIATRY OF WEALTH, SUCCESS, AND HAPPINESS," and another book, "LEARNING AND LIVING THE ABC'S OF LOVE FOR YOU AND YOUR CHILD."

affection. Language delay is typically *far* more severe than would be expected from "difficulty paying attention" in ADHD kids. Mild to moderate cases of ADHD usually show hyperkinetic kids who can be emotionally trying but still have an emotional bonding to their parents.

Many of them sit happily on my couch right next to their parents during a portion of the interview—wiggling all the time. Autistic kids, on the other hand, don't really seem to care if their parents are there or not and can be coolly distant —even with devoted and nurturing parents.

The magnitude of difference between the symptoms of ADHD and autism can at times, however, be difficult to ascertain. Family history is frequently helpful in making or excluding a diagnosis. If grandpa, pa, and aunts, uncles, nephews and nieces are all wigglesome, hyperactive entrepreneur types, chances are it's most likely a severe case of ADHD.

A medication trial can frequently be helpful in distinguishing the two. Stimulant medications, in particular, can make autistic children much more unstable, irritable, quarrelsome, and possibly combative; whereas it can calm down and stabilize kids with ADHD.

Care should be taken that a child with autism is not left on a stimulant for a long time, however, as many studies indicate that stimulant medications can actually permanently worsen the clinical course of a child with autism (because it delays developmental tasks even further), whereas there is clear indications of the effectiveness of stimulants in most children with severe ADHD.

ADD vs. Autism

Autism and ADD, Tourette Syndrome and other disorders share so many symptoms that it can be frustratingly difficult to tell them apart. In this discussion, parents and a teacher share ways to tell the difference.

Hi, everyone,

I know I've asked this question before, but now that I'm a little more educated about autism, I'll ask it again. (grin)

How would an average everyday mom of an ADD kid know the difference between ADD and autism?

Is there any one characteristic of autism that just is not there for the ADDers? Or vice-versa?

(I have a new theory.)

—*B. J. Yahr*

B.J., You have a good question there.

Could it be mind-reading?

Say . . . I get a can of Heinz Baked Beans from the cupboard and I open a drawer. I expect an ADDer to "know" I am looking for a can opener, but not a high-functioning autistic like my son. I call what the ADDer is doing "mind reading." I mean he figures out what I am looking for, while an autistic child would not be able to tell.

—*Vicky*

B.J.,

The diagnosis of autism is made on this criteria: The child's social and language development is delayed and disordered significantly more than his/her overall development would indicate.

For example, I have an 9-year-old autistic student. His academic level is 3rd grade, (except for math, which is 1st grade), his language/social level is between 5 and 6 years. The language/social development is not just delayed, but disordered. In other words, he has some skills at a 6-year-old level, and some at a 4-year level.

Also, recently, doctors here have added the criteria that the child has disordered sensory development. These children have problems tolerating and processing input from their senses.

Clear as mud?

—*Anne*

Anne, yes, it's clear as mud!

Re: *"The diagnosis of autism is made on this criteria: The child's social and language development is delayed and disordered significantly more than his/her over all development would indicate."*

This looks like severe ADD to me!

What about high-functioning autistics?

Somebody told me that a telltale symptom of autism is the "stare right through you." The "far away look." Thing is . . . again, what about high-functioning autistics? Or extremely high-IQ autistics? (Sheesh, Carly and I, who have ADD without the H, stare like that without Ritalin!) And what about autistic adults, don't they catch up in their development?

Sensory:

Re: *"Also, recently, doctors here have added the criteria that the child has disordered sensory development. They have problems tolerating and processing input from their senses."*

Ah . . . tactile defensive! All three of us in this family, diagnosed w/ADD, have this problem!

Now. Another question: Do you know of any families where there are genetic siblings, one autistic, one ADD?

As for my new theory: I've noticed that most ADD students benefit greatly from rhythm. Learning reading as though it were poetry (as my kids did) works so well. I've used it to calm ADHD kids many times. I see a definite connection here. I'm just trying to revolutionize education, here, pardon me! :-)

B. J. Yahr

B. J.,

I'll try some more! Sorry if I'm not clear, I've been around autistic kids so much, I can almost pick them out of a crowd! So it's perfectly clear to me!

Re: *"This looks like severe ADD to me!"* and *"What about high functioning autistics?"*

The 9-year-old I described earlier is a very high functioning autistic child. There is a difference between functioning ability and cognitive ability. His language/social skills are very impaired, but his academic, daily living, self-care type skills are well within the normal range.

Re: *"A telltale symptom of autism is the stare-right-through-you. The far-away look."*

Nab, autistic kids may do this, but like you said, so do other people. Besides it is correlatively easy to teach eye contact. I have known many autistic kids who wouldn't look at you, who looked at you too intensely, or didn't know when to stop looking at you. You see, with autism, the skills can be taught. It's the pragmatics, how to use the skills that is difficult!

Re: *"Ah . . . tactile defensive! All three of us in this family, diagnosed w/ADD, have this problem!"*

No, sorry, this is not what I meant. Tactile defensive may be part of it, but autistic people process sensory input differently. What they see, is not necessarily what you see; what they hear may be painful, or not heard at all (despite functional ears); what registers on you as a loving hug, can be a outrageously painful experience for an autistic kid! Smells and tastes, too, are different experiences for autistic people.

Re: *"And what about autistic adults, don't they catch up in their development?"*

Absolutely not! Autism is a lifelong disorder. Autistic kids can learn things. Some learn more than others. Some grow up to have jobs and live independently, but the autism is still there and needs to be compensated for.

I can tell you this; I have 5 students in my class, ages 8-11. One of these is a student 11 years old, who is not autistic, but with some language development impairment and the most extreme ADHD anyone has ever seen in this lifetime! No drugs have been able to touch his ADHD, although some have "drugged" him enough to slow his kinetic output, but haven't really helped his ADHD. Anyway, his ADHD is very severe. But visitors in my room who know anything about autism interact with him for 5 minutes and then say to me, "Why is he here? He's not autistic!"

So you see, there is a very clear difference between autism and ADD!

We also have a son with TS [Tourette Syndrome]. I think this disability is different from autism in degree, not in kind. But I can very clearly see a difference between my son and my students!

Although these disabilities (ADD, autism, TS, etc) may be on the same continuum, it seems there is usually a very clear difference between them.

More mud?

—Anne

B.J.,

Re: *"Do you know of any families where there are genetic siblings, one autistic, one ADD?"*

We have one of each. Also, probable ADD-dad. One kid who's plain vanilla too. Oddly, the plain vanilla kid has some of the more "traditional" autistic characteristics: spins without dizziness, lined things up as a kid (ever seen a Mr. Potato Head warehouse? (grin)), has trouble with change.

My ADD child and my autistic child are each in their own worlds, but those worlds are on totally different planets . . . still clear as mud?

—*Erica*

Anne,

Re: *"I'll try some more! Sorry if I'm not clear, I've been around autistic kids so much, I can almost pick them out of a crowd! So it's perfectly clear to me!"*

Sounds like me with ADD kids!

I think we're getting somewhere. If only I could be around some kids that I knew for sure were autistic. I'm sure that would help a lot.

Re: *Tactile defensive*

Maybe *I* can teach you something here. This term sounds so . . . fluffy.

It's not.

The sound of a staple gun is *excruciating* to Carly.

Colin hates tags in any clothing. He prefers t-shirts and sweatpants or elastic-waist shorts. He hears everything from the crickets walking on the brick on the outside of his bedroom wall to the clock ticking in the kitchen when he's trying to go to sleep. He also sees all.

Carly is uncomfortable eating lunch in the lunchroom (the size of a basketball gym) *because of all those people.*

Both kids go barefoot as often as possible.

We've given up on sheets and blankets for the kids' beds. They sleep in sleeping bags. They're sensitive to the texture of the linens.

Carly's audio processing problem is not a hearing disorder. It's the way the brain processes the sounds. I have it too. I suspect Colin may have it. It's sort of like dyslexia of the hearing system. I captured a thread a long time ago on this . . . several people talking about their experiences. It really gets the point across.

—B. J. *Yahr*

Boy! Does this sound familiar. My 7+ year old daughter, Sheryl, is not ADD and she's not autistic, but she does have a sensory integration problem and has severe tactile defensiveness, although OT [occupational therapy] has improved it a lot.

Re: *Both kids go barefoot as often as possible.*

Interesting. Sheryl will go barefoot only under duress. She HATES the feel of the carpet (and particularly of sand or grass). She has definite opinions on how particular shoes fit the bill though.

Sheryl also has trouble in crowds. She's very musical and sings in a choir. She's terrific in rehearsal where the children are not close to each other and are not facing a crowd, but she often "spaces out" to cope when they perform.

—*Kate Eisen*

Even though *reading* about autism and ADD sometimes will give the impression that there are a lot of similarities, in my experience people with autism are much more disordered in these areas. I don't mean they're more severely affected, I mean they're further away from "normal."

—*Elisa Davis (Sysop)*

B.J., I loved all the descriptions of tactile defensiveness! Sounds like my TS son (won't sleep w/ sheets either).

But with autism, I'm not talking just defensiveness, I'm talking a different perception.

Re: *"Carly's audio processing problem is not a hearing disorder. It's the way the brain processes the sounds."*

This is getting closer yet! Autistic kids seem to actually perceive sensory input differently. The clearest example of this I can think of is a student I had a couple of years ago. If I played catch with him and threw the ball slightly to his left side, he would reach over to his right side to try and catch it!

I had another student who couldn't lay on a wedge, he kept falling off! The position was so different for him, he couldn't process the proprioception* and figure out where his body was!

Theoretically, that's what all the flapping, rocking, etc., is about; a way of self-treating the sensory deficit. The flapping etc., stimulates or calms sensory input.

This is, as I said, a part of autism, about which we are just learning. So, some of this is theory, but theorized by some of the best experts in the world.

Also. some new research is showing that whereas ADD kids switch their attention very rapidly, autistic kids get "stuck" and have difficulty changing their attention. This difference can be seen very clearly by two kids in my room; one who is classically autistic, and [one] ADHD kid.

Re: *"If only I could be around some kids that I knew for sure were autistic."*

Yup, probably would help. The next best thing would be to read some books by autistic authors. I can recommend you start with EMERGENCE, LABELED AUTISTIC by Temple Grandin. If you want more, I can dig up a few more titles for you.

—*Anne*

---

* *Proprioception*: The ability to know where your body, or parts of your body, are in space; knowing how your body moves and how to make it move the way you want it.

Anne,

Re: *"I had another student who couldn't lay on a wedge, he kept falling off! The position was so different for him, he couldn't process the proprioception and figure out where his body was!"*

This can be true of children who are not autistic but simply have sensory integration problems. My daughter used to (and occasionally still does) pull the disappearing child trick. One moment she's on her chair and the next she's under the table and she's not sure how she got there. When interacting with her, one has to protect oneself from her head, elbows, and knees because she isn't exactly sure where they are. She is surprised, for example, when she turns and whacks me in the nose.

I've also worked with autistic kids (at residential summer camps when I was a teenager) and they have some of the same problems. Yet they seem much more severe and concentrated. They also seem to interfere more with social interaction than I've seen with kids with fairly straightforward sensory integration problems.

You know, Elisa said:

"Even though *reading* about autism and ADD sometimes will give the impression that there are a lot of similarities, in my experience people with autism are much more disordered in these areas. I don't mean they're more severely affected, I mean they're further away from 'normal.' "

I'd like to add this: I've met people with autism, with ADD, and with straight sensory integration problems. I think what Elisa means by further away from "normal" is that those with ADD at least seem to have some idea where the "normal world" is even if they can't remain in it for very long at any given moment.

Those with autism seem not to grasp where the "normal world" actually is. They are so different (and perhaps their sensory functioning is so different) that, for them, theirs is nothing like our "normal world." Those with straight sensory integration problems have some problem grasping the "normal world" but are so much, much closer than those with autism.

—*Kate Eisen*

Hi Everyone,

In following this thread I see so many common factors of ADD, Autism, TS, and BD's [behavior disorders]. I think we can all learn much about our individual experiences from the related themes.

—*Sherry Griswold*

If you are wondering about autism, the questions to ask are: Is his language/ social development disordered, and significantly lower than the rest of his development?

—Anne

Anne.

I think these are all related in some way. My TS son is also mild ADHD, OCD, very anxious, has motor planning problems and his tics are not obvious. It's a miracle he is diagnosed. My nephew is PDD/autistic. A meaty book that describes this whole thread is by Dr. Comings (a geneticist) called TOURETTE SYNDROME AND HUMAN BEHAVIOR. The scope of the book is astounding . . . the role of different neurotransmitters, different behaviors, medications, etc. If I only had one book in my library (and I've done a bunch of reading) it would be this one.

—Joanie

Top Files from The ADD Forum On CompuServe

The following is a sample listing from an inventory of over 1,000 library files currently available in the ADD Forum on CompuServe.

Adult ADD

ADCOL3.TXT   For a "Hunter" with ADD, what comes next? by Nina B.

EXCUSE.TXT   What to do when people use ADD as an excuse—forum discussion

FIDGET.TXT   Do you use fidgets?—forum discussion

FUTURE.TXT   Creating Your Future—forum discussion

HAPPY.ZIP   Can You Make Someone Happy?—forum discussion

HYPER2.TXT   ADD & Hypersensitivity: Is there a connection? by Mary Jane Johnson

MUSIC.TXT   Do you have music running through your head?—forum discussion

TIME.TXT   Article on ADD sense of time by Dave deBronkart for THE ADDED LINE

Biofeedback & Attention Training

EAST.TXT NASA—Extended Attention Span Training System

Diagnosis and Treatment Information

ADDBRO.TXT ADD: A Difficult Diagnosis by Mark S. Roth, M.D.

ADDTST.TXT ADHD testing—forum discussion

BIPOLR.TXT Distinguishing between ADD and bipolar disorder—forum discussion

DIGNOS.TXT How to diagnose ADD: a discussion online w/doctors

EARINF.ZIP Is there a link between ear infections and ADD?—forum discussion

GENERI.TXT Are generic drugs effective for ADD?—forum discussion

MEDIC1.ASC How I Medicate Patients with ADD/ADHD (Part 1) by Paul T. Elliott, M.D.

RATEYNP2.TXT Ratey Neuropsychiatry Text/Chapter abstracts

RITALN.TXT Facts About Ritalin by Patti Meadows

STIMNEED.TXT Stimulants as Needed?—forum discussion

THERPY.TXT Discussion of psychotherapy for ADD/ADHD—forum discussion

Diet

FEINGO.TXT Feingold diet—forum discussion

Education

ADHDGF.TXT ADHD And Children Who Are Gifted—an ERIC Digest, Educational Resources Information Center, U.S. Dept of Education

COMP.TXT Accommodations for ADHD students by Linda Dannemiller

EDFUND.TXT Why do so many smart kids with ADD fail in public school? by Thom Hartmann

H-WORK.TXT Homework Help—forum discussion

HOMSCH.TXT Homeschooling the ADD Child by Joy Kutz

186

INTERV.TXT	Intervention Strategies for Educators by Ronald E. Jones, P.A.-C.
SCHOOL.TXT	August 95 Forum Conference on Back to School
STUDY.TXT	Studying with ADD—forum discussion

Forum Conferences

H&R516.TXT	Hallowell & Ratey conference Edward M. Hallowell M.D. & John J. Ratey M.D. answer forum members' questions.
KIDSCO.ZIP	Transcript of 3/11/95 "Ask the Experts" Kid's Conference
NRATEY.TXT	Nancy Ratey Conference Transcript 6/23/94 "ADD in the Workplace"
THOMCO.TXT	Transcript of Thom Hartmann Conference on 2/12/94— discussing his book FOCUS YOUR ENERGY: HUNTING FOR SUCCESS IN BUSINESS WITH ADD

Newsletters

AN0294.TXT	ADDult News Online, An Online Newsletter—for ADD adults, published by Parents of Hyperactive/ADD Children and edited by Mary Jane Johnson
LINE14.TXT	Volume 1, No. 4 of THE ADDED LINE
NEWSLTR.JUL	July CH.A.D.D./NYC Newsletter by Hal Meyer
CONCTF95.TXT	ADD Connection—Fall 1995. Published by LDA of Washington-Olympia; edited by Janie Bowman

Parenting

8PRINC.TXT	Eight Principles to Guide ADHD Children by Russell A. Barkley, PH.D.
ANSEXC.TXT	Hallowell—To Be Here and There and Everywhere
ALLOW.TXT	Allowance ideas for children over 9 years old—forum discussion
BRAT.TXT	"Is this kid ADD or just a brat?"—forum discussion
CHIPS.TXT	"Chips in the jar" behavior mod method—forum discussion

EMOTIONS.TXT   From Emotions to Advocacy: The Parents' Journey by
               Pamela Darr Wright, L.C.S.W.

NOFRND.TXT   "Dad, I have no friends."—forum discussion

PADDTN.TXT   Parenting ADD Teens

SIB.TXT   ADD and Siblings

Research

NIH-ADHD.TXT   ADHD—Decade of the Brain [National Institutes of Health]

NIMH.TXT   National Institute of Mental Health-Funded Research on ADHD

Resources

Where Do I Turn?

A Resource Directory of Materials about Attention Deficit Disorder

This document was developed by the Chesapeake Institute, Washington, D.C., as part of contract #HS92017001 from the Office of Special Education Programs, Office of Special Education and Rehabilitative Services, United States Department of Education. The points of view expressed in the books, videos, programs, and other materials in this publication are those of the authors and do not necessarily reflect the position or policy of the U.S. Department of Education. The materials listed were not selected, approved, or reviewed in any way; nor does mention of trade names, commercial products, or organizations imply endorsement by the U.S. government. Neither the inclusion or omission of any item is intended to be taken as any indicator of its quality. Many of the included titles can be ordered through a local book store as well as through the sources listed here. We encourage the reproduction and distribution of this directory.

Choosing Materials

Reading these lists of resources, educators and parents may wonder how they can tell which materials would best suit their needs. Douglas Carnine, director of the National Center to Improve the Tools of Educators (funded by the U.S. Department of Education's Office of Special Education Programs), suggests that schools and individuals follow a six-step process of evaluation. Before choosing a new book or program, potential purchasers should ask themselves:

1. Are the approach and its outcomes clearly defined?

2. Do instructional research findings indicate that the method is effective?

3. Is an accountability system for teaching and learning built into the method?

4. Is the method sustainable?

Published by Division of Innovation and Development, Office of Special Education Programs, Office of Special Education and Rehabilitative Services, U.S. Department of Education

5. For which groups of students is the method equitable?

6. Are the costs of the method and its implementation reasonable?

The claims of publishers and other producers should be carefully examined and substantiated before implementing any new approach. Parents and teachers should not assume any one source is the final word. Instead, they should examine the information from several sources. The most reliable information will be the consensus among these different sources.

National Organizations

ADDult Support Network
2620 Ivy Place
Toledo, OH 43613
(419) 472-1286

American Federation of Teachers (AFT)
555 New Jersey Avenue, N.W.
Washington, D.C. 20001
(202) 879-4400

Association for Childhood Education
International (ACEI)
800 Roosevelt Road
Glen Ellyn, IL 60137
(800) 442- 4453

Attention Deficit Information Network
(AD-IN)
475 Hillside Avenue
Needham, MA 02194
(617) 455-9895

Attention Deficit Disorder Association
(ADDA)
P.O. Box 972
Mentor, OH 44061
(800)-487-2282
Support Group Referral & General
Information line

Attention Deficit Resource Center
Suite 14, 1344 East Cobb Drive
Marietta, GA 30068

Children with Attention Deficit
Disorders (CH.A.D.D.)
499 N.W. 70th Avenue, Suite 308
Plantation, FL 33317
(305) 587-3700

Council of Administrators of Special
Education Inc.
615 16th St., NW
Albuquerque, NM 87104
(505) 243-7622

Council for Exceptional Children (CEC)
1920 Association Drive
Reston, VA 22091
(703) 264-9474

Council for Learning Disabilities
PO Box 40303
Overland Park, KS 66204
(913) 492-8755

Federation of Families for Children's
Mental Health
1021 Prince St.
Alexandria, VA 22314
(703) 684-7710

Higher Education and Adult Training
for People with Handicaps (HEATH)
National Clearinghouse on Post-
secondary Education for Handicapped
Individuals
One Dupont Circle, NW
Suite 800
Washington, DC 20036-1193
(800) 939-9320

Learning Disabilities Association of
America (LDA)
4156 Library Road
Pittsburgh, PA 15234-1349
(412) 341-1515

National Association of School
Psychologists
8455 Colesville Road, Suite 1000
Silver Spring, MD 20910
(301) 608-0500

National Center for Learning
Disabilities (NCLD)
381 Park Avenue, Suite 1420
New York, NY 10016
(212) 545-7510

National Education Association (NEA)
1201 16th St., NW
Washington, DC 20036
(202) 833-4000

National Information Center for
Children and Youth With Disabilities
(NICHCY)
PO Box 1492
Washington, DC 20013-1492
(800) 695-0285, (202) 884-8200

National Parent Network on Disabilities
16000 Prince Street, Suite 115
Alexandria, VA 22314
(703) 684-6763

Professional Group for ADD and
Related Disorders (PGARD)
28 Fairview Road
Scarsdale, NY 10583
(914) 723-0118

General Sources of Information About ADD

A.D.D. Pamphlet briefly describes ADD, its effects, causes, diagnosis, and treatment.
2pp. ADDA

ABOUT ATTENTION DEFICIT DISORDER. Bete, Channing. Short booklet provides brief
information about ADD. ($19.50) for 25 copies. ADD Warehouse

ADD/ADHD: WHAT IS IT? Simple explanation of ADD, its associated characteristics and
the myths about ADD. 3pp. (free) ADDA

ADD AND CHILDREN WHO ARE GIFTED. ERIC Digest E522. Shows the similarities between
ADD behavior and gifted behavior, and how to distinguish between the two. It includes
information on what to do if a child with ADD is also gifted. 2pp. ($1) ERIC

THE ADD HYPERACTIVITY WORKBOOK FOR PARENTS, TEACHERS, AND KIDS. Parker, Harvey.
Describes ADD and treatment. Includes worksheets to help with behavioral management. 108pp. ($12.95) Impact Publications

ADHD. National Center for Learning Disabilities. Explains the characteristics of
individuals with ADHD. Includes "Understanding Attention Deficit-Hyperactivity
Disorder" by Larry Silver and "A Basic Discussion" by Simon Epstein, and "The
Confusion Relating to Ritalin" by Silver. 15pp. (free) NCLD

ADHD/HYPERACTIVITY: A CONSUMER'S GUIDE. Gordon, Michael. Explains principles
that enable parents and teachers to understand and work with children with ADD.
178pp. ($16) GSI Publications

ALL ABOUT ATTENTION DEFICIT DISORDER. Phelan, Thomas. Brief manual on symptoms of ADD and methods of diagnosis and treatment. 45pp. ($14) ADD Warehouse

ASSESSMENT AND CHARACTERISTICS OF CHILDREN WITH ATTENTION DEFICIT DISORDER.
Dykman, Roscoe; Ackerman, Peggy; and Raney, Thomas. Arkansas Children's Hospital
Research Center. This document synthesizes research on the definition, possible causes,
and behavioral characteristics of ADD. It reviews different assessment methods and
evaluates commonly used rating scales. 130pp. ERIC

Attention Deficit Disorder. ERIC Digest #E445. Short explanation of ADD and teaching directions. 2pp. ($1) ERIC

Attention Deficit Disorder: ADHD and ADD Syndromes. Jordan, Dale. Chapters include: Forms of Attention Deficit Disorder; How Attention Deficit Disorder Disrupts One's Life; How to Help Individuals Who Have ADHD; and Hope for the Future. 121pp. ($14) LDA

Attention Deficit Disorder: Adding Up the Facts on ADD. Office of Special Education Programs. This publication provides an introduction to ADD: explaining its definition, characteristics, identification, causes, and treatments. It also outlines the role of the school and its legal obligations. 4pp. ERIC

Attention Deficit Disorder: Beyond the Myths. Office of Special Education Programs. This publication rebuts ten commonly BELIEVED myths about ADD and explains the facts. 2pp. ERIC

Attention Deficit Disorder: A Different Perception. Hartmann, Thom. This book's perspective is that people with ADD are "Hunters in a Farmer's World." It describes ADD and analyzes why some children and adults with ADD are more successful than others. Provides practical advice and specific techniques. 160pp. ($9.95) The Added Line

Attention Deficit Disorder: What Parents Should Know. Office of Special Education Programs. This publication explains to parents steps they should take if they believe their child might have ADD, provides an overview of medication in the treatment of ADD, and describes interventions that can be used at home. 3pp. ERIC

Attention Deficit Disorder: What Teachers Should Know. Office of Special Education Programs. This publication provides advice for teachers who suspect students in their classrooms might have ADD. It sketches effective strategies to use to help teach and manage the behavior of children with ADD. 4pp. ERIC

Attention Deficit Disorder in Teenagers and Young Adults. Sloane, Mark; Assadi, Laurie; and Linn, Linda. This booklet describes the course of ADD in young adults. ($3.00) LDA

Attention Deficit Hyperactivity Disorders. Barkley, Russell. Comprehensive analysis of the history of ADHD, its symptoms, theories of its nature, associated conditions, developmental course and outcome, and family context. The book emphasizes assessment and treatment. 747pp. ($50) Guilford Press

Attention Deficits: The Diverse Effects of Weak Control Systems in Childhood. Levine, Melvin. This reprint from Pediatric Annals explains to doctors the technical details and symptoms of ADD. It includes a sample inventory of symptoms and information on control systems, associated manifestations, complications, evaluation, and management. 9pp. ($3) LDA

Attention Deficit Disorder in Children and Adolescents. Fadely, Jack and Hosler, Virginia. Describes the course of the disorder in children and teenagers. 292pp. ($49.75) Charles Thomas

Briefing Paper: ADD. National Information Center. Answers common questions about ADD, its causes, the signs of ADD, self-esteem and Special Education. Explains behavior management, medication, and appropriate educational programs. Includes bibliography and list of organizations. 8pp. (free) National Information Center

CHILDREN WITH ATTENTION DEFICIT DISORDERS: ADD FACT SHEET. CH.A.D.D. Briefly describes the characteristics, identification, and treatment of children with ADD. 2pp. (free) CH.A.D.D.

CHILDREN WITH ADD: A SHARED RESPONSIBILITY. Based on a report by CEC's Task Force on ADD, this booklet goes into detail on the prevalence and characteristics of ADD, the evaluation process, the use of intervention, teacher assistance teams, multidisciplinary approaches and professional collaboration, and communication between parents and professionals. It also tells how to create a positive school climate, work on school staff development, and help the child in the classroom. Includes focusing strategies. 35pp. ($8.90) CEC

CREATIVE APPROACHES TO ADHD: MYTHS AND REALITY. Hunter, Christine. This guide identifies and responds to 13 common myths about ADHD. It includes a list of additional resources. ($4) LDA

DR. CROOK DISCUSSES HYPERACTIVITY AND THE ATTENTION DEFICIT DISORDER. Crook, William. Crook discusses ADHD and his controversial theory that it is caused by food allergies and yeast. 32pp. ($3.50) LDA

EXECUTIVE SUMMARIES OF RESEARCH SYNTHESES AND PROMISING PRACTICES ON THE EDUCATION OF CHILDREN WITH ATTENTION DEFICIT DISORDER. Office of Special Education Programs. This set of research summaries provides an overview of the research syntheses on ADD funded by the Division of Innovation and Development, Office of Special Education Programs, Office of Special Education and Rehabilitative Services, U.S. Department of Education at the five ADD Centers. 56pp. ERIC

GIFTED BUT LEARNING DISABLED: A PUZZLING PARADOX. ERIC Digest E479. This digest explains that since students' learning disabilities are separate from their intelligence, children can be both ADD and gifted. 2pp. ($1) ERIC

THE HYPERACTIVE CHILD BOOK. Kennedy, Terdal and Fusetti. Guide to treating, educating, and living with an ADHD child. ($19.95) St. Martin's Press

THE HYPERACTIVE CHILD, ADOLESCENT, AND ADULT: ADD THROUGH THE LIFESPAN. Wender, Paul. Information on causes of ADD, symptoms, differences between ADD and learning disabilities, evaluation methods, and treatment approaches. 162pp. ($12) Oxford Press

HOW TO OWN AND OPERATE AN ATTENTION DEFICIT KID. Maxey, Debra. Written by a parent of an ADD child, this booklet provides general information and ways to help the child with ADD. 43pp. ($10) HADD

ISSUES IN THE EDUCATION OF CHILDREN WITH ADD. McKinney, James; Hocutt, Anne; and Montague, Marjorie. EXCEPTIONAL CHILDREN Special Issue Vol 6 No 2. Contains articles on ADD. 96pp. ($8.50) CEC

LEARNING DISABILITIES AND YOUNG ADULTS. American Academy of Pediatrics. This brochure describes the different types of learning disabilities and how to help young people cope with associated problems at school and work. 5pp. (free with SASE, 100 for $27.50) American Academy of Pediatrics

A NEW LOOK AT ATTENTION DEFICIT DISORDER. Nichamim, Samuel J. and Windell, James. This booklet outlines how ADD is treatable. It includes information on the symptoms and signs of ADD. ($3.25) LDA

STRESS MANAGEMENT FOR THE LEARNING DISABLED. ERIC Digest #E452. Short explanation of achievement stress and how it affects children with learning problems. 2pp. ($1) ERIC

SUCCEEDING AGAINST THE ODDS: HOW THE LEARNING DISABLED CAN REALIZE THEIR PROMISE. Smith, Sally. A guide for helping people with LD and ADD achieve. It includes useful strategies, guidance, and inspiration. 304pp. ($13) ADD Warehouse

A SYNTHESIS OF RESEARCH LITERATURE ON THE ASSESSMENT AND IDENTIFICATION OF ATTENTION DEFICIT DISORDER. McKinney, James; Montague, Marjorie; and Hocutt, Anne. University of Miami Center for Synthesis of Research on Attention Deficit Disorder. This document is a synthesis of research related to the assessment and identification of children with ADD. It describes the characteristics of children with ADD, their co-occurring disabilities, and multicultural characteristics. 200pp. ERIC

WHO, WHAT, WHERE, AND WHEN: A CALENDAR OF CONFERENCES AND SPEAKERS ON ATTENTION DEFICIT DISORDER. Office of Special Education Programs. This calendar lists events and speakers on ADD, ranging from speakers at local support groups to national conferences focusing on ADD. 12pp. ERIC

WHY JOHNNY CAN'T CONCENTRATE: COPING WITH ATTENTION DEFICIT PROBLEMS. Moss, R. and Dunlap, H. Explains the problems of children with ADHD for the general reader. ($10) LDA

Resources for Parents

ADD: WHAT PARENTS NEED TO KNOW. Office of Special Education Programs. This publication explains ADD to parents to help them determine if their child shows signs of having ADD. It is a step-by-step guide to identification, the role of the school, the laws pertaining to ADD, and medication. It also describes some simple strategies to help parents with their child's behavior at home. 4pp. ERIC

ADHD AND LEARNING DISABILITIES: BOOKLET FOR PARENTS. Silver, Larry. This booklet provides a general overview of ADHD and learning disabilities, including the various types of disabilities, effects of ADD, emotional and social problems. Includes information on how parents can help. 16pp. ($2) LDA

ATTENTION DEFICIT HYPERACTIVITY DISORDER: QUESTIONS AND ANSWERS FOR PARENTS. Greenberg, Gregory S. and Horn, Wade F. Answers frequently asked questions about ADD. Includes behavior management and cognitive therapy techniques. 134pp. ($11.95) Research Press

ATTENTION DEFICIT DISORDERS, HYPERACTIVITY AND ASSOCIATED DISORDERS—A HANDBOOK FOR PARENTS AND PROFESSIONALS. Coleman, Wendy. This book describes ADD & ADHD and includes information for parents and teachers. Calliope Books

ATTENTION DEFICIT-HYPERACTIVITY DISORDER: A GUIDE FOR PARENTS. LDA. Pamphlet provides a brief overview of ADD and its treatment. 2pp. (free) LDA

ATTENTION, PLEASE! Copeland, Edna, and Love, Valerie. Written by parent professionals, this guide for successfully parenting children with ADD emphasizes real-life experiences and proven solutions. 352pp. ($20) Resurgens Press

COPING WITH THE HYPERACTIVE. Cima, Kathleen. Describes hyperactive (ADHD) behavior and provides some suggestions for parents of young children. 5pp. ($1) LDA

CORRECTING WITHOUT CRITICIZING: THE ENCOURAGING WAY TO TALK TO CHILDREN ABOUT THEIR MISBEHAVIOR. Taylor, John. This booklet addresses often-overlooked ways adults can become more effect in confronting children about misbehavior. 34pp. ($4.50) Sun Media

CREATIVE ANSWERS TO MISBEHAVIOR: GETTING OUT OF THE IGNORE-NAG-YELL-PUNISH CYCLE. Taylor, John. This booklet contains 29 categories of response to misbehavior. 32pp. ($4.50) Sun-Media

DR. LARRY SILVER'S ADVICE TO PARENTS ON ADHD. Silver, Larry. Answers common questions about ADHD and explains the methods of treatment. It focuses on what parents can do to help their child. 240pp. ($17.95) American Psychiatric Press

GUIDELINES FOR LIVING WITH A HYPERACTIVE CHILDREN. Ente, Gerald. A list of 12 simple things parents can do. 2pp. ($.50) LDA

HELPING YOUR HYPERACTIVE CHILD. Taylor, John. Includes information on a multi-modular approach including nutritional, educational, psychological and medical techniques. 466pp. ($20) LDA

HOUSE RULES ABOUT HOMEWORK. ADDA. List of suggestions of ways for parents to make sure that homework is done. 1pp. (free) ADDA

HYPERACTIVITY: WHY WON'T MY CHILD PAY ATTENTION. Goldstein, Sam and Michael. Explains ADHD, reviews the treatments and provides guidelines. Helps parents work with their children. 240pp. ($20) ADD Warehouse

HYPERKINESIS. Centerwall, Siegried & Willard. Explains what hyperkinesis means and what causes hyperactive behavior. Also covers how to treat hyperactivity and how it affects children's future. ($2.50) LDA

IF YOUR CHILD IS HYPERACTIVE, IMPULSIVE, DISTRACTIBLE. Garber, Stephen and Marianne, Spizman, Robyn. Practical program for changing the behavior of ADD children from diagnosis to a step by step program to improve the child's attention span. 235pp. ($20) ADD Warehouse

KEYS TO PARENTING A CHILD WITH ADD. McNamara, Barry and Francine. Guide to working with a child's school, managing the child's behavior and acting as an Advocate. 165pp. ($5.95) Barron's Educational Series

LEARNING DISABILITIES AND CHILDREN: WHAT PARENTS NEED TO KNOW. American Academy of Pediatrics. Alerts parents to the early signs of learning disabilities. De-scribes the causes of the problem and emphasizes the need for early detection and proper treatment. 5pp. (free with SASE, 100 for $27.50) American Academy of Pediatrics

LEARNING TO PARENT THE HYPERACTIVE CHILD. Hafner, Claire. This book contains entries from a journal kept by a nurse and mother of a hyperactive son. The book provides a personal perspective on hyperactivity and how to control it. ($8.95) LDA

MAYBE YOU KNOW MY KID: A PARENT'S GUIDE TO IDENTIFYING, UNDERSTANDING & HELPING YOUR CHILD WITH ADD. Fowler, Mary. The story of the author's son who has ADD and the effects his ADD has had on the family. It tells how to help children with ADD and how to become an activist for their education. ($14) Birch Lane Press

THE MISUNDERSTOOD CHILD. Silver, Larry. Includes a general overview of learning disabilities and positive treatment strategies. 322pp. ($10) McGraw-Hill

NEGOTIATING THE SPECIAL EDUCATION MAZE. Anderson, Chitwood, and Hayden. Contains information about programs and legislation. Shows how to find the best program. 250pp. ($15) ADD Warehouse

NEW SKILLS FOR FRAZZLED PARENTS. Amen, Daniel. Workbook and 8 cassettes help teach parents to establish rules and manage misbehavior. Helps in thinking clearly and logically in dealing with a difficult child. Taped live from an actual parenting class. ($104.50) Center for Effective Living

A PARENT'S GUIDE: ATTENTION DEFICIT HYPERACTIVITY DISORDER IN CHILDREN. Goldstein, Sam and Michael. Basic information on ADD for parents and health professionals. 24pp. ($28 for ten) ADD Warehouse

A PARENT'S GUIDE TO ATTENTION DEFICIT DISORDERS. Blain, L. Helps parents to understand their child with ADD and to find the appropriate treatment and support for the disorder. It includes sections on causes, diagnosis, treatment, therapy, and living with ADD. ($10) LDA

THE PARENTS' HYPERACTIVITY HANDBOOK: HELPING THE FIDGETY CHILD. Paltin, David. This book explains the symptoms of ADHD and its possible link to minimal brain dysfunction or genetic disorders. 300pp. ($27.50) Insight Books

PARENT PACKET. AD-IN. This package contains many different articles and information sheets. It includes technical articles on ADD as well as lists of resources, strategies, and legal rights. ($15) AD-IN

PARENTING ATTENTION DEFICIT DISORDERED TEENS. Landi, Patricia. Booklet describes how the normal problems of adolescents are radically altered by ADD. ($3.95) LDA

SOLVING THE PUZZLE OF YOUR HARD-TO-RAISE CHILD. Crook, William. This book claims that much unsatisfactory behavior results from improper or inadequate nutrition and advises parents how to improve their children's behavior by improving their diet. ($17.95) LDA

SOMETHING'S WRONG WITH MY CHILD! Rose, Harriet Wallace. Subtitled: A straightforward presentation to help professionals and parents to better understand themselves in dealing with the emotionally-charged subject of disabled children. 210pp. ($35.75) Charles Thomas

SOMETIMES I GET ALL SCRIBBLY: LIVING WITH ADHD. Neuville, Maureen. The mother of an ADHD child portrays what life with ADD is like for the child and family. 116pp. ($9.95) Sun Media

YOUR HYPERACTIVE CHILD: A PARENT'S GUIDE TO COPING WITH ADD. Ingersoll, Barbara. Includes a general overview of ADHD, diagnosis, causes, treatment, daily life, special problems, school, and behavior modification. 219pp. ($10) ADD Warehouse

Resources for Children With ADD

THE DON'T GIVE UP KID. Gehret, Jeanne. Illustrated. Story of a child with learning disabilities who gains an understanding of his problem. ($8.95) Sun Media

EAGLE EYES. Gehret, Jeanne. Illustrated. Story of a child who uses nature to understand and work on his ADD. 40pp. ($10) Verbal Images

FIGHTING INVISIBLE TIGERS: A STRESS MANAGEMENT GUIDE FOR TEENS. Hipp, Earl. This book presents easy-to-understand guidelines for assertion, friendship skills, relaxation methods, etc., for adolescents. 120pp. ($10) Sun Media

HIGH SCHOOL HELP FOR ADD TEENS. Chesapeake. This booklet contains academic strategies and tips for students with ADD. 30pp. ($7.95) Chesapeake Psychological Services

I WOULD IF I COULD: A TEENAGER'S GUIDE TO ADHD/HYPERACTIVITY. Gordon, Michael. This book helps teenagers understand ADD and its effects. ($12) GSI

I'M SOMEBODY TOO. Gehret, Jeanne. A book length story that explains ADD to siblings of children with ADD and shows how one girl handles her feelings when her parents give more attention to her brother with ADHD. 170pp. ($12) Verbal Images Press

JUMPIN' JOHNNY GET BACK TO WORK!: A CHILD'S GUIDE TO ADHD/HYPERACTIVITY. Gordon, Michael. This is the story of impulsive Johnny and how his family and school work with him to make life easier. 30pp ($11) GSI Publications

KEEPING AHEAD IN SCHOOL: A STUDENT'S BOOK ABOUT LEARNING DISABILITIES AND LEARNING DISORDERS. Levine, Mel. Explains how people learn and the causes of learning problems. Shows how to understand their strengths and weaknesses. Ages 9-15. 297pp. ($27) Educator's Publishing Service

LEARNING TO SLOW DOWN AND PAY ATTENTION. Nadeau, Kathleen and Dixon, Ellen. Illustrated. Explains to children how to identify ADD related problems and how their parents, teachers, and doctor can help. Ages 6-14, ($11) LDA

MAKING THE GRADE: AN ADOLESCENT'S STRUGGLE WITH ADD. Parker, Roberta. This is the story of a seventh grader's life with ADD. Includes a section on commonly asked questions and answers about ADD. For ages 9-14. 47pp. ($10). Impact Publications.

MY BROTHER'S A WORLD-CLASS PAIN. Gordon, Michael. Story of an older sister's efforts to understand and live with a brother with ADHD. ($11) GSI

OTTO LEARNS ABOUT HIS MEDICATION. Galvin, Matthew. Illustrated. Fidgety car visits mechanic who gives him special medicine. Ages 5-10. ($8.00) Magination Press

PUTTING ON THE BRAKES. Quinn, Patricia and Stern, Judith. This book explains the problems of students with ADD. Includes techniques and coping strategies. For ages 8-12. 64pp. ($9) Brunner/Mazel

"PUTTING ON THE BRAKES" ACTIVITY BOOK FOR YOUNG PEOPLE WITH ADHD. Quinn, Patricia and Stern, Judith. This companion book uses pictures, puzzles, and mazes to teach problem solving, organizing, setting priorities, planning, and maintaining control. 88pp. ($14.95) Brunner/Mazel Publishers

SCHOOL SURVIVAL GUIDE FOR KIDS WITH LEARNING DIFFERENCES. Cummings, Rhoda, and Fisher, Gary. This book is designed to help school adjustment and study skills. It includes sections with advice for specific subjects and tips on social skills. 172pp. ($10.95) Sun Media

SHELLY THE HYPERACTIVE TURTLE. Moss, Deborah. Illustrated. Hyperactive turtle learns what "hyperactive" means and is given special medicine. For Ages 3-7, 24pp. ($12.95) Woodbine House

SLAM DUNK: A YOUNG BOY'S STRUGGLE WITH ADD. Parker, Roberta. This is the story of an inner city fifth grader and his problems caused by ADD. It shows how behavioral, medical, and classroom interventions help him. It includes a section with questions and answers about ADD. Ages 8-12. ($10) ADD Warehouse

THE SURVIVAL GUIDE FOR KIDS WITH LEARNING DIFFERENCES. Cummings, Rhoda, and Fisher, Gary. This book explains some problems of children with learning problems and how to handle the problems and the feelings that come with them. 98pp. ($9.95) Sun Media

TROUBLE WITH SCHOOL. Dunn, Kathryn and Allison. This picture book, written by a mother/daughter team from their own experience, follows a young girl from discovering problems in the first grade to developing a treatment plan. Illustrated. For ages 6-10. ($10) ADD Warehouse

THE YOUNG PERSON'S GUIDE TO UNDERSTANDING ADHD. This book explains ADD to children from 7-14 and gives advice on how to become better organized. ($8.95) Magination Press

Resources for Adults with ADD

ADD IN ADULTS. Epstein, Samuel. Describes ADD in adults, the diagnosis, and the effects of drugs. 2pp. (free) LDA

ADD ADULT PACKET. AD-IN. This packet contains many different articles and information sheets. The articles range from technical information about ADD to practical strategies on living with one's ADD. Includes information about college. ($10)AD-IN

THE ADULT WITH ADD. CH.A.D.D. Special Edition. Contains six articles on adults with ADD. Includes "Paying Attention to Attention in Adults", "Adult Attention Deficit Hyperactivity Disorder, Residual State," "Coping Strategies for ADHD Adults," "The Emotional Experiences of ADD," "Coming Out of the Closet... Confessions of an ADD? Mother," and "ADD Adult Strategies." 15pp. (free) CH.A.D.D.

ATTENTION DEFICIT DISORDER IN ADULTS. Weiss, Lynn. Explains what ADD is, how it manifests itself in adults, and what can be done to cope with it. 217pp. ($13) LDA

THE GIFT OF ADD. Allen, Richard. A psychologist's autobiography of his personal victory over his ADD and Learning Disabilities. 14pp. ($4.95) Attention Deficit Resource Center

HYPERACTIVE CHILDREN GROWN UP. Weiss, Gabrielle and Hechtman, Lily. Based on a McGill University study following children with ADD as they grew up. Describes treatments and changes in these young adults. 473pp. ($10.95) Guilford Press

INSIDE ADD. Alfultis, Susan. The autobiography and journal of a woman with ADD. Includes techniques she has used to compensate for her disability. ($16) ADDult Support Network

PROBLEMS OF ATTENTION DEFICIT DISORDER IN ADULTS. Landi, Patricia. Includes information about the problems of adults with ADD including job problems, psychological problems, and relationship problems. ($3.95) LDA

YOU MEAN I'M NOT LAZY, STUPID, OR CRAZY. Kelly, Kate and Ramundo, Peggy. Written by ADD adults for ADD adults, the book provides information on identifying, understanding, and managing the dynamics of ADD in Adults. Includes practical "how- to's" and moral support. 448pp. ($19.95) Tyrell & Jerem Press

Resources for Educators

ATTENTION DEFICIT DISORDERS: A GUIDE FOR TEACHERS. CH.A.D.D. Defines ADD and gives specific recommendations for teaching students with ADD. 6pp. (free) CH.A.D.D.

ADD HYPERACTIVITY HANDBOOK FOR SCHOOLS. Parker, Harvey. Explains current education policies and their effects on children with ADD. Includes methods of evaluation and helping to teach children with ADD and sample IEPs. 330pp. ($25) Impact Publications

THE ATTENTION DEFICIT HYPERACTIVE CHILD IN THE CLASSROOM: STRATEGIES FOR THE REGULAR CLASSROOM TEACHER. Martin, Lucy. Suggested practical interventions for teachers to use when working with ADHD children. 20pp. ($2.08)Chesapeake Psychological Services

ATTENTION DEFICIT HYPERACTIVITY DISORDERS IN CHILDREN: CLINICAL AND TREATMENT ISSUES. Teeter, Phyllis, ed. This special issue of the School Psychology Review features articles on ADD, its basis, criticism, and assessment. It also includes the effects of medication, behavioral interventions and training models. ($12.50) NASP

ATTENTION DEFICIT HYPERACTIVITY DISORDER (ADHD): TEACHER HANDOUT. Waddell, Debby. Describes ADHD and what teachers can do to help students. It has suggestions for elementary and secondary students. 3pp. (free) NASP

THE ATTENTION DEFICIT/HYPERACTIVE STUDENT AT SCHOOL: A SURVIVAL GUIDE. Taylor, John. This booklet is a quick reference for teachers that explains ADD and how teachers can help. 48pp. ($10.95) Sun Media

ADD: HELP FOR THE CLASSROOM TEACHER. Buchoff, Rita. Explains how teachers can identify ADD and how to help manage a child with ADD in the classroom. Gives specific suggestions on organization, directions, classroom management, and self-esteem as well as how to establish a cooperative parent-teacher relationship. 5pp. ($2.75) Association for Childhood Education International

ADHD AND LEARNING DISABILITIES: BOOKLET FOR THE CLASSROOM TEACHER. Silver, Larry. This booklet provides a general overview of ADHD and LD including the various types of disabilities, effects of ADD, emotional and social problems. Includes information on how teachers can help. 16pp. ($2) LDA

ATTENTION WITHOUT TENSION. Copeland, Edna and Love, Valerie. A handbook on ADD for teachers including ADD characteristics, causes, treatments, and classroom management strategies. It also contains 80 pages of reproducible masters. 180pp. ($22) Resurgens Press

BEYOND MALADIES AND REMEDIES. Riegel, Mayle, and McCarthy- Henkel. Based on suggestions from 900 teachers, this book demonstrates ways to adapt instructional methods or materials to children with special needs. 127pp. ($37) ADD Warehouse

CH.A.D.D. EDUCATORS MANUAL. Fowler, Mary. This book, written by several leaders in the ADD field, explains ADD and the best ways to educate students with ADD to teachers, school administrators and others in education. Sections include: "The

Disability Named ADD," "ADD Goes to School," "Factors that Compromise Learning," "Identification and Assessment," "Interventions: Principles and Practices," "Behavioral Interventions," "Parents and Schools Working Together," and "ADD: A Brief Legal Summary" 84pp. ($10) CH.A.D.D.

CHILDREN WITH EXCEPTIONAL NEEDS IN REGULAR CLASSROOMS. Cohen, Libby G., ed. This book presents emerging trends and preferred practices for teaching exceptional students in regular classrooms, as well as the legal requirements governing their education. 184pp. ($11.95) NEA

COMPLETE LEARNING DISABILITIES HANDBOOK. Hartwell, Joan. This book outlines a referral and identification process, intervention strategies, classroom management and ways to help with weak areas. Its emphasis is on suggestions and ready-to-use materials. 206pp. ($30) ADD Warehouse

DIFFICULTIES THAT CHILDREN WITH ADHD MAY HAVE IN SCHOOL. Lists some of the problems children with ADD have in school. 1pp. (free) ADDA

DIVERSE TEACHING FOR DIVERSE LEARNING. Copeland, Edna and Walker, Ronald. This book presents a model for effectively teaching at-risk students in regular education including classroom strategies and medical management of ADD. ($24) Resurgens Press

EDUCATORS' PACKET. AD-IN. This package contains many different articles and information sheets. It includes technical articles on ADD as well as lists of resources, classroom strategies, and legal rights of children with ADD. ($10) AD-IN

HANDWRITING WITHOUT TEARS (WORKSHOP SERIES, TEACHING GUIDE, AND STUDENT WORKBOOK). Olsen, Jan. This workshop series and accompanying instructional materials present a structured program to teach manuscript and cursive writing skills. The program employs both multi-sensory techniques and hand-writing manipulatives. For example, the child learns to manipulate wooden puzzle pieces to form letters of the alphabet. The child then practices writing these letters on a small, hand-held chalkboard. The Teaching Guide provides directions for conducting handwriting lessons, while the Student Workbook provides sample practice sheets for elementary school students. (Instructional materials are free to workshop participants). Jan E. Olsen Potomac (MD)

THE HYPERACTIVE CHILD. Black, Bob. Describes the hyperactive child and how to understand him. 2pp. ($.50) LDA

HOW TO REACH AND TEACH ADD/ADHD CHILDREN. Rief, Sandra. This book focuses on practical techniques, strategies and interventions for helping children with attention problems and hyperactivity. 245pp. ($27.95) CEC

POSITION STATEMENT: STUDENTS WITH ATTENTION DEFICITS. National Association of School Psychologists. The official policy of NASP regarding ADD. It lists effective interventions and recommendations for medication. 2pp (free)NASP

THE PREPARE CURRICULUM. Goldstein, Arnold. Contains ten course length interventions on problem solving, interpersonal skills, situational perception, anger control, moral reasoning, stress management, empathy, recruiting supportive models, cooperation, and understanding and using groups. 700pp. ($40) ADD Warehouse

THE PRE-REFERRAL INTERVENTION MANUAL. McCarney, Wunderlich, and Bauer. This book contains ways schools can help children with ADD focus and learn within regular education settings. 504pp. Hawthorne Educational Services

200

A PRIMER ON ATTENTION DEFICIT DISORDER. Fouse, Beth and Brians, Suzanne. The authors define this often elusive condition and describe its characteristics at different age levels. They then offer a variety of behavior modification strategies for coping with ADD. 40pp. ($1.25) Phi Delta Kappa

PROMISING PRACTICES IN IDENTIFYING AND EDUCATING CHILDREN WITH ATTENTION DEFICIT DISORDER. Burcham, Barbara and Carlson, Laurance. University of Kentucky's Federal Resource Center. This document describes assessment and intervention policies and practices used by schools. It includes in-depth studies of nine schools. 180pp. ERIC

PROVIDING AN APPROPRIATE EDUCATION TO CHILDREN WITH ADD. ERIC Digest E462. Briefly describes the school responsibilities and federal laws affecting children with ADD. 2pp. ($1) ERIC

RESEARCH SYNTHESIS ON EDUCATION INTERVENTIONS FOR STUDENTS WITH ATTENTION DEFICIT DISORDER. Fiore, Thomas; Becker, Elizabeth; and Nero, Rebecca. Research Triangle Institute, Attention Deficit Disorder Intervention Center. This document is a synthesis of research on behavioral and Educational interventions for children with ADD. The report evaluates several strategies and educational techniques for educating children with ADD. 117pp. ERIC

SCHOOL-BASED ASSESSMENTS AND INTERVENTIONS FOR ADD STUDENTS. Swanson, James. Based on a model school program at the University of California, this book includes information on behavior modification, social skill training and cognitive therapy. ($22) ADD Warehouse

SIMPLY PHONICS—QUICK AND EASY. Rief, Sandra. This structured program teaches basic phonics skills to elementary school students. Recommended instructional strategies include suggestions for teaching (a) word and pattern recognition, (b) specific sounds/phonemes, and (c) letter/sound associations. Strategies for integrating phonics instruction and "whole language" reading methods within a comprehensive language arts program are featured. The manual includes 43 individual lessons with accompanying "black-line" ditto masters. 135 pgs. EBSCO Curriculum Materials Birmingham (AL)

STUDENTS WITH SPECIAL NEEDS: RESOURCE GUIDE FOR TEACHERS. Shinsky, F. John. Practical descriptions, instructional and behavioral strategies for working with students with disabilities. Contains information on several disabilities areas including ADHD. ($9.95) Michigan

A TEACHER'S GUIDE: ATTENTION DEFICIT HYPERACTIVITY DISORDER IN CHILDREN. Goldstein, Sam and Michael. This booklet briefly describes ADHD, the problems it causes in the classroom, and practical behavioral interventions. 24pp. ($28 for ten) ADD Warehouse

TEACHER TRAINING PROGRAM. Dwyer, Kevin. This computer disk contains all the materials from the National Association of School Psychologists teacher training course on ADD. (at-cost, call) NASP

TEACHING CHILDREN WITH ADD. ERIC Digest #462. Defines the two forms of ADD and includes tips on establishing the proper learning environment, giving instructions to students with ADD, giving assignments, and enhancing self-esteem. 2pp. ($1) ERIC

TEACHING STRATEGIES. Office of Special Education Programs. This publication helps teachers by describing several schools' methods of teaching children with Attention

Resources   **201**

Deficit Disorder. It includes ways to modify existing lessons and ways to plan new strategies to meet the special needs of children with ADD. ERIC

TEACHING STUDENTS WITH ADD: A SLIDE PROGRAM FOR IN-SERVICE TEACHER TRAINING. Parker, Harvey and Gordon, Michael. Provides an overview of ADHD and practical help in working with students and parents. It includes handouts and presenter's manual. 42 slides. ($150) ADD Warehouse

TECHNIQUES FOR INCLUDING STUDENTS WITH DISABILITIES. Shinsky, F. John. A "step by step" guide with organizational, instructional, and behavioral strategies. Contains reproducible charts and 17 building checklists. 425pp. ($59.95) Michigan

THINKING SMARTER. Crutsinger, Carla. This book contains 127 lessons designed to teach students how to assimilate, process and retain information. Includes Teacher Manual and Student Black Line Masters. ($44) ADD Warehouse

TOUCH MATH: THE TOUCHPOINT APPROACH TO TEACHING BASIC MATH COMPUTATION (Video Tape, Instructional Guide, and Five Instructional Kits). Innovative Learning Concepts. This special instructional program uses kinesthetic techniques to help children learn basic computation facts by touching and counting strategically placed "touchpoints" on the numerals one through nine. The Video Tape and accompanying Instructional Guide demonstrate how to use Touch Math techniques with elementary school students. The five Instructional Kits review (a) number concepts, (b) addition, (c) subtraction, (d) sequence counting, and (e) multiplication and division. Each kit contains an instructional manual, recommended teaching aides, and over 150 "black-line" ditto masters. (Kits range in price from $58.50 to $87.50). Innovative Learning Concepts Boulder (CO)

TOUGH TO REACH, TOUGH TO TEACH: STUDENTS WITH BEHAVIOR PROBLEMS. Sylvia Rockwell. Describes children with behavior problems and suggests ways of gaining their cooperation in their own learning. 106pp. ($20) CEC

WHY CAN'T THEY PAY ATTENTION? ADD: WHAT TEACHERS NEED TO KNOW. Office of Special Education Programs. This publication explains ADD to teachers and describes how they can help identify children with ADD. It lists some simple strategies teachers can use to help students focus more in class, and describes some programs adopted by successful schools. 4pp. ERIC

Legal Rights of Children with ADD

ADD/ADHD: EDUCATION AND PARENTS' RIGHTS. ADDA. Lists the rights of parents in their child's education. Includes information about IEPs and suggestions for communicating with the school. 3pp. (free) ADDA

ATTENTION DEFICIT DISORDER AND THE LAW. Latham, Peter and Patricia. Addresses the rights of ADD under federal and state law. Includes protection under the Constitution, court decisions, Rehabilitation Act of 1973, the Individuals with Disabilities Education Act and the Americans with Disabilities Act. ($25) JKL Communications

CLARIFICATION OF POLICY TO ADDRESS THE NEEDS OF CHILDREN WITH ADD. U.S. Department of Education. This is the official position of the Education Department on A.D.D. It outlines what schools are required to do for students with ADD. 4pp. (free) NICHCY

GETTING PARENTS INVOLVED IN THE EXCEPTIONAL EDUCATION PROCESS. Messina, James and Constance. This handbook guides parents through the Special Education procedures under Public Law 94-142. It includes a glossary and key court cases. 148pp. ($11.95) Sun Media

GUIDE TO SECTION 504: HOW IT APPLIES TO STUDENTS WITH LEARNING DISABILITIES AND ADHD. LDA. This guide explains the section of the Rehabilitation Act of 1973 which applies to persons with disabilities. Explains the definition of "Handicap", the types of discrimination prohibited and what school districts are required to provide. 2pp. (free) LDA

HOW TO PARTICIPATE EFFECTIVELY IN THE IEP PROCESS. LDA. Explains the Individual Education Plan that schools must develop for children with special needs. Outlines how to participate in the IEP meeting, what the IEP should contain and what to do if parents disagree with the plan. 2pp. (free) LDA

PROVIDING AN APPROPRIATE EDUCATION TO CHILDREN WITH ADD. ERIC Digest E462. Briefly describes the school responsibilities and federal laws affecting children with ADD. 2pp. ($1) ERIC

WHEN YOUR CHILD NEEDS TESTING: WHAT PARENTS, TEACHERS, AND OTHER HELPERS NEED TOO KNOW ABOUT PSYCHOLOGICAL COUNSELING. Shore, Milton; Brice, Patrick; and Love, Barbara. This book explains about the purpose and method of psychological testing and what to do if parents disagree with the results. 192pp. ($20) ADD Warehouse

YOU, YOUR CHILD, AND SPECIAL EDUCATION: A GUIDE TO MAKING THE SYSTEM WORK. Cutler, Barbara. This books shows parents how to maneuver the Special Education system. It explains the rights of children, how to develop a partnership with teachers and administrators, and how to make the IEP process work. 249pp. ($22) ADD Warehouse

Medication and Other Treatments

1-2-3: MAGIC: TRAINING YOUR PRESCHOOLER AND PRETEEN TO DO WHAT YOU WANT THEM TO DO. Phelan, Thomas. Discipline program with specific instructions. 57pp. ($14) Child Management

ADD/ADHD: MEDICAL TREATMENT. ADDA. Simple explanation about medication written for parents. Includes information about side effects. 3pp. (free) ADDA

THE ATTENDING PHYSICIAN: ADD. Copps, Stephen. This guide for pediatricians who treat ADD explains the tools necessary to identify and treat patients with ADD. 180pp. ($26) Resurgens Press

ATTENTION DEFICIT-HYPERACTIVITY DISORDER: A CLINICAL GUIDE TO DIAGNOSIS AND TREATMENT. Silver, Larry. A guide for medical professionals. ($23.50) American Psychiatric Press

ATTENTION DEFICIT DISORDERS AND HYPERACTIVITY IN CHILDREN. Accardo, Blondis and Whitman, editors. This anthology emphasizes diagnosis and treatment from a medical point of view. 424pp. ($45) ADD Warehouse

ATTENTION DEFICIT DISORDER AND LEARNING DISABILITIES: REALITIES, MYTHS, AND CONTROVERSIAL TREATMENTS. Ingersoll, Barbara and Goldstein, Sam. Two experts present a guide to help parents and professionals recognize the symptoms of ADD and evaluate the various treatments. Includes information on scientifically validated and controversial interventions. 240pp. ($13) ADD Warehouse

CHOOSING A DOCTOR FOR YOUR CHILD WITH LEARNING DISABILITIES OR ATTENTION DEFICIT DISORDERS. Ripley & Cvach. Advice for selecting a doctor. Learning Disabilities Project

COGNITIVE-BEHAVIORAL THERAPY WITH ADHD CHILDREN: CHILD, FAMILY AND SCHOOL INTERVENTIONS. Braswell, Lauren and Bloomquist, Michael. A model for treating ADD integrating cognitive behavioral techniques and the home/school environment. 391pp. ($40) Guilford

CONTROVERSIAL TREATMENTS FOR CHILDREN WITH ADHD. Goldstein, Sam, and Ingersoll, Barbara. This article shows the lack of evidence for and the faults in the claims of several controversial "treatments" (controlled diet, megavitamins, anti-motion sickness medication, Candida yeast, EEG Biofeedback, Applied Kinesiology, and optometric vision training.) 4pp. (free) CH.A.D.D.

DEFIANT CHILDREN: A CLINICIAN'S MANUAL FOR PARENT TRAINING. Barkley, Russell. Outlines a specific training program to teach parents of children with ADD. It focuses on ways parents can use behavioral management. 195pp. ($28) Guilford

DIAGNOSING LEARNING DISORDERS. Pennington, Bruce. Includes information on diagnosing and treating ADHD (and several other disorders.) 224pp. ($25) ADD Warehouse

THE EFFECTS OF STIMULANT MEDICATION ON CHILDREN WITH ATTENTION DEFICIT DISORDER: A REVIEW OF REVIEWS. Swanson, James. University of California at Irvine ADD Center. This document synthesizes research from many different studies about the effects of stimulant medication. 74pp. ERIC

GOAL CARD PROGRAM. Parker, Harvey. Program for school or home to provide structure and positive reinforcement. ($14.95) ADD Warehouse

HOW TO CURE HYPERACTIVITY: A BLUEPRINT INVOLVING NUTRITION. Wild, C. The author suggests an eight point plan to turn hyperactivity into productive activity. It includes information on body chemistry and how to use effort effectively. ($11.95) LDA

INDEPENDENT STRATEGIES FOR EFFICIENT STUDY. Rooney, Karen. Program of educational intervention including strategies for time management, reading, testing and note taking. 102pp. ($28) ADD Warehouse

LISTEN, LOOK AND THINK: A SELF-REGULATION PROGRAM FOR CHILDREN. Parker, Harvey. Contains a looped tape cassette that beeps at a variable interval to remind the child to pay attention. ($19.95) ADD Warehouse

MANAGEMENT OF CHILDREN AND ADOLESCENTS WITH ATTENTION DEFICIT HYPERACTIVITY DISORDER. Friedman, Ronald and Doyal, Guy. Discusses ADD and hyperactivity. Gives practical applied guidance for managing and teaching children with ADD. ($24) LDA

MANAGING ATTENTION DISORDERS IN CHILDREN: A GUIDE FOR PRACTITIONERS. Goldstein, Sam and Michael. Contains technical information about ADD and an interdisciplinary approach to treatment incorporating drugs and behavior modification. Includes a section on training parents. 449pp. ($52.50) ADD Warehouse

MEDICAL MANAGEMENT OF CHILDREN WITH ADD. Parker, Harvey and Storm, George. Answers medical questions about ADD including extensive explanations about medication and their effects. 4pp. (free) CH.A.D.D.

MEDICATIONS FOR ATTENTION DISORDERS (ADHD/ADD) AND RELATED MEDICAL PROBLEMS. Copeland, Edna. Describes the neurophysiological basis of ADHD and the effect of medication. Includes advice on how to choose the right medication. 420pp. ($35) Resurgens Press Inc.

THE OVERACTIVE CHILD. Eisenberg, Leon. Reprint of Hospital Practice article describing hyperkinetic children (now called ADHD) and what physicians can do. Includes information on working with teachers, suggestions for parents, and information about drugs. 8pp. ($1) LDA

PARENTS ARE TEACHERS. Becker, Wesley. A child management program stressing the use of clear instructions. 200pp. ($16) ADD Warehouse

RITALIN: THEORY AND PATIENT MANAGEMENT. Greenhill, Laurence and Osman, Betty. This book is for physicians and health care professionals and contains technical information about the drug Ritalin. 320pp. ($95) ADD Warehouse

SOS: HELP FOR PARENTS. Clark, Lynn. Helps parents learn skills for child management. 246pp. ($10) Parents Press

THE GOOD KID BOOK: HOW TO SOLVE THE 16 MOST COMMON BEHAVIOR PROBLEMS. Sloane, Howard. Each chapter presents a common problem (homework, interrupting, cleaning one's room) and a step-by-step behavior guide to solve it. 350pp. ($20) ADD Warehouse

THERE ARE BETTER WAYS TO HELP THESE CHILDREN. Crook, William. Crook explains his controversial theory that diet and yeast causes everything from hyperactivity and attention deficits to school failure and juvenile delinquency. 32pp. ($5.50) LDA

Magazines and Newsletters

ADHD Report. Bi-monthly. ($65) Guilford

The ADDed Line. Bi-monthly. ($69) ADDed Line

ADDendum. Quarterly. ($12.00) Chesapeake Psychological Services

ADDvisor. Bi-monthly. ($36) Attention Deficit Resource Center

ADDult News: An Adult Newsletter. Quarterly ($8.00) ADDult Support Network

Attention Please. Bi-monthly. Attention Please

CHADDer Box. Bi-monthly. (Included with membership) CH.A.D.D.

CHADDer. Semi-annually. (Included with membership) CH.A.D.D.

Challenge. Bi-monthly. ($20) ADDA

Exceptional Child Education Resources. Quarterly. ($60) CEC

Exceptional Children. Bi-monthly. (Included with membership) CEC

Inclusion Times. Quarterly. ($29.95) National Professional Resources, Inc

LDA Newsbriefs. Bi-monthly. ($13.50) LDA

Learning Disabilities. Semi-annually. ($25) LDA

Strategies for Success. ($19) Strategies

Teaching Exceptional Children. Quarterly. (Included with membership) CEC

Videos

1-2-3 MAGIC: TRAINING YOUR PRESCHOOLER AND PRETEEN TO DO WHAT YOU WANT THEM TO DO. Phelan, Thomas. Discipline program with specific instructions on how to manage behaviors. Includes book. ($40) Child Management

THE ABC's OF ADD. Quinn, Patricia; Lavenstein, Bennett; and Latham, Peter and Patricia. This video covers medical, legal, and personal strategies from childhood to adulthood. :30 ($29) JKL Communications

ACADEMIC AND SCHOOL-RELATED PROBLEMS OF STUDENTS WITH ADHD AND ADD. Copeland, Edna and Walker, Ronald. This video is part of the Diverse Teaching for Diverse Learning Series. It addresses the difficulties of students with ADD. Includes participant's guide. :45 ($35) Resurgens Press

ADD ADULTS PANEL. Dr. Harrison, Walter et. al. Panel discussion at AD-IN's Third National Conference on ADD. 1:00 ($30) AD-IN

ADD ADULT WORKSHOP: THE THRILL OF IT ALL. Dr. Hallowell, Edward, and Dr. Ratey, John. From AD-IN's Fourth National Conference on ADD. 1:00 ($30) AD-IN

ADD ADULT WORKSHOP: WHY CAN'T YOU LISTEN? PROBLEMS IN COUPLES AND RELA-TIONSHIPS. Dr. Hallowell, Edward, and Dr. Ratey, John. From AD-IN's Fourth National Conference on ADD. 1:00 ($30) AD-IN

ADD FOR BEGINNERS: A PRIMER FOR MEDICATIONS. Dr. Bass, Jonathan. Information on medication from AD-IN's Fourth National Conference on ADD. 1:00 ($30) AD-IN

THE ADD CHILD IN THE CLASSROOM: ADDITIONAL TECHNIQUES TO IMPROVE BEHAVIOR. Lavoie, Richard. More classroom strategies. 1:00 ($30) AD-IN

THE ADD CHILD IN THE CLASSROOM: SPECIFIC TECHNIQUES TO IMPROVE BEHAVIOR. Lavoie, Richard. Classroom strategies from AD-IN's Second National Conference on ADD. 1:00 ($30) AD-IN

ADD GOES TO COLLEGE PANEL. Cavanaugh, Faigel, Goldberg, and Muncaster. Panel discussion from AD-IN's Fourth National Conference on ADD. 1:00 ($30) AD-IN

ADD: A SENSORY INTEGRATION PERSPECTIVE. Koomer, Jane. From AD- IN's Fourth National Conference on ADD. 1:00 ($30) AD-IN

ADHD/ADD FROM THE STUDENT, PARENT & ADULT PERSPECTIVES. Copeland, Edna and Walker, Ronald. This video is part of the Diverse Teaching for Diverse Learning Series. It highlights the difficulties faced by students and parents as they attempt to address the facets of ADD. Includes participant's guide. :45 ($35) Resurgens Press

ADHD IN ADULTHOOD: A CLINICAL PERSPECTIVE. Arthur Robin. Explains the symptoms and diagnosis of ADHD in adults and gives intervention and medication strategies. 1:00 ($59) Professional Advancement Seminars

ADHD IN ADULTS. Barkley, Russell. Explains the symptoms and treatment of adult ADHD and how it differs from that of children. Shows the lives of four adults with ADHD. :30 ($95) Guilford Publications

206

ADHD IN THE CLASSROOM: STRATEGIES FOR TEACHERS. Barkley, Russell. Combines interviews with hands-on demonstrations of techniques for the classroom and strategies for working with the parents and school system. Includes discussion on the legal aspects and obligations. :30 ($95) Guilford Publications

ADHD—WHAT CAN WE DO? Barkley, Russell. Explains techniques parents and educators can use. It can be rented through Fanlight Productions. :45 ($75) Guilford Publications

ADHD—WHAT DO WE KNOW? Barkley, Russell. Describes ADHD, the problems of children with ADD, and the medical treatment. Interviews parents, teachers and children. It can be rented through Fanlight Productions. :35 ($75) Guilford Publications

ALL ABOUT ADD. Explains the symptoms of ADD and their effects, causes of ADD, treatment of ADD (counseling, interventions, behavioral management, medication) and ways to predict the child's future. 3:15 ($50) Child Management

ANSWERS TO ADD: THE SCHOOL SUCCESS TOOL KIT. Taylor, John. Techniques and practical solutions for parents and teachers. Includes advice on homework, organization, note taking and the "Three R's". 1:42 ($39.95) Sun Media

APPROACHING COLLEGE FOR STUDENTS WITH ADD. This video features for college students with ADD who present their own experiences and address what students need to know before they get to college. It explains the implications of being a college student with ADD. ($30) Pediatric Development Center

AROUND THE CLOCK: PARENTING THE DELAYED ADD CHILD. Goodman, Joan, and Hoban, Susan. This video is for parents who have children with ADD who are also developmentally delayed. This video shows the lives of two families and the symptoms, coping, and acceptance of the problem. :30 (150) Guilford

ATTENTION DISORDERS: THE SCHOOL'S VITAL ROLE. Copeland, Edna. This package includes "Understanding ADD: Preschool to Adulthood" (:42) which portrays typical life with ADHD children and adults and discussion of the behavior. It also has "The School's Key Role in ADHD/ADD" (:77) which shows ADD students in the classroom and ways to educate them. Includes Instruction Manual. ($190) Resurgens Press

BEHAVIOR MANAGEMENT OF ADD. Dr. Barkley, Russell. Clinical discussion of ADD at AD-IN's First National Conference on ADD. 1:00 ($30) AD-IN

CAUSES OF ADD. Copeland, Edna and Walker, Ronald. This video is part of the Diverse Teaching for Diverse Learning Series. It addresses the neurological basis of ADD and the genetic, social, emotional, educational, and environmental risk factors. Includes participant's guide. :45 ($35) Resurgens Press

CHARACTERISTICS OF ADD. Copeland, Edna and Walker, Ronald. This video is part of the Diverse Teaching for Diverse Learning Series. It provides an overview of ADD. Includes participant's guide. :45 ($35) Resurgens Press

CLASSROOM INTERVENTIONS FOR BEHAVIORALLY AND SOCIALLY DIFFICULT STUDENTS. Copeland, Edna and Walker, Ronald. This video is part of the Diverse Teaching for Diverse Learning Series. It addresses the motivations of control, attitudes toward authority and principles and strategies that work. Includes participant's guide. :45 ($35) Resurgens Press

CLASSROOM ORGANIZATION AND STRUCTURE. Copeland, Edna and Walker, Ronald. This video is part of the Diverse Teaching for Diverse Learning Series. How to maximize learning and cooperation through the environment. Includes participant's guide. :45 ($35) Resurgens Press

DEVELOPING COPING SKILLS: A WORKSHOP FOR ADULTS WITH ADD. Schultz, Jerome. Workshop at AD-IN's Fourth National Conference on ADD. 1:00 ($30) AD-IN

DIALOGUE WITH DR. WEISS. Dr. Weiss, Gabrielle. Discussion with an expert on adults with ADD at AD-IN's Fourth National Conference on ADD. 1:00 ($30) AD-IN

EDUCATING INATTENTIVE CHILDREN. Goldstein, Sam and Michael. Provides educators with information to identify and evaluate classroom problems and practical guidelines to educate students with ADD. 2 hours ($90) ADD Warehouse

AN EDUCATOR'S PERSPECTIVE ON ADD: IF YOU DON'T STAND UP FOR SOMETHING, YOU'LL FALL FOR ALMOST ANYTHING. Lavoie, Richard. Lecture at AD-IN's Second National Conference on ADD. 1:00 ($30) AD-IN

THE EFFECTIVENESS OF DEALING WITH THE ENTIRE FAMILY WHEN TREATING THE ADD CHILD. Dr. Weaver, Robert. Lecture at AD-IN's Fourth National Conference on ADD. 1:00 ($30) AD-IN

HOW PARENTS CAN DEVELOP A BETTER RELATIONSHIP WITH THEIR ADD CHILDREN AND IMPROVE THEIR SELF-ESTEEM. Weaver, Robert. Lecture on the role of parents from AD-IN's Second National Conference on ADD. 1:00 ($30) AD-IN

INCLUSION OF CHILDREN AND YOUTH WITH ATTENTION DEFICIT DISORDER. Buehler, Bruce and Evans, Joseph. Video focuses on causes, diagnosis and treatment for ADHD as well as home based and school interventions. :42 ($99) National Professional Resources

IT'S JUST ATTENTION DISORDER: A VIDEO FOR KIDS. Goldstein, Sam and Michael. MTV style video designed to help the child learn about his problem and its treatment. Includes manual and study guide. ($90). ADD Warehouse

JUMPIN' JOHNNY GET BACK TO WORK!: THE VIDEO. Gordon, Michael. Based on the children's picture book, this animated video tells the story of a boy with ADHD. :30 ($45) ADD Warehouse

LANGUAGE AND LITERACY ACROSS THE ELEMENTARY SCHOOL CURRICULUM: WHAT TO LOOK FOR, WHAT TO DO. Franciscan Children's Hospital Speech and Language Pathologists. A panel discussion on elementary school. 1:00 ($30) AD-IN

LIVING WITH ADD. Efforts to support families with ADD children. The parents on the tape are all members of an ADD group. :55 ($10 rent) LDA

MEDICAL INTERVENTIONS FOR ADHD AND THE SCHOOL'S VITAL ROLE IN MEDICAL MANAGEMENT. Copeland, Edna and Walker, Ronald. This video is part of the Diverse Teaching for Diverse Learning Series. It provides an overview of current medical treatments. Includes participant's guide. :45 ($35) Resurgens Press

MEETING THE ATTENTIONAL AND EMOTIONAL NEEDS OF STUDENTS. Copeland, Edna and Walker, Ronald. This video is part of the Diverse Teaching for Diverse Learning Series. It shows how teachers and parents can meet the needs of students with ADD. Includes participant's guide. :45 ($35) Resurgens Press

MODIFYING THE CLASSROOM FOR SUCCESS: PRACTICAL TECHNIQUES FOR WORKING WITH THE CHILD WHO HAS ADD. Schultz, Jerome. In-service training for teachers at AD-IN's Fourth National Conference on ADD. 1:00 ($30) AD-IN

MULTISENSORY STRATEGIES FOR TEACHING LANGUAGE ARTS. Copeland, Edna and Walker, Ronald. This video is part of the Diverse Teaching for Diverse Learning Series. Discusses effective multisensory approaches and accommodations in testing procedures. Includes participant's guide. :45 ($35) Resurgens Press

MULTISENSORY TEACHING METHODS FOR MATHEMATICS. Copeland, Edna and Walker, Ronald. This video is part of the Diverse Teaching for Diverse Learning Series. Discusses effective multisensory approaches and accommodations in testing procedures. Includes participant's guide. :45 ($35) Resurgens Press

NEUROLOGICAL ISSUES FOR ADD/LD. Dr. DeBassio, William. Lecture at AD-IN's Fourth National Conference on ADD. 1:00 ($30) AD-IN

PARTNER SYSTEMS FOR OPTIMUM LEARNING OF CONTENT AND VALUES. Copeland, Edna and Walker, Ronald. This video is part of the Diverse Teaching for Diverse Learning Series. It discusses how cooperative learning can help ADD students. Includes participant's guide. :45 ($35) Resurgens Press

PEER SUPPORT: ADHD/ADD TEENS SPEAKOUT! Lambert, Laura Teens Speak out with other teens and share thoughts on self management, communication, medication, ability, success. Shows how to form a peer support group. 1:20 ($40) Starbase One

POSITIVE TEACHER STRATEGIES TO FOCUS STUDENTS AND ENHANCE ATTENTION. Copeland, Edna and Walker, Ronald. This video is part of the Diverse Teaching for Diverse Learning Series. It provides positive reinforcement strategies. Includes participant's guide. :45 ($35) Resurgens Press

PRINCIPLES OF BEHAVIOR MANAGEMENT FOR OPTIMUM STUDENT PERFORMANCE AND ESTEEM. Copeland, Edna and Walker, Ronald. This video is part of the Diverse Teaching for Diverse Learning Series. It provides an overview of behavior management for emotional and educational behavior. Includes participant's guide. :45 ($35) Resurgens Press

STRATEGY INSTRUCTION: THE MISSING LINK FOR THE ADD/LD STUDENT. Amico, Kathleen. Lecture from AD-IN's Fourth National Conference on ADD. 1:00 ($30) AD-IN

SUCCESS STRATEGIES FOR ADD ADULTS. Melear, Larry. Health educator shares tips for family and career based on his own experience as a person with ADD and information from studies of ADD adults. Audio tape only. ($14.95) Attention Deficit Resource Center

UNDERSTANDING ATTENTION DEFICIT DISORDER. Dr. Epstein, Simon. A general introduction to ADHD Including history, symptoms, methods of diagnosis, Special Education, medication, therapy, and self- esteem. :45 ($23.50) CACLD

UNDERSTANDING HYPERACTIVITY. Psychiatric Support Services, Inc. Explains the symptoms and consequences of hyperactivity through the experiences of one family. :25 ($40) ADD Warehouse

THE VIDEO SOS: HELP FOR PARENTS. Clark, Lynn. Video helps teach parents skills for child management. Includes book, handouts and Leader's Guide. 1:07 ($150) Parents Press

WHY WON'T MY CHILD PAY ATTENTION? Goldstein, Sam and Michael. Familiarizes parents with ADD behaviors and the problems they can cause. It explains the effects these behaviors have on children and provides guidelines to help parents and professionals 1:16 ($30) ADDA

Organizations and Publishers

ADD Warehouse (ADDW)
300 NW 70th Ave
Plantation, FL 33317
(800) 233-9273

The ADDed Line
3790 Loch Highland Parkway
Roswell, GA 30339
(800) 982-4028

ADDult News: An Adult Newsletter
Mary Jane Johnson, Editor
2620 Ivy Place
Toledo, OH 43613

499 N.W. 70th Avenue, Suite 308
Plantation, FL 33317
(800) 233-4050

Connecticut Association for Children
with Learning Disabilities (CACLD)
18 Marshall Street
South Norwalk, CT 06854
(203) 838-5010

Council of Administrators of Special
Education Inc.
615 16th St., NW
Albuquerque, NM 87104
(505) 243-7622

Council for Exceptional Children
(CEC)
1920 Association Drive
Reston, VA 22091
(703) 264-9474

Educational Resources
19900 Ten Mile Road
St. Clair Shores, MI 48081
(313) 776-2949

Educators Publishing Service
75 Multon St.
Cambridge, MA 02138
(617) 547-6706

ERIC Clearinghouse for Handicapped
and Gifted Children
Council for Exceptional Children
1920 Association Drive
Reston, VA 22091
(703) 264-9474

Fanlight Productions
47 Halifax Street
Boston, MA 02130
(617) 524-0980

GSI Publications
PO Box 746
DeWitt, NY 13214
(315) 446-4849

Guilford Publications, Inc
72 Spring Street
New York, NY 10012
(800) 365-7006

HADD
4231 Colonial Ave SW
Bldg E, Suite 6
Roanoke, VA 24018

Impact Publications
300 N.W. 70th Ave
Plantation, FL 33317
(305) 792-8944

Insight Books
Plenum Publishing Corporation
233 Spring Street
New York, NY 10013
(800) 221-9369

JKL Communications
1016 16th St. NW, Suite 700
Washington, DC 20036
(202) 223-5097

John Wiley & Sons
Eastern Distribution Center
1 Wiley Drive
Somerset, NJ 08873
(908) 469-4400

Learning Disabilities Association of
America (LDA)
4156 Library Road
Pittsburgh, PA 15234-1349
(412) 341-1515

Learning Disabilities Project,
Interstate Research Association
26 Jones Branch Suite
1100 McLean, VA 22102

Magination Press
Dept. QC
19 Union Square West
New York, NY 10003
(800) 825-3089

Michigan Products Inc.
PO Box 24155
Lansing, MI 48909-4155
(800) 444-1773

National Association of School
Psychologists
8455 Colesville Road, Suite 1000
Silver Spring, MD 20910
(301) 608-2514

National Information Center for
Children and Youth with Disabilities
(NICHCY)
PO Box 1492
Washington, DC 20013
(800) 999- 5599

National Professional Resources Inc.
25 South Regent St.
Port Chester, NY 10573
(800) 453-7461

Parents Press
PO Box 2180
Bowling Green, KY 42102
(502) 842-4571

Pediatric Development Center
3268 Arcadia Place, NW
Washington, DC 20015

Phi Delta Kappa Educational
Foundation
408 N. Union
PO Box 789
Bloomington, IN 47402-0789
(800) 766-1156

Professional Advancement Seminars
One Dix Street
Worcester, MA 01609
(508) 792-2408

Professional Group for ADD and
Related Disorders (PGARD)
28 Fairview Road
Scarsdale, NY 10583
(914) 723-0118

Research Press
2612 North Mattis Avenue
Champaign, IL 61821
(217) 352-3273

Resurgens Press, Inc.
1770 Old Spring House Lane,
Suite 111
Atlanta, GA 30338
(800) 526-5952

Starbase One Ltd.
PO Box 2217
Jasper, OR 97438

Strategies
1633 Babcock Suite 231
San Antonio, TX 78229

St. Martin's Press Publishers
Book & Audio
PO Box 070059
Staten Island, NY 10307
(800) 288-2131

Sun Media
1095 25th Street S.E. Suite 107
Salem, Oregon 97301
(800) VIP-1ADD

Charles Thomas, Publisher
2600 South First Street
Springfield, IL 62794-9265
(800) 358-8980
(217) 789-8980

Tyrell & Jerem Press
PO Box 20089
Cincinnati, OH 45220
(800) 622- 6611

Underwood-Miller, Inc
708 Westover Drive
Lancaster, PA 17601

Verbal Images Press
19 Fox Hill Drive
Fairport, NY 14450
(716) 377-3807

Woodbine House
5615 Fishers Lane
Rockville, MD 20852
(301) 468- 8800

ADVOCACY CHECKLIST

Emergency! Crisis! Help!

If you are a parent with a child with learning or attention differences, it is vitally important that you learn everything you can about your child's special needs and legal rights. This will aid you in working with the school to provide your child with an appropriate educational program.

In a crisis, parents often experience anger, guilt, confusion, frustration and helplessness. The key to success in obtaining a successful educational program for your child, whether you initiate Special education litigation or not, is Preparation, Preparation, & more Preparation! Civil cases that are well-prepared for trial are usually settled and rarely, actually go to trial.

"The issues are the same—only the names and dates change."

A crisis can hit without warning! How do you prepare? Join several organizations in order to receive their national, state and local newsletters. Read about and understand the law. Know how to write an IEP (Individualized Education Plan) and become an expert in the global nature of your child's abilities, disabilities, the law, IEP's, tests & measurements.

Where Do I Begin?

❑ Call the national organizations listed and request membership and order publication material.

❑ Call your state and local educational departments and Advocacy /support groups and request information that they have available.

❑ Request copies of your child's entire cumulative and confidential files from the Special education Department of your local school district and from all other public or private agencies that may have information on your child. Arrange in chronological order in a loose-leaf notebook. Date each document lightly, in pencil, in the lower right-hand corner.

Does This Sound Familiar?

☛ "We don't recognize your private sector evaluation that identifies your child as needing Special education services. . . ."

Written for Parent Advocates of Students with Learning Disabilities and Attention Deficit Disorder Adapted from "THE PARENT/ADVOCATE: FIRST STEPS"—A Special Education Attorney's First Response To The Parent's Initial Frantic Telephone Call © 1994 by Peter W. D. Wright, Attorney at Law, Courthouse Commons, 4104 East Parham Road, Richmond, VA 23228-2734. Office: (804) 755-3000; voice mail box: (804) 257-0857; fax: (804) 755-3003. CompuServe: 75116,364

☛ "Your child's real problems lie within a dysfunctional family. Besides, he's just not motivated. . . ."

☛ "The services your child needs are simply not available at our school. . . ."

☛ "Your child is not benefiting from the program and doesn't really need it anyway. . . ."

☛ "Your child's true problem is that he's emotionally disturbed, not learning disabled. . . ."

Knowledge equals *empowerment* equals *success!*

Document everything! Including all written correspondence and telephone calls.

❏ Learning Disabilities Association of America (LDA) (PA) (412) 341-1515
  • State LDA Office
  • Local LDA Chapter

❏ Orton Dyslexia Society (MD) 1-800-222-3123
  • Branch Office

❏ National Center for Learning Disabilities (NY) (212) 545-7510

❏ CH.A.D.D. (Children & Adults with Attention Deficit Disorders) National Office (FL) 1-800-233-4050
  • Local Chapter

❏ TAPP/PTI Office (Technical Assistance for Parent Programs Project/Parent Training & Information Projects) Check with your state or local LDA office or call the Federation for Children with Special Needs (MA) (617) 482-2915

❏ National Association of Protection & Advocacy Systems (legal information & support) (202) 408-9514

❏ Local Special education Attorney

❏ HEATH (National Clearinghouse on Post-secondary education for for Individuals with Disabilities) (Washington. D.C.) 1-800-544-3284

❏ NICHCY (National Information Center for Children and Youth with Disabilities (Washington, D.C.) 1-800-695-0285

❏ ERIC Clearinghouse for Handicapped and Gifted Children, Council for Exceptional Children (VA) (703) 264-9474

❏ Office for Civil Rights (Contact your state LDA or TAPP/PTI Office)

❏ Local School
  •School Psychologist
  •Other school personnel
  • Superintendent

❏ State Superintendent
  • State Special Education Department

Other Resources

❏ Check with your nearby law school library for "INDIVIDUALS WITH DISABILITIES EDUCATION LAW REPORTER" (IDELR) published by LRP Publications in Horsham, PA. Look for the "Topical Index" for cases similar to yours.

❏ Read "YOUR CHILD'S IEP: PRACTICAL AND LEGAL GUIDANCE FOR PARENTS" written by Pamela Darr Wright. It is available in the Legal/Advocacy Library on CompuServe's ADD Forum under the file name IEPS&C.TXT or directly from Peter Wright. (CompuServe Information Service 1-800-524-3388, GO ADD) To quickly search for all articles written by Peter & Pamela Wright, use the CompuServe ID: 75116,364.

❏ Purchase: "UNDERSTANDING LEARNING DISABILITIES: A PARENT GUIDE AND WORKBOOK" from the Learning Disabilities Council, P.O. Box 8451, Richmond, VA 23226 (804) 748-5012 Cost: $21.70 Prepaid.

Books

Check with your local public library or support group.

❏ THE MISUNDERSTOOD CHILD by Larry Silver, M.D. (recent, revised edition)

❏ ATTENTION DEFICIT DISORDER: A DIFFERENT PERCEPTION by Thom Hartmann

❏ SOMETHING'S WRONG WITH MY CHILD by Richardson, Brutten & Mangel.

❏ ATTENTION DEFICIT DISORDER IN ADULTS by Lynn Weiss, PH.D.

❏ DRIVEN TO DISTRACTION by Edward M. Hallowell, M.D. & John J. Ratey, M.D.

❏ NO EASY ANSWERS and SUCCEEDING AGAINST THE ODDS by Sally Smith

Groups

CH.A.D.D. (Children and Adults with Attention Deficit Disorders)

499 N.W. 70th Avenue, Suite 101, Plantation, FL 33317, 1-800-233-4050

CH.A.D.D. publishes a magazine and newsletter, puts on an annual conference, and has affiliated groups all across the United States and Canada. It's the primary, and probably the best, international resource for parents of children with ADD.

National Center for Learning Disabilities—NCLD

381 Park Avenue Suite 1420, New York, New York 10016, (212) 545-7510. Internet: ncld@paltech.com.

A voluntary not-for-profit organization providing national information, referral services and educational programs for people with learning disabilities and attentional differences.

The Learning Disabilities Association of America—LDA.

4156 Library Road Pittsburgh, PA 15234-1349, (412) 341-1515, (412) 341-8077, Fax (412) 344-0224. A nonprofit, membership organization providing information and support for individuals with learning and attention differences.

LDA STATE OFFICES

LDA of Alabama
PO Box 1588
Montgomery, AL 36111
(205) 277-9151

LDA of Alaska
Contact Colleen Deal
19400 Verdant Cir.
Eagle River, AK 99577
(907) 694-7907

LDA of Arizona
PO Box 30606
Phoenix, AZ 85046
(602) 495-1175
Fax: (602) 495-1176

LDA of Arkansas
PO Box 7316
Little Rock, AR 72217
(501) 666-8777
M-F 8-5 P.M.

LDA of California
Jane Bagley
655 Lewelling Blvd. #355
San Leandro, CA 94579
(415) 343-1411
T-W-Th, 1-5
Fax (415) 343-1854

LDA of Colorado
1045 Lincoln St., #106
Denver, CO 80203
(303) 894-0992

LDA of Connecticut
100 Constitution Plaza Ste. 710
Hartford, CT 06103
(203) 560-1711

LDA of District of Columbia
PO Box 6350
Washington, DC 20015
(202) 667-9140

Florida ACLD
Cheryl Kron, Ex. Sec.
331 East Henry St.
Punta Gorda, FL 33950
(813) 637-8957

LDA of Georgia
PO Box 965505
Marietta, GA 30066
(404) 514-8088

LDA of Hawaii
Jennifer Shember-Lang
200 N. Vineyard Blvd. Suite 310
Honolulu, HI 96817
(808) 536-9684
Fax: (808) 537-6780

LDA of Idaho
Michelle Arnold
12160 N. Forrest Rd.
Hayden, ID 83835
(208) 762-3170
Ginny Hughes
1308 Circle Dr.
Hayden Lake, ID 83835-9503
(208) 762-2316

LDA of Illinois
Diane Laporte
10101 S. Roberts Rd. Suite 205
Palos Hills, IL 60465
(708) 430-7532

LDA of Indiana
PO Box 20584
Indianapolis, IN 46220
(317) 898-5751

LDA of Iowa
PO Box 665
Indianola, IA 50125
(515) 280-8558

LDA of Kansas
PO Box 4424
Topeka, KS 66604
(913) 272-0033

LDA of Kentucky
Catherine Senn
2210 Goldsmith Lane. #104
Louisville, KY 40218
(502) 473-1256
Fax: (502) 459-9287

LDA of Louisiana
Contact Barbara Duchardt
Northwestern State University
Teacher Ed. Ctr, Room 105-A
Natchitoches, LA 71497
(318) 357-0784
Fax: (318) 357-6275

LDA of Maine
2E Mechanic St.
PO Box 385
Gardiner, ME 04345
(207) 582-2866
Fax: (207) 437-2837

LDA of Maryland
76 Cranbrook Rd., Ste 300
Cockeysville, MD 21030
(410) 265-8188
Fax: (410) 265-5739

LDA of Massachusetts
1275 Main St.
Waltham, MA 02154
(617) 891-5009
T-W-Th, 9:00-2:00 p.m.

LDA of Michigan
200 Museum Dr., Ste. 101
Lansing, MI 48933
(517) 485-8160
Fax: (517) 485-8462

LD of Minnesota
400 Selby Ave., Ste. D
St. Paul, MN 55102
(612) 222-2696
(800) 488-4395

LDA of Mississippi
State Office (800) 661-9074

LDA of Missouri
Eleanor Scherff
PO Box 3303
1942 E. Meadowmere, #104
Springfield, MO 65804
(417) 864-5110
Fax: (417) 864-7290

LDA of Montana
President Maureen Ferrell
4026 Pine Cove Rd
Billings, MT 59106
(406) 656-7138

LDA of Nebraska
PO Box 6464
Omaha, NE 68106

LDA of New Hampshire
PO Box 7118
Concord, NH 03301
(800) 794-9700

LDA New Jersey
PO Box 187
Oceanport, NJ 07757
(908) 571-1221

LDA of New Mexico
6301 Menaul, NE #556
Albuquerque, NM 87110

LDA of New York
90 S. Swan Street
Albany, NY 12210
(518) 436-4633

LDA North Carolina
Box 3542
Chapel Hill, NC 27515
(919) 493-5362
M-W-F 8:30-4:00

LDA of North Dakota
PO Box 2339
Bismarck, ND 58502
(701) 247-2667

LDA of Ohio
Stephanie Richley
1380 Pearl Road Ste 203
Brunswick, OH 44212
(216) 273-7388
1-800-543-7532 (Ohio & 412 in PA)
Fax: (216) 225-0228

LDA of Oklahoma
Box 2315
Stillwater, OK 74076
(405) 743-1366

LDA of Pennsylvania
Toomey Building Eagle, Box 208
Uwchland, PA 19480
(610) 458-8193

LDA of Puerto Rico
President Elisa Blum
76 Kings Ct. Apt. 701
Santurce, PR 00911
(809) 728-5166

LDA of Rhode Island
PO Box 6685
Providence, RI 02940
(401) 232-3822

LDA of South Carolina
PO Box 112881
Charleston, SC 29422

LDA of Tennessee
PO Box 381107
Germantown, TN 38183

LDA of Texas
Ann Robinson
1011 W. 31st Street
Austin, TX 78705
(512) 458-8234
Fax: (512) 458-3826

LDA of Utah
Joyce Otterstrom
PO Box 112
Salt Lake City, UT 84110
(801) 355-2881
Fax: (801) 467-2148

LDA of Vermont
Contact Christina Thurston
PO Box 1041
Manchester Ctr., VT 05255
(802) 362-3127

LDA of Virginia
PO Box 573
Springfield, VA 22150
(703) 451-5007

LDA of Washington
7819 159th PL NE
Redmond, WA 98052-7301
(206) 882-0792
(206) 882-0820 (Business Line)
1-800-536-2343 (within WA only)
Fax: (206) 861-4642

LDA of West Virginia
Jane Crist
PO Box 602
Ansted, WV 25812
(304) 658-4910

LDA of Wisconsin
15738 W. National Ave.
New Berlin, WI 53151
(414) 821-0855

International ADD Support Groups

Learning Disabilities Association
of Canada
323 Chapel Street
Ottawa, Ontario K1N 7Z2
President: Linda Jeppesen
Phone: (613) 238-5721
Fax: (613) 235-5391

LADDERS
Stan Mould
95 Church Rd.
Bradmore
Wolverhampton WV3 7EW
United Kingdom

ADD-ADHD Family Support Group
Mrs. G. Mead, President
1a, High Street
Dilton Marsh
Westbury, Wilts. BA13 4DL
Tel: 01373 826045
Mr. B. Tuffill
93 Avon Road
Devizes, Wilts, SN10 1PT
Tel: 01380 726710
This support group provides informa-
tion internationally.

Hyperactive Children's Support Group
Sally Bunday
71 Whyke Lane
Chichester, West Sussex P019 2LD
England
Phone: +(44) 903-725-182
(This group may lean toward natural
remedies)

Hyperactivity/Attention Deficit
Association (N.S.W.)
29 Bertram Street
Chatswood 2067
Australia

Hyperactive Childrens Support
Group—Ireland
Stephanie Mahony
25, Lawnswood Park
Stillorgan Co.
Dublin, Ireland
Phone: 44-288-9766

Moscow, Russia
Kim Palchikoff, +(7) 095 971-4944
Internet: palc@glas.apc.org
Sylvia Naumovski +(7) 095 415-4302
Please note: There is an 8-hr time
difference between Moscow and EST.
Moscow is ahead. (9am in Seattle =
noon in New York = 8pm in Moscow.)
If you call Moscow, please plan ahead
so you don't call in the middle of the
night.

South Wales ADD / ADHD
Support Group
Mrs Linda Cook
13, Eton Place
Cardiff CF5 1PB
United Kingdom
Tel: 01222 383279
CompuServe 100552,3226

Books of Interest

The following is a collection of books, listed in random order, that many forum members find helpful in understanding attention deficit disorder. They can be ordered through any local bookstore.

DRIVEN TO DISTRACTION by Edward M. Hallowell, M.D. and John J. Ratey, M.D.

ATTENTION DEFICIT DISORDER IN ADULTS, by Lynn Weiss, PH.D.

YOU MEAN I'M NOT LAZY, STUPID OR CRAZY? by Kate Kelly and Peggy Ramundo

THE ADHD PARENTING HANDBOOK by Colleen Alexander-Roberts

ATTENTION DEFICIT DISORDER: A DIFFERENT PERCEPTION by Thom Hartmann

ANSWERS TO DISTRACTION by Edward M. Hallowell, M.D. and John J. Ratey, M.D.

WOMEN WITH ATTENTION DEFICIT DISORDER by Sari Solden, M.S., M.F.C.C.

ADHD AND TEENS: A PARENT'S GUIDE FOR MAKING IT THROUGH THE TOUGH YEARS by Colleen Alexander-Roberts

ADD SUCCESS STORIES: A GUIDE TO FULFILLMENT FOR FAMILIES WITH ATTENTION DEFICIT DISORDER by Thom Hartmann

A COMPREHENSIVE GUIDE TO ATTENTION DEFICIT DISORDER IN ADULTS: RESEARCH, DIAGNOSIS AND TREATMENT edited by Kathleen G. Nadeau, PH.D.

ADD Forum Sysop Roster

LIKE MOST FORUMS ON COMPUSERVE, the ADD Forum is staffed almost entirely by volunteers who generously donate their time and energies to building a productive, supportive community. Your staff members include:

Thom Hartmann (76702,765) The Primary Sysop for the ADD Forum is Thom Hartman. Thom is the founder (with his wife, Louise) and former Executive Director of the New England Salem Children's Village in Rumney, New Hampshire, a residential treatment facility for children in the White Mountains. He's also the author of "ATTENTION DEFICIT DISORDER: A DIFFERENT PERCEPTION" and "ADD SUCCESS STORIES" published by Underwood Books, and "FOCUS YOUR ENERGY" published by Pocket Books. Thom is the parent of an ADD teenager.

Elisa Davis (74431,117) Elisa is the mother of two boys and lives in the NYC suburbs. She used to be a financial analyst and strategic planner, now she is an amateur expert on neurobehavioral disorders because of her children. Her older son has a variety of behavior difficulties, and her younger son has been diagnosed with high-functioning autism. Both children have been in a variety of special and regular education programs. In addition to being one of our most active sysops on the board in general, Elisa is one of the key figures in the TS/PDD/Aut/NBD section. (Her husband Seth is a four-time champion on Jeopardy; do NOT play Trivial Pursuit with him.)

Elisa is also the Primary Sysop for the New York Magazine Online Forum (GO NYFORUM) and can be found listed in the Magazine's masthead among the Assistant Editors.

Susan Burgess (72662,3107) Susan Burgess is the Public Relations Sysop on the ADD Forum and handles online publicity for a large number of forums on CompuServe. Before starting her company, Communications Today, she was an award-winning journalist. Communications Today won a national PR award in its first year. She also does research on the Internet's World Wide Web.

Morgan Adcock (74777,3462) (Beth Ann) Morgan Adcock is a RN. Nothing rang any bells when she studied "hyperkinesis" in nursing school — but hearing Dave deBronkart describe what it's like to have ADD struck home immediately. (Her having left her food at the drive thru window after paying for it—yet again—earlier that day probably had something to do with that.) She had a difficult time convincing her family doctor that she needed a workup for ADD because he considers her a highly capable person, and that didn't fit into his antiquated view of ADD. Once seen by a specialist knowledgable in ADD, however, she was quickly diagnosed.

Morgan is also the mother of an ADD high school junior, who has been an honor roll student since sixth grade. Her (very patient) husband teaches at a residential treatment facility, where many of his students have ADD.

Cj Bowman (72614,1003) Cj Bowman, a home schooled ADDer, was born in 1979 and has an avid interest in the electronic frontier. He was the youngest (12) to enroll in a high school vocational skills center where he studied Computer Programming/Data Processing. In the summer of 1993, Cj, at age 13, became one of the youngest Sysops on CompuServe, joining the Sysop team on the ADD Forum. When Cj isn't sleeping, he's on the computer (and the telephone).

Janie Bowman (72662,3716) Janie Bowman is a volunteer for the Olympia Chapter, L.D.A. of Washington (state), and editor of her local LDA newsletter, *"ADD Connection!."* As a home schooling parent of two wonderful ADD children and non-ADD spouse to a fantastic ADD husband, she readily admits that her B.S. Degree in Family & Consumer Studies and Certificate in Social Welfare did not prepare her for such an exciting life!

Dave deBronkart (76702,1140) Dave deBronkart is a successful ADD adult who didn't discover the trait until he was 42; he then scored 10/14 on the DSM-III-R diagnostic criteria, and discovered why he hadn't "just grown up." A black-belt troubleshooter in computerized graphic arts, he's known for his ability to analyze complex problems from several angles at once—sometimes indulging in three-day sleepless binges, though he's tried to avoid this in recent years(g). A Board member of the New England Salem Children's Village, "deB" is writing "HYPERTHINK: THE EDISON TRAIT," which documents that Thomas Alva Edison's "kaleidoscopic mind," as he called it, was almost certainly ADD. deB's main interest in ADD is finding ways to harness the trait's strengths.

Dale Hammerschmidt, M.D. (72662,76) Dale Hammerschmidt, M.D. is an Associate Professor of Medicine at the Univ. of Minn., and is Senior Editor of the *Journal of Laboratory and Clinical Medicine*. He is on the Board of the Minn. Tourette Syndrome Assn., and on one of the medical advisory panels of TSA/ National. He and his wife (Dr. Mary Arneson) run a support group for families with neurobehavioral disorders (ADD, OCD, Pervasive Developmental Disorder and Tourette's), and are the parents of two children with TS. But don't be intimidated by credentials; Dale has a pony tail, a bushy beard, an eccentric interest in 3-D photography and a tendency in his Walter Mitty moments (when he answers to "Velo-Mann") to ride a racing bike and pretend he's 30 years younger!

Wendy Hoechsetter (76300,363) Wendy Hoechsetter started her professional life with a BS in Spanish and Linguistics, then spent 10 years or so as a paramedic and in other areas of allied health. She first discovered ADHD in adulthood while a sales rep for Abbott Labs, selling one of the meds used to treat the condition, but did not explore the issue further for herself until some 7 years later. She thought all she needed was "more discipline." After a stint selling insurance with Northwestern Mutual Life, she finally realized she needed more help, and was diagnosed as severely ADHD as well as having mild Tourette's Syndrome, and OCD, and discovered she has some learning disabilities. Aided by these discoveries, she is now back in school studying the basic sciences so she can pursue her lifelong dream, becoming a doctor. After her own diagnosis, she was unable to find any support services, and so started the ADD support group on Edforum on CIS in mid 1992.

Hal Meyer (71333,2770) Hal Meyer is on the Board of Directors of CH.A.D.D.® (Children and Adults with Attention Deficit Disorders) and, together with his wife Susan founded CH.A.D.D. of New York City which they both coordinate. Hal is a past chairman of Big Brothers/Big Sisters, a former Board Member and current committee member at the Jewish Board of Family & Children's Services. He is on the Board of Kaplan House, a residential treatment facility for adolescents. Active in the NYC Public School system, Hal serves on special education committees in his District and is the President of his community school board. Hal and Susan frequently lecture on helping teach and reach students with Attention Deficit Disorders, when they are not running a company specializing in marketing and mailing list management on computers. Hal's main interest is early childhood and elementary education.

Carla Nelson (73020,1421) Carla Nelson, mother of two ADD children with a "roving mind" of her own, is a communications consultant with a degree in Psychology from UC Berkeley who assists clients across the country with research and writing projects. The self-styled "computer addict and cyberspace cruiser" has also played an active role in local civic and charitable efforts, including stints as communications adviser to the county foster parent program, founding president of a nonprofit group providing school age day care for elementary students, library foundation board member, and positions on boards concerned with local planning issues.

Linda Rawson (76702,3547) Linda Rawson lives in northern New Mexico, in an entirely ADD household. Her very varied [read ADD!] background includes 10 years' work as a corporate lawyer, as well as professional work in foreign language translation and interpretation, in Spanish and Russian. Linda now runs a computer consulting business. She also spends time advocating for her son and other children with neurological disabilities in the local school district and belongs to a state-wide study group on special education. She is working to educate her local school district on educational issues related to neurological disorders covered in this forum. For recreation, Linda's family has two ADD Spaniels, on whom she practices behavior modification techniques. Linda also enjoys gardening, with a serious weakness for old garden roses.

Mark Snyder, M.D. (73317,3426) Not diagnosed with ADD until he was 46, Mark was 20-for-20 on the D2D question list. By the time he was diagnosed, he'd been in and out of two branches of the military; been an undercover police officer as well as a uniformed officer; had started and succeeded (or failed miserably!) at several businesses (including one that did advertising with an aircraft!) . . . and had had *many* ADD-related difficulties in school, up to and including medical school, as well as in 3 years of a 4 year psychiatry residency. He's also a video producer (currently limited to ADD-related topics), marketing consultant, and entrepreneur. While he's had lots of experience in his residency program, he's currently not in practice, but plans to be again in Q4 of 1995. Currently he's focused on assisting another Forum Sysop in developing an ADD instructional lecture series for physicians and therapists... This Sysop has been *there!*

In addition to the Sysops in the ADD Forum, we are very fortunate to have active Staff members. They include:

Veronica Deane (100045,1227)   John Shumate (71644,3107)

Steve Foust (70632,3177)   Janet Whipple (76375,3470)

Sherry Griswold (75202,431)   Alysia Wurst (71621,2021)

Elna Hensley (74631,276)   Carol Yudis (76731,1671)

Pam Jacobs (73144,224)   Rose Zagaja (72643,3712)

Harlan Lampert (71643,2050)

Acknowledgments

WHAT WAS IT LIKE for a non-ADD person to work with so many ADD people in the compilation of this book? Intriguing, of course! And while I always felt that ADD people are giving and compassionate, I was not prepared for the extent of their generosity, that of their families, and the professionals who work with them.

If you're familiar with ADD people, you'll know how 'allergic' they can be to paperwork, so it was natural for my role to be the handler of what they termed the 'boring' and 'tedious' aspects of the book—collecting the information, getting permission to use material, acting as liaison among the people involved., and dealing with the thousand and one details that came up.

As I compiled THINK FAST! I used whimsical antics and zany poetry to get their attention. Occasionally, I varied that with prompts and deadlines. As you know, ADD people often procrastinate until a deadline is on top of them . . . and then, well, look out! They'll compress a week's work into five hours and do a great job of it, too!

Very few people, though, have had the privilege of experiencing a collective ADD hyperfocus. After months of passing edited files through electronic mail, faxes, phone calls, and general preparation, we suddenly got a firm commitment to publish the book and a deadline. Instantaneously, everyone shifted into overdrive! Files didn't pass through email, they flew through email. Phone calls increased. Ideas magically appeared everywhere! There was a vibrant feeling in the air!

What happened, of course, is that all the ADD people I was working with decided to hyperfocus at the same time, because the time was 'NOW!' leaving me, the non-ADDer, saying, 'WOW! Hey, wait for me!'

This anthology would not have been possible without the commitment of close to eighty individuals and professionals from the ADD community who graciously supported our efforts to compile one of the most complete books available on the ADD experience. Our sincere thanks to those whose works are included within.

A special thank you to

Dave deBronkart: for your support and technical expertise. You have such incredible insight and knowledge. How could we have compiled this anthology without you?

Susan Burgess: for your diligence and extraordinary editing skills, which became evident as we passed the manuscript back and forth on the many nights we watched the clock push past midnight.

Don Arnoldy: for your creative talents. You worked magic with our manuscript.

Elisa Davis: for your creative suggestions, archiving and caring support. You are greatly appreciated.

Additionally, many other individuals contributed their encouragement, inspiration, ideas and support. They include (but are not limited to) Jody Falco, Colleen Alexander-Roberts, Carl & Jean Hartmann, Dorothy Smith, Jim Butler, Linda Robertson, Mary Jane Johnson, Tim & Deborah Underwood, Patti Meadows, Linda Dannemiller, Mark S. Roth, Ronald E. Jones, Harvey Parker, Lisa Poast, Debbie Sorrells, Howard Morris, Mary T. Zakis, Clinton & Margaret Bowman, Pieter Bowman, Beth Odekirk, Anne Bennett, Jerry Waters, Glenda Serpa, Morgan Adcock, Dale Hammerschmidt, Wendy Hoechstetter, Hal Meyer, Carla Nelson, Linda Rawson, Mark Snyder, Veronica Deane, Steve Foust, Elna Hensley, Pam Jacobs, Harlan Lampert, John Shumate, Alysia Wurst, Rose Zagaja, Carol Yudis, Anita Diamant, Sherry Griswold, Janet Whipple.

Thanks to CompuServe, whose software and networking made the ADD Forum possible in the first place. Without their technology, none of the wonderful interactions you'll see in this book would have happened.

Our families also deserve our sincere appreciation. Louise, Kindra, Justin, & Kerith Hartmann; Clint, Cj and Shane Bowman. Thank you for walking with us as we brought together the wit and wisdom of the ADD experience.

—Janie Bowman

Index

232

X, Y, Z

0488